Olódùmarè

God in Yoruba Belief

BY

E. BOLAJI IDOWU

A New Introduction
By
Iyanla Vanzant

A&B BOOKS PUBLISHERS
Brooklyn, New York
11201

To
MY BELOVED
GRANDMOTHER
ADEOLA

Omiji
Omiji Aminiwon Ogun
Omidiji Aminiwon Egbogi

COVER DESIGN: A&B BOOKS PUBLISHERS
COVER ILLUSTRATION: JOEY HART
LETTERING: INDUSTRIAL FONTS & GRAFIXS

ISBN 1-881316-96-3

Reprinted 1994
by

A&B BOOKS PUBLISHERS
149 Lawrence Street
Brooklyn, New York, 11201
(718)596-3389

97 96 95 94   4 3 2 1

Contents

Plates

As a child, my grandmother taught me about two very separate and distinct Gods. The first one, she talked about. The other, she lived. Hearing her relate the awesome possibilities of God's vengeful wrath, while she conducted her daily life affairs according to nature and universal law. I became somewhat confused and frightened of the "being" I was taught to believe was God. Had it not been for my exposure to the philosophy, traditions and culture of the Yoruba people, I would have suffered from the same malady as my Granny; spiritual schizophrenia.

My grandmother is the offspring of a second generation, American born Nigerian father and a Native American Black Foot mother. Her father, born into slavery, elevated to a sharecropper, taught Granny about God in compliance to the dogma he learned from his "masters". This God, the one of which my Granny spoke, was powerful yet punishing; forgiving but judgmental; compassionate while being jealous; merciful and condemning at the same time. This God meted out rewards to the chosen, those who feared Him and lived to exemplify His obviously loathsome view of human capability and morality. Granny learned about this God through her father's interpretation of the Bible. He told her what this Holy book said, how it was to be applied; and, the wrathful results that would befall her if one "rule" was broken. The most astounding thing about this biblical interpretation was, neither my great-grandfather or my Granny could read.

In contrast, Granny learned about the presence and essence of God from her mother. This God was wise and loving; so wise, He shared rule of the universe with the forces of nature. More importantly, the essence of this God was present in all mankind. From her mother, Granny learned that God ruled not by fear, but by "law and order." Universal laws of nature which were exact and impersonal and gave rise to a divine order in the flow of life. From her mother, Granny learned to honor the energy of the seasons as they represented God's plan for man's life. She knew the wisdom and necessity of honoring the sun and the moon. She knew which direction the head of the bed should face; the time of the day the sun was best for the plants; which direction to face when you prayed; and which plants, teas and herbs would soothe your "female" problems.

Dr. Yosef Ben Jochannan said:

"Every time I had the good fortune to research into someones religion, I found "God" to be in the image of the people to whom the religion belongs."

My Granny met her God through the eyes of her parents. Her father's eyes, stripped of their heritage, saw God from the perspective of others who believed his spiritual detriment was based on his being born a descendant of Africans. His salvation, according to them, was based on his ability to live as they lived; think as they thought. Her mother's eyes, lived in defiance of all the Biblical precautions to honor the essence of God present in all things everywhere. She was however a "squaw", so to listen to her, to maintain the culture, was to be damned to hell for practicing heathenism. The eyes of the people have been shut. The minds of the people have been colored.

Far too many descendants of Africans born in the Americas have inherited, from their well meaning ancestors, conflicting philosophies and constructs regarding God. Having been denied the opportunity to see God through their own eyes, they embraced a God who loathed them by offered salvation, if they would be something other than they were—Africans. If religion is culture specific, one must have a cultural base from which to approach religion and ultimately God. The importance of this work is that it views God, Olódùmarè, through the eyes of an African people, bringing together their ancestral culture and philosophy in a way which supports spiritual and cultural continuity.

It is truly divine order that Olódùmarè is the premiere work to reveal an African philosophy of God. 86.7% of the slaves transported to the Americas were captured in the southwestern region of Nigeria; the land of the Yoruba people. Consequently, the largest percentage of African Americans living the Judeo-Christian ethics are Yoruba descendants. Whether we choose to practice our ancestral spiritual heritage is one thing. We have, however, a right and a "need", at the very least, to "know" what it is. Olódùmarè is an important work for the descendants of Africans in so far as it expands the ideas of God to include the concepts embraced by our greatest grandparents. Whether we realize it or not, those concepts are still alive at the core of our being; the DNA, the genes, which continue to keep us Africans.

In 1983, I was initiated into the Priesthood of the Yoruba culture. After many years of conflict trying to decipher the mixed messages I received from my grandmother, I found one thread of truth I could embrace and actualize; God created me to be what I am. I am the descendant of African people. I may have lost contact with the land and the language, but the culture has been preserved. The Native American held a part, the old wise women held a part, and the biggest part was alive in me; it was the part of my spirit which came alive with the sights and sounds of the practice of this ancient culture.

It was frightening at first, to stand in defiance of the Bible. Eventually, I realized, I was not rebelling against or relinquishing that part of my life, I was merely reinterpreting the information to include a part of myself which had been denied. Africans did not always speak English. How was I to know that Orish'nla was not Jesus, or Esu was not Paul; or Orunmila was not Moses unless I did my own independent investigation. My search bore out one truth, how people see, approach and relate to God is colored by the culture and language to which they subscribe. In embracing my ancestral culture, I found God who looked and sounded like the ancient echoes in my soul. For me that was good enough.

As you read this work, maintain an open mind. Investigate not only the words and concepts, but the philosophy behind the practices related. Like me, you will surely recognize some of the things your Granny said and did. Certain ideas will intrigue you; others will be quite appalling. Remain open. Openness promotes growth and evolution. As we each grow in our consciousness of who we are, and from where we have come, who we are shall evolve. At our divine core, we are all children of God, the Supreme Creator. Ask yourself, would God have made us all so different and deemed only one correct way to approach Him? I for one think not.

Iyanla Vanzant, born in Brooklyn, New York, is a Yoruba Priestess, lawyer and empowerment specialist. Cofounder of Inner Visions Spiritual Life Maintenance Network, she lives in the Washington D.C. area with her daughters and grandchildren.

July 1994

Preface

In all the previous works which have reference to the religion of the Yoruba, the Deity has been assigned a place which makes Him very remote, of little account in the scheme of things. Very few people who really know the Yoruba can escape the uneasy feeling that there is something inadequate, to say the least, about such a notion; and it is that "uneasy feeling" that led to my investigation of what the Yoruba *actually* know and believe about the Deity.

This book thus presents a new study of the belief of the Yoruba with the specific aim of emphasising their concept of the Deity.

In order to do this objectively, I have endeavoured throughout, as much as possible, to let the Yoruba themselves tell us what they know and believe, as they are so well able to do through their myths, in the recitations of their philosophy, with their songs and sayings, and by their liturgies.

To translate Yoruba verses and sayings into English and yet preserve their exact meaning is not an easy task. I have, however, tried to meet the difficulty by being rather literal and keeping very close to the original in my translations.

Throughout this work, I have reserved the title "Deity" for the Supreme Being alone, where I am not calling Him by His Yoruba name; and for the "gods many and lords many" I have used either the generic designation of "divinity" (or "divinities" as the case may be), or call them by their Yoruba generic name, *orìṣà*, when I am not using their individual names.

One secondary aim which I seek to fulfil through this book is to supply one of our deeply felt needs in the matter of good standard textbooks on Yoruba beliefs and thoughts. It is thus my hope that the book will be of value to teachers and students.

At this point I like to borrow the words of my Tutor, Dr. A. C. Bouquet of Cambridge: "But if anyone should ask: 'How can a padre be expected to produce an impartial treatise on a subject

PREFACE

concerning which he is bound to have definite denominational convictions'—my answer would be at once: 'I believe that truth shines by its own light. I have faith that if my own creed is in any true sense absolute, it cannot suffer from an unprejudiced and dispassionate exposition of the history of religion'. And so I have striven to write as a scientist, not as an advocate. Whether I have succeeded the public must judge." To this I do not need to add any comment.

I wish to express my gratitude to those who have so generously helped me by giving me of their valuable time and wisdom for the purpose of this book.

My thanks go first to all the friends throughout the country whose aid has been invaluable to me in the onerous and bewildering task of collecting material. In this connection I should like to mention especially my brother, Mr. Ogunlẹyẹ Idowu, and Mr. Rufus Awojọdù of Ile-Ifẹ̀. I thank Mrs. Mabel Nwachuku for typing most of the draft, Mr. F. Olubọ́rọ̀de Ogunyẹmi, who patiently and skilfully prepared the complete typescript, and Mrs. F. A. Ogunṣẹyẹ, who kindly prepared the map. I am also grateful to Rev. G. S. Todd, Immanuel College, Ibadan, for reading the work throughout in typescript or manuscript and giving me the benefit of his constructive and helpful criticism; to Miss Molly M. Mahood, Professor of English, University College, Ibadan, Mr. Ulli Beier, of the Extra-mural Department, University College, Ibadan, and Mr. M. B. Ranson, Nigerian College of Science and Technology, for reading portions of the typescript and making very helpful suggestions; to Miss Eva Richardson of the United Missionary College, Ibadan, and to my dear wife, both of whom so carefully and helpfully read the proofs.

It remains for me to add that this book is based on a Thesis presented to the University of London in 1955 for the Degree of Doctor of Philosophy in the Faculty of Theology. In this connection, I record my deep gratitude to Rev. Dr. E. Geoffrey Parrinder, who inspired and supervised my thesis throughout; to Miss Monica Humble, of the Methodist Girls' High School, Lagos, and Mr. H. Ulli Beier, who read the thesis and helped me with their criticisms with a view to its publication.

I send out this book in the hope that it will be a contribution to the study of the "ways and wisdom" of our beloved Africa.

E. Bọlaji Idowu

University College,
Ibadan.
April, 1960.

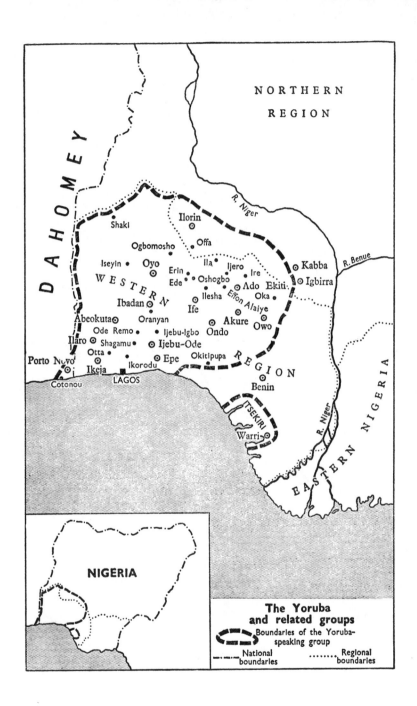

The Yoruba
and related groups

Boundaries of the Yoruba-speaking group

National boundaries

Regional boundaries

x

I

" In All Things . . . Religious "

"Bunter," said Lord Peter, . . . "do you know why I am doubtful about the success of those rat experiments?"

"Meaning Mr. Hartman's, my Lord?"

"Yes, Dr. Hartman has a theory. In any investigation, my Bunter, it is most damnably dangerous to have a theory."

"I have heard you say so, my Lord."

"Confound you—you know it as well as I do! What is wrong with the doctor's theories, Bunter?"

"You wish me to reply, my Lord, that he only sees the facts which fit in with the theory."[1]

This detective dialogue is apposite here as we open the first chapter on a work which involves careful scientific study. It is of supreme importance to bear in mind that it is a compulsory prerequisite of successful scientific investigation to keep a clear, open mind. This is, however, one of those injunctions which, in consequence of the vagaries of the human mind, have often been taken as counsels of perfection. Especially is it important in our field of investigation to avoid the pitfalls of prejudice and preconceived notions; for, in the words of William Temple, "Where conditions are prescribed beforehand, honest study is impossible."[2]

A Yoruba folktale tells of an enchanted garden where small gourds grew in profusion. On entering the garden, one heard the clamour of several of the gourds inviting one in the most winning, persistent, almost compulsive way, "Pluck me! Pluck me! Pluck me!" There were, however, others which were perfectly calm and remarkably silent. He who was wise and would be successful in life must ignore the alluring invitations of the clamorous ones; for in them were contained all that baffled, all that embarrassed, all that stung, all that caused suffering.

[1] *A Treasury of Sayers' Stories*, by Dorothy L. Sayers (London, Victor Gollancz Ltd., 1958), p. 254.

[2] Quoted by E. C. Dewick in *The London Quarterly and Holborn Review* (The Epworth Press, January 1959), p. 7.

Let him pluck of the calm, silent ones; for on smashing them, wealth and prosperity became his lot.

For those who cannot be lured away from the path of principles by the clamour and glitter of things, there is the reward which steadiness of purpose and patient search bring.

In our field, there will be many alluringly clamorous and fanciful things; but since our quest is the truth, we must reject everything else, however tempting or sensational, which does not minister to the truth. We must guard against finding facts to fit in with certain theories.

"Mere collections of information are apt to be misleading about anything, but are certain to be about what is living and organic like religion."[1] It is important that one should be able to use the collections wisely and profitably, and that inevitably involves interpretation. To interpret objectively is a difficult task, however. It has been to many an investigator " A gulf profound as that Serbonian bog, Betwixt Damiata and Mount Casius old, where armies whole have sunk."[2] There are at least three pitfalls which are there for his undoing.

First, there is the besetting temptation to take appearance for reality without adequate verification. To avoid this has been by no means easy, especially for those who study the ways and wisdom of peoples who live in worlds of ideas and beliefs which are different from those on which they have been brought up. More often than not, errors of judgment have resulted from most investigations conducted by such people. For example, the word *fetich* has been widely used to describe the religion of West Africa. According to the history of the word, it was first introduced by the Portuguese to describe the charms and sacred emblems of West Africa. The word signifies "that which is made". Some of the explorers described the whole of Africa as a place governed by "insensible fetish".[3]

Another label which has been flung about indiscriminately is *juju*.[4] The French must have thought that the cult objects of West Africa were no more than ridiculous playthings; for the word is said to be derived from the French *jou-jou*, which means "toy". It has, however, been

[1] *The Natural and The Supernatural*, by John Oman (Cambridge University Press, 1931), p. 485.

[2] *Paradise Lost*, Book II, 591–594.

[3] *The Voice of Africa*, by Leo Frobenius (London, Hutchinson, 1913), vol. I, p. xiii.

[4] For further comments on the two words, *fetichism* and *juju*, see Chapter 7, p. 64.

employed extensively as a comprehensive expression which purports to convey all that is meant by religion in West Africa.

By these two illustrations, we see that the idea which has been circulated abroad and widely accepted is that the religion of West Africa is something without any real value—something in which barbaric crudeness is mercifully relieved by a touch of the ridiculous. The works of writers like R. S. Rattray and E. Geoffrey Parrinder have aimed a strong blow at this erroneous idea; but how successful they have been is still very much to be seen.[1]

Secondly, the question of origin is a very tempting one. There have been those who have eagerly traced the origin of every element in our native belief and culture to sources outside ourselves. The ancient civilisation of Egypt has been irresistible to such investigators, so attractive that it has become impossible for them to think even of the breath of our nostrils without going all the way to Egypt for its source! This is an excess to which a Yoruba national in his eagerness to prove the nobility of his ancestry and the soundness of his culture may easily fall victim.[2] But an unwary European explorer may be tripped up here also. Leo Frobenius became so enamoured of the religion of the Yoruba that he plainly saw in Ile-Ifẹ [3] the "Lost Atlantis" of Plato's romance![4]

Thirdly, in trying to avoid the first two errors, one is likely to fall into another, which, though less obvious, is equally dangerous. That is the mistake of morbidly shrinking from any suggestion of similarities or identification between one category of religious terminologies and another. In his book, *The Dawn of Religion*, Eric S. Waterhouse practically condemns Father Schmidt, without due trial, of illegitimately exporting Christian theological terms for the purpose of describing the concept of the Supreme Being among "primitive races". "The attributes which are recorded by Schmidt," says he, "seem to be interpreted too readily in terms of *our* (italics mine) theology, for he gives them as eternity, omniscience, beneficence, morality, omnipotence, and creative power."[5] Waterhouse seems to think that other races apart from the Europeans are incapable of apprehending the Deity in those terms. Surely, there are no ideas and categories which are created to be the

[1] See *Ashanti*, by R. S. Rattray, and *West African Religion*, by E. Geoffrey Parrinder (London, The Epworth Press, 1949), pp. 12 ff.
[2] *The Religion of the Yorubas*, by Dr. J. Olumide Lucas (Lagos, C. M. S. Press, 1948), appears to savour too much of this tendency.
[3] See Chapter 2.
[4] *The Voice of Africa* (London, Hutchinson, 1913), Vol. I, pp. 344 f.
[5] Op. cit., pp. 39 f.

exclusive monopoly of any particular race? Why should it be impossible for the Deity to reveal Himself to other races and to the Europeans in similar ways? Is there any reason why what has been thought and practised in one place could not occur in another without any previous contact between the two places? This is a question about which we cannot be too careful, for there is no point at all in creating distinctions where they do not exist merely because we fear that we may be accused falsely of employing foreign categories where they do not apply. If we find that the Yoruba have religious doctrines and practices similiar to, or identical with, doctrines and practices among the Hebrews or the Etruscans, it should be legitimate to employ in reference to the former such terminologies as have been used in describing the latter, provided they are found to be appropriate. There should be nothing to prevent us from using adequate tools with which theology or anthropology has provided us; it would be dishonest not to call things by their proper, known names.

These are points which must be carefully weighed as one undertakes a work so delicate. Otherwise, there is the danger of the confusion which arises from "mere collections of information" or of erroneous judgment which is the outcome of the wrong attitude. Already signs of these are showing themselves in a new way. There is a "modern" school of investigators who claim to be free from the handicaps and prejudices of the earlier writers—handicaps and prejudices which, according to them, include the Christian faith. By and large, however, they tend not to know exactly what to make of their collections, to rationalise, to refuse to admit that other people besides themselves are capable of thinking, and to pooh-pooh anything that is not in agreement with their own particular views. In consequence of this attitude they are likely to remain for ever like those against whom St. Paul warns Timothy: "Ever learning, and never able to come to the knowledge of the truth."[1]

We see, then, the predicament of the modern investigator who sets out upon an objective study of the belief and culture of any nation. If, however, he follows the safe course—safe but arduous—of patiently and courageously avoiding the "clamorous gourds" of fancy and preconceived notions, of bringing his predilections under proper control, of waiting patiently for and accepting the real revelations of truth as it is vouchsafed to him, he will reach a safe haven.

In our study, therefore, our main task is to go to the Yoruba in order that they may reveal themselves to us; to see them "from the inside",

[1] II Timothy 3:7.

and so learn from themselves what they know and believe with regard to the supreme matter of religion. So let us look and listen.

The Yoruba comprise several clans which are bound together by language, traditions, and religious beliefs and practices. The question of their origin is still a debatable subject, since we do not yet possess adequate material out of which we can build up the history of their beginning.

In the main, the Yoruba claim to be descendants of a great ancestor.[1] There is no doubt at all that they have been a great race. They are; and they appear in some ways to be detrimentally over-conscious of their great ancestry and long, noble traditions. Indeed, they are the progeny of great war lords, efficient kingdom builders and astute rulers. They have been enjoying for centuries a well-organised pattern of society, a pattern which persists basically in spite of all the changes consequent upon modern contacts with the Western World. Their kings have, from a very long past, worn costly beaded crowns and wielded royal sceptres. And no one remembers a time when the Yoruba have not worn clothes. Truly, then, they have their reasons for being proud of their race.

However, the real keynote of the life of the Yoruba is neither in their noble ancestry nor in the past deeds of their heroes. The keynote of their life is their religion. In all things, they are religious. Religion forms the foundation and the all-governing principle of life for them. As far as they are concerned, the full responsibility of all the affairs of life belongs to the Deity; their own part in the matter is to do as they are ordered through the priests and diviners whom they believe to be the interpreters of the will of the Deity. Through all the circumstances of life, through all its changing scenes, its joys and troubles, it is the Deity who is in control. Before a child is born, the oracle is consulted and due rites observed; when the child is born, the oracle gives directions about it; at every stage of life—puberty, betrothal, marriage, taking up a career, building a house, going on a journey and, in fact, the thousand and one things which make up human existence here on earth—man is in the hands of the Deity whose dictate is law, and who is waiting on the other side of this life to render to him as he deserves.

The religion of the Yoruba permeates their lives so much that it expresses itself in multifarious ways. It forms the themes of songs, makes topics for minstrelsy, finds vehicles in myths, folktales, proverbs and sayings, and is the basis of philosophy.

[1] See Chapter 3, pp. 22 ff.

5

As there are no written records of the ancient past of the people, all that has been preserved of their myths, philosophy, liturgies, songs and sayings, has come down to us by word of mouth from generation to generation. And all this together we shall call "Oral Traditions". These oral traditions are our only means of knowing anything at all of their theogony and cosmogony and what they think and believe about the relationship between heaven and earth. The oral traditions enable us to see that questions fundamental to religion have been asked and answered in the past, and that it is in consequence of those questions and answers that the body of oral traditions now available to us has come into being.

Two things must be pointed out at once. It will be observed, upon critical analysis, that there are groups of these oral traditions which must be pieced together as facets of one central doctrine. Failure to recognise this fact from the beginning may result in confusing, partial truths. On the other hand, there are several of them which appear to us to be mutually contradictory or inconsistent. This is often due to situations created by past and long-forgotten events and not to the fact that the Yoruba are in love with "tension but not precision" as it was once expressed in a lecture, when it was suggested rather unfairly that the Yoruba deliberately or even mischievously created tensions and contradictions where they did not originally exist. For that is very untrue. The truth is that the Yoruba are only being honest about the facts of their experiences and are often involved, like any other peoples, in the problem of interpretation. They know that life is full of paradoxes and contradictions and do not seek cleverly to blink at the truth. Here is another fact which *must* be recognised in order to make the right use of elements from this category. As H. U. Beier[1] once observed, what appear to the critical investigator as contradictions and inconsistencies do not appear so to the generality of the Yoruba, as their religion knows no dogma. Beier is quite right. The Yoruba live *in* all these elements taken together, and they form the warp and weft of their belief.

This does not mean that in our study we must suspend judgment. We only need to make a careful note of this important warning, so that we may avoid the temptation of making things too smooth by rejecting one type of material in favour of another, merely because the latter is more plausible or happens to be more suited to some pet theory. Contradictory, or apparently contradictory, traditions may in themselves

[1] H. U. Beier is a tutor in the Extra-Mural Department of the University College, Ibadan.

6

be of real value, as in them we may discern that there are probably two or more parallel or supplementary schools of doctrine on the same subject.

Now, let us look in some detail at the various elements which in sum total form the body of oral traditions.

First, the myths. From the character of our myths, they appear to be, in the main, explanatory answers to the questions posed to man by the very facts of his confrontation with the physical universe and his awareness of a world which, though unseen, is yet sufficiently palpable to be real to him. Certain phenomena stand out as unavoidable question-marks: these demand of the mind answers as to the whence and wherefore, why and how, of things. The mind of man also, however naïve, has always been an explorer into the mysteries of existence, ever roaming and recounting the results of its exploration. Children ask questions: in order to subdue their natural curiosity, something acceptable by way of answer must be given to their questions.

In the myths, therefore, we have stories ranging from the simple explanation of common occurrences related to the fact of human existence, to answers to serious riddles like those involved in the phenomena of birth, human life in all its phases, and death; questions with reference to the Deity, the whence and wherefore of the unseen world in which man feels himself enveloped, which rules, guides, or molests him. The myths thus serve the manifold purposes of statements of doctrinal beliefs, confirmation of faith in the mind, liturgical credo, simple metaphysics, and the provision of something ready to say "when thy son asketh thee in time to come saying, What is this?"

Secondly, the Odù corpus. This is a body of recitals which belong to the intricate system of divination connected with the cult of Ọ̀runmìlà.[1] They are believed to be the responses vouchsafed by the oracle through the priests to devout enquirers and suppliants, and constitute, in a systematic way, the religious philosophy of the Yoruba, which is a pragmatic one. As they are, they belong to the most fixed and reliable[2] section of the oral traditions.

We cannot tell exactly how many of the recitals there are within the corpus. However, we know that they are well grouped under headings to which are given the generic name of Odù.[3] There are two hundred and

[1] Ọ̀runmìlà is the oracle divinity. See Chapters 8, pp. 75 ff; and 10, pp. 138 ff.
[2] See Chapter 15, p. 210.
[3] Odù in this case means "heading", "section", or "chapter". See pp. 33 ff for further comments.

fifty six of these *Odù*; and to each of them, according to the *baba'láwo*,[1] are attached one thousand six hundred and eighty stories or myths, called pathways, roads, or courses.[2]

Each *Odù* has its own name and character, and falls into three distinct sections. First, there is a pithy saying which is conveyed in a verse. This verse should be clearly linked and related to the two sections which follow it, while those sections should be its amplification. This is often the case, but it is not always so; for, true to the type of an oracular utterance, it may even appear to be absolutely irrelevant or unintelligible in the context in which it is set. The reason for this may be that it has a deeper meaning than that which appears immediately on the surface; but it is often due to the textual dislocations which have taken place in the corpus in consequence of the limitations of mental records. Nevertheless, each verse has its own intrinsic value for our study, as it invariably holds some theological, philosophical, or proverbial expression. Here is an example—This *Odù* is *Iwòrì-Méjì*:

> *Ọpǎ nlá ní 'yọ agogo idẹ l' ẹnu;*
> *Òjò nlá l' ó p' èkìtì n' pẹtẹ;*
> *Ọṣun Ẹwùjì l' ó fẹ́ jẹ, l' o fẹ́ mu,*
> *L' ó rá 'rd wọ 'nú omi lọ.*

A thick rod it is that troubles the brass gong;
A heavy rain it is that reduces the anthill to mud;
Ọṣun of Ẹwùjì it is who finished eating, finished drinking,
And crawled deliberately away into the river.

The second section which follows the verse is a story; and it is the kernel of the recital from the point of view of divination. It is introduced by *O dá fún*, or *O d' ifá fún*, which means "Thus declares the oracle to or about . . ." or "This is the oracle's declaration for or about . . ." These words of introduction at the same time link up the story with the preceding verse. The story tells of a mythological character or characters to whom the oracle had spoken before under circumstances similar to

[1] This is the generic title given to the diviners who are connected with the cult of Ọrunmìlà; it means literally, "father of the cult" or "father who is versed in the mystery".

[2] *Yoruba Heathenism*, by Rev. James Johnson (England, James Townsend, 1899), p. 19.

those of the present enquirer. Thus, the lines which follow the above
verse go as follows:

> O dá fun Ẹhìn-Ìwà:
> Tí 'ṣe ẹgbọ́n Ònì
> Èrò Isìnpẹ̆, nitori Ẹhìn-Ìwà
> L' a ṣe nṣ' Ònì l' ọ̃re.

Thus declares the oracle to Ẹhìn-Ìwà ("After-Being", personified)
Who is the senior of Ònì ("To-day", personified).
O ye people of Isìnpẹ̆, it is on account of Ẹhìn-Ìwà
That we are hospitable to Ònì.

Often the story is clearly and sufficiently implied in lines as in this one
just quoted, or told in a full narrative. In either case, it leads immediately to the third section which is its practical application, its purpose
being analogical. Thus the baba'láwo tells the enquirer that he must
always be hospitable that he may have a good After-Life.[1]

It is particularly of value that the Odù corpus contains the names and
appellations of, and stories about, the Deity and the divinities. Thus, they
give us valuable material on Yoruba theogony.[2]

Thirdly, the liturgies. Here again, we feel that we are on reasonably
sure ground because the liturgies have been preserved for us almost
undisturbed for generations. We owe this to their sacredness, and the
belief of the Yoruba that the efficacy of worship depends on the correctness of their conduct. In Yoruba worship, there is nothing of the non-
conformists' go-as-you-please style. A priest approaches his appointed
task with awe, ever conscious of the dreadful fact that if the wrong step
should be taken or the right order of service be not followed, everything
might be lost and his own life and the life of the worshippers jeopardised.
We have reason, therefore, to be fairly certain that in the liturgies we have
what has been handed down intact—that is, as far as the human mind
could make it—from generation to generation.

The liturgies are the people's means of communication with their
objects of worship. It is an ingrained habit in man to call his object of
worship by attributive names. The Yoruba are especially fond of appellations and personal epithets even in their dealings between man and
man. In the old days, and to a great extent today, the kings and the
nobles have people whose main duty is to sing their praises; the nobler
and more heroic a person's ancestry, the longer the list of his praise-

[1] See Chapter 14, pp. 196 ff.   [2] See Chapters 3, p. 18; 7 and 8.

9

names and appellations. This list includes a survey of his ancestral origin, the circumstances of his ancestors and their connections and heroic deeds, and a call to him to live up to the noble tradition and prestige of his lineage. What happens on this human level happens also when the Yoruba communicate with their objects of worship. Thus, in the liturgies we learn much about the names of the Deity and the divinities, their origins or no-origins, their circumstances, their attributes and capabilities, and the hopes which are reposed in them.

Fourthly, the songs. The Yoruba are a singing people. In their singing, which comprises songs, lyrics, ballads, and minstrelsy, they tell stories of their past, the circumstances of their present, and their hopes and fears of the future. If all that a Yoruba clan has ever sung could be collected, there is no doubt that a fairly accurate history of that clan could be built up. And their songs are permeated with their beliefs. We know how often it happens that what is ineffable in consequence of the limitations of prosaic speech rides forth easily on the vehicle of poetry. For that reason, the Yoruba can put their doctrinal and philosophical thinking into expression through singing.

A good many of the songs are ancient and fixed in character. Of these are the hymns used at worship and which are, therefore, parts of the cults. This category includes also the epics and the tales of history which have been reduced to poetry. These are all informative and meaningful for our purpose.

Lastly, there are those gems of Yoruba language—the proverbs, adages, and epigrams—which have become the *sine qua non* of Yoruba speech and often convey deep theological or metaphysical meaning.

All these various elements taken together enable us to study the indigenous belief of the Yoruba "from the inside": to know what they *actually* think and believe, and not what we think that they should think and believe, in due deference to some pet theories. To achieve this study "from the inside", it is necessary to go to the people, to meet them, to see them as they *really* are, to enter sympathetically into their feelings and thus to understand that which is the keynote of their life. In order to reach the heart of the Yoruba in this way, the first place of importance for us to go is Ile-Ifẹ̀, their Ancestral Home, their Holy City. After this, and only after it, should we look elsewhere. And so, let us pay a visit to that Ancient City!

2

Our Ancestral Home

Ile-Ifẹ̀: the first of creation here below; the original home of all things; the place from which the day dawns; the enchanted, holy city; the home of divinities and mysterious spirits! That was the multifarious picture of Ile-Ifẹ̀ which used to form part of our childhood knowledge. Even today, in spite of several years of Western sophistication, the city still has a certain enchantment for the Yoruba people, if only because it is the heart which sets the religious blood coursing through their national veins.

Until comparatively recently, when easy communication has made it possible to travel almost all over the country safely and quickly, Ile-Ifẹ̀ used to be the sacred loadstone which filled the Yoruba people everywhere with a deep yearning for pilgrimage. There was ever in evidence something nostalgic in everyone, always a community of interest everywhere, about the city.

Our elders used to have (they still have) many stories—entertaining, enchanting, or hair-raising—to tell about its manifold mysteries. They told of places and things of great interest, of things permissible to the young to see, of things which not even an elder, and none at all except the initiated, might see on pain of grievous perils. For example, there was the grove of Ọlọ́fẹ́fúra: he was a divinity reputed to have the habit of hailing and welcoming visitors even from the distance with laughter and spontaneous joy as one does an old, long-missed, beloved friend. If, however, any visitor responded correspondingly, his facial features would remain permanently fixed in the contortion of mirthless laughter. How could a young, unwary, person visit such a perilously tantalising place without endangering his face! Or the shrine of the "Moon". There the "Moon" lay in the shape of a flat slab of stone. The visitor took a small piece of stone and rubbed hard on its surface. As he rubbed, he was sure, within a short time, to observe the movements of certain shadows: these were shades of people who had departed from this earth, among whom he was sure to recognise someone! He must not be startled or frightened, however, or his life would be in great danger. Therefore, that was another place out of bounds for the young and the nervous. The "moon-rubbing" might not be undertaken by anyone at all during the appearance of the moon in the sky as it was then unconditionally dangerous to do so.

A young person who was lucky enough in those days to be taken by his parents to Ile-Ifẹ̀ would approach the city with feelings which baffled analysis. He was bound to be assailed on entering the city with successive waves of emotion. He would be almost afraid to look; for at every turn might be walking or lurking, for all he knew, some divinities or ghosts!

He would be shown several places and things, however. A very impressive one would be Ọpá Ọrǎnyàn—"The staff of Ọrǎnyàn". Ọrǎnyàn, as the oral traditions have it, was a powerful hero, a warrior son of the great Odùdúwà, the royal, deified progenitor of the Yoruba.[1] When he became very old, he withdrew himself from the abode of men and lived in seclusion in a grove. From there, he exercised a quasi-divine supervision over the affairs of his children, the Ifẹ̀. In the case of an invasion, he went to their aid and, single-handed, defeated their enemies. The Ifẹ̀ were forbidden to panic, fire a single shot, or try to defend themselves in any way in such a crisis. They should rather sing and dance, after they had given out the shout, Ọrǎnyàn, ogun mà dé o!—"O Ọrǎnyàn, we are being attacked!" Ọrǎnyàn would then go forth on a charger and put the invading army to rout with much slaughter. One day, however, during a great festival, when the city was thronged with people all celebrating and rejoicing, in consequence of which wine had flowed very freely, some frivolous Ifẹ̀ became inspired with alcohol, and without knowing the harm they were causing shouted, "O Ọrǎnyàn, we are being attacked!" Immediately, the fierce warrior, blinded with the passion for carnage, came out on his charger, sword unsheathed, and began the ghastly work of wholesale massacre. (It is said that, habitually, he only stopped killing when "his charger was fetlock-deep in blood"!) He had already destroyed many before an old sage shouted to him from a respectful distance, "O Ọrǎnyàn! You are destroying your own children!" It was then that his eyes cleared as if scales had fallen from them and he realised what havoc had been done. He was deeply grieved; he sheathed his sword, turned the head of his horse and rode in silence, with drooping head, towards his grove. At the entrance, he paused and, after cool deliberation, made a solemn vow that, henceforth, he would

[1] See Chapter 3, pp. 22 ff.

never go out again in visible form to champion the cause of his children; he would defend them in future from his seat in the grove. So he planted his warrior's staff in the ground on the spot where he made the vow, and this immediately turned into stone. He then rode into the grove: there, in a sitting posture on his charger, he metamorphosed himself into rigid granite, together with his wife who in a kneeling position held up to him a welcoming calabash of cool drink. On the staff which stood several feet high were some hard metal studs which the elders described as the bullets which had been fired at the great warrior during his campaigns.

The young visitor would be taken to see *Bàbá Şìgìdì*. This would be described to him as an Ifè warrior of antiquity who, instead of dying in the normal way, converted himself to stone. *Bàbá Şìgìdì* is the granite bust of an aged personage wearing a raffia hat. The young visitor would be assured that *Bàbá Şìgìdì* still breathed faintly and winked his eyes just perceptibly and, because an elder said so, he would discern some signs of faint breathing and some just perceptible signs of winking! From the example of *Bàbá Şìgìdì* it would be explained further to the young visitor that in the old days several of the great and strong men did not die in what had now become the normal way, but changed themselves into stone or walked through a cave into heaven.

The entrance to that cave would be pointed out to him. He would see that it had been sealed up and would be told the interesting story connected with its closure. According to the story, the entrance had been sealed up because too many people were finding their way to heaven prematurely. Originally, the cave-entrance was used by both those who were old and ripe enough to go and live permanently in heaven and those who only paid visits there in order to beg for some favour or blessing. In course of time, however, people became greedy and wanted too many things in a hurry. They would go to heaven and ask for these things; and if they were told that according to their destiny they would have to wait a long time for what they wanted, or that their stores of earthly goods had been exhausted, they would become heartbroken and refuse to return to the earth. Hence it was considered expedient to seal up the passage.

Another story about the dead that would be told to the visitor was that since Ile-Ifè was the original home of all, any person who died, wherever it might be, must visit Ile-Ifè immediately in order to receive instructions about what to do next. There, he would be told whether he should go directly to heaven, in which case his feet would be set along the way; or whether he should still remain here on earth, in which case he would be told where to abide and what to do. Such a "person", when going to Ile-Ifẹ̀, must be dressed in white and hold a white fowl. At Ile-Ifẹ̀, there was a particular shrine which was the reception place for the newly deceased.

Yes, Ile-Ifẹ̀, according to the beliefs of the Yoruba, is the earthly origin and fountain of all; it is also the earthly end to which all must return in order to be told what to do next. The Yoruba are still largely positive about that. Ile-Ifẹ̀ is the origin and centre, not only of the Yoruba world but also of the whole world of nations and peoples. At one time, a stone "shoe" could be seen there, and it was said to be the primeval shoe, the archetype of the shoes worn by Europeans. There are two bodies of water in the city: one is called Ọsàrà (Ọ̀sà)—"The Lagoon" and the other Òkun—"The Sea". These are said to be respectively the original sources from which the world's lagoons and seas and oceans derived. Olókun, "The Goddess of the Sea" (a female Neptune) is one of the divinities of Yorubaland. When Leo Frobenius, the German explorer, visited Yorubaland, he was so impressed by the cult of the goddess and the whole set-up of Yoruba religion that he concluded that Ile-Ifẹ̀ was the "Lost Atlantis" rediscovered and that the Yoruba were descendants of that legendary kingdom.[1]

Today, the "mysteries" of Ile-Ifẹ̀ are being closely investigated. It is now known that Ọ̀pá Ọrănyàn was the product, with many other things of similar nature, of an ancient civilisation the full bearing of which on Yoruba history we are still to know. It is a worked, granite obelisk. There have been many suggestions about its origin, but nothing is yet known for certain. The iron studs on it are suggestive of several things. It seems, because they are set in the shape of a trident, that the obelisk was originally connected with the cult of Olókun—"The Goddess (or was this a god originally?) of the Sea". Or is it a gigantic phallus, as its shape suggests? There is also, towards its top, just before its pyramidal apex, some engraving which was probably part of an inscription; but since a part of this has been chipped off, there seems to be no knowing what it originally was.[2]

The "Moon" was only a slab of special stone which sparkled when its surface was being rubbed with another piece of stone. It was taken away a few years ago by an unscrupulous investigator, we are told. Thus

[1] Op. cit.
[2] But see *The Religion of the Yorubas*, by J. Olumide Lucas (Lagos, C.M.S. Bookshop, 1948), pp. 305 ff on the subject.

one could go on to explain that there is little mystery about many things which were once regarded with awe in Ile-Ifẹ̀.

But when all these have been said and admitted, many of the old stories about Ile-Ifẹ̀ remain substantially an expression of the belief of the Yoruba about their ancient, holy city. The religion of the Yoruba is closely related to the religion of Ile-Ifẹ̀. Most Yoruba people refer themselves back in tradition to Ile-Ifẹ̀ as their original home. The work of scientific investigators has enhanced, rather than diminished, the significance of Ile-Ifẹ̀ with regard to the history and culture of the Yoruba, even when some of her erstwhile mysteries have been stripped of their superstitious or sentimental wrappings. With the discovery there of bronzes and works of ancient art which are unique in the whole of Nigeria, the city has come into a new prominence. It is now known for certain, through her traditions and the archeological discoveries made there from time to time, that Ile-Ifẹ̀ was the home of a centuries-old culture.

The King of Ile-Ifẹ̀ is regarded by most of the Yoruba as the Father of the race as well as their spiritual leader. It is generally believed that he derives his status from *Odùdúwà*[1] whom the Yoruba believe to be their original ancestor and a priest-king of Ile-Ifẹ̀. There is traditional evidence that in the ancient days, the priest-king of Ile-Ifẹ̀ was the one in whom resided all authority, religious and secular, and that he held a pontifical sway over all. Even after the sceptre had branched off and part-authority went to Ọ̀yọ̀ and elsewhere, the Yoruba continue to look upon Ile-Ifẹ̀ as "the Home", the unique, sacred spot which was the source and fountain of all. Many kings of Yorubaland rule today because their sceptres derived from Ile-Ifẹ̀. In Yorubaland, there is a cultural organisation, known as Ẹgbẹ́ Ọmọ Odùdúwà, which has considerable influence in the country. The organisation represents the whole race and has given fresh emphasis to the importance of Ile-Ifẹ̀ as the holy city of the Yoruba.

It is clear, then, that a modern and new study of the religion of the Yoruba should centre round Ile-Ifẹ̀, although the investigator must take account of all the other important religious and civic centres of Yoruba life; for it is necessary to know also the manifold variations which obtain from place to place in order to present a balanced view of the subject.

In this connection, the town of Ọ̀bà[2] calls for special mention, because

[1] See Chapter 3, pp. 22 ff.
[2] Ọ̀bà is a village about four miles away from Àkǔrẹ́. It is called either Ọ̀bà-Ilé or Ọ̀bà Àkǔrẹ́ to distinguish it from the other places called Ọ̀bà in Yoruba country.

it too lays claim to being the origin of the earth. A careful study of its tradition has revealed, however, that there is confusion somewhere; and this has resulted from its strong attachment to the cult of Orìṣà-nlá, the arch-divinity of the Yoruba.[1]

The tradition of Ọ̀bà shows that the first Ọlọ́bà (the king of Ọ̀bà) was a member of an expedition which Ọ̀rǎnyàn[2] led into the Edo country[3]; when Ọ̀rǎnyàn was returning to Ile-Ifẹ̀ from this expedition, the Ọlọ́bà chose to stop at the place which is now called Ọ̀bà. It appears, however, that it was Ọ̀rǎnyàn who stationed him there because the place was considered an outpost between Ile-Ifẹ̀ and Benin suitable as an observation post for the safety of his kingdom. However, the Ọlọ́bà remained there and founded a town.

The Ọlọ́bà must have taken with him the cult of Orìṣà-nlá from Ile-Ifẹ̀. But this is the point at which the tradition of Ọ̀bà is rather confused. It is claimed by the Ọ̀bà people that the first Ọlọ́bà was the founder of the earth. It was he whom Olódùmarè sent, with Odùdúwà as his companion, to go and establish the earth; to him was given the loose earth in a snail's shell; and it was he who came hanging down by a chain and accomplished the work, beginning at the place which is today called Ile-Ifẹ̀. This, of course, identifies the Ọlọ́bà with Orìṣà-nlá.[4]

The question then is, if Orìṣà-nlá and the Ọlọ́bà are one and the same, how came it that the Ọlọ́bà was a follower of, or at least subordinate to, Ọ̀rǎnyàn? For Ọ̀rǎnyàn was definitely the leader of the expedition to the Edo country. How came it also that the Ọlọ́bà was stationed or chose to stop at a place of considerably less importance than Ile-Ifẹ̀, while Ọ̀rǎnyàn went back to the more important place? It is certain that Orìṣà-nlá was in every way superior to Ọ̀rǎnyàn; he was a divinity "of the heavens" while the latter was a human hero, though he became deified later. The living Ọlọ́bà today worships Orìṣà-nlá who is known in Ọ̀bà as Orìṣà Ọlọ́bà—"The Divinity who owns Ọ̀bà", or "The Divinity whom the Ọlọ́bà worships". According to the present Ọlọ́bà, Orìṣà-nlá is the supreme owner of *Kábíyèsi*—"His Majesty"—here on earth.

Our conclusion, therefore, is that the first Ọlọ́bà was a priest-king whose divinity was Orìṣà-nlá. He went from Ile-Ifẹ̀ to Ọ̀bà with both

[1] See Chapter 8, pp. 71 ff.   [2] See above, pp. 12 f; and Chapter 8, p. 92.
[3] According to history, Ọ̀rǎnyàn reigned in Benin City for a short while and then decided to return to Ile-Ifẹ̀. He promised to give the Benin a king of their own blood. He therefore took a Benin woman to wife, and the product of that union was Ewekà I of Benin City.
[4] See Chapter 3.

the cult of the divinity and the tradition connected with it. His subjects were told that their divinity was the head over all the Yoruba divinities as well as the founder of the earth. We can see the easy transition from this original belief to the tradition that the place where the founder of the earth dwelt was, in fact, the origin of the earth. And, of course, when the first Ọlọ́bà died and became an ancestral cult object, he gradually became merged, in the thought of the people of Ọ̀bà, with Orìṣà Ọlọ́bà who also was, and still is being addressed simply, and in easy abbreviation, as Ọlọ́bà. It is worthy of note that in spite of their proud tradition, the people of Ọ̀bà continue to refer to Ile-Ifẹ̀ as their original home.

3

In the Beginning

What are we taught by our forbears, according to the oral traditions, about the world in which we live? Who made this world and all its fullness? And how are the affairs of the world managed?

Someone who has made a careful study of all the material which our sources afford will have no hesitation in asserting that Olódùmarè is the origin and ground of all that is.[1] That is the fact which impresses itself upon us with the force of something incontrovertible. From all the evidence which we gather from the traditions, the Yoruba have never, strictly speaking, really thought further back than Olódùmarè, the Deity. There is no doubt that they have had their occasional worries, like all believers and thinkers all down the ages, with regard to the origin of Olódùmarè Himself; but whenever that question has raised its head, it has been nipped in the bud as the dangerous beginning of irreverent inquisitiveness.[2] The existence of Olódùmarè eternally[3] has, for all practical purposes, been taken for granted as a fact beyond question. It is upon this basic faith that the whole superstructure of Yoruba belief rests.

Then there are the divinities,[4] especially the principal ones. All the indications which have come down to us are that they were all brought into existence by Olódùmarè that they might be His ministers in carrying out, each in his own office, the functions connected with the creation and theocratic government of the earth. But as to when they began to be, we have little information. They are first introduced to us in connection with the creation of the earth and the arrangement of its equipment.

And what about the creation of the original man or woman? When did this take place, or how? Here again, we are lost in the wilderness. All that is clear is that they were made by Olódùmarè, who also fixed their destiny.[5] According to the oral traditions, some "creatures" who

---

[1] See Chapter 4.   [2] See Chapter 5, p. 46.
[3] See Chapter 5, p. 46.   [4] See Chapters 7 and 8.
[5] See Chapter 13, pp. 173 ff.

formed the nucleus of the human occupation of the earth had been in existence even earlier than the earth. The myths speak about them and refer to them simply as human beings. There have been scattered suggestions, too, that the divinities were the original occupants of the earth at its foundation, and that it was from these that its present inhabitants derived. This theory makes the divinities no more than deified ancestors, and it must have stemmed from their myths which show them very often engaged in human activities here on earth. We have little to make us doubt, however, that there are divinities who are clearly and essentially "of the heavens", quite distinct from deified ancestors, although there have been ancestors who, by the sheer force of their character, absorbed into themselves, at their apotheosis, attributes which used to belong to some of the pure divinities and so qualified themselves for the pantheon.[1]

We shall now proceed to tell the story of the creation of the earth and its fullness. What is now our earth was once a watery, marshy waste. Up above was the skyey heaven which was the abode of Olódùmarè and the divinities, with some other beings. The watery waste constituted, in a way, the sporting place for those dwellers above. Upon it they used to descend by strands of spider's web which also formed bridges by which they walked over it. Some of them came down from time to time for the purpose of hunting.

What moved Olódùmarè to think of creating the solid earth, no one knows. However, He conceived the idea and at once carried it into effect. He summoned Orìṣà-nlá, the arch-divinity,[2] to His presence and charged him with the duty: for material, He gave him a leaf packet of loose earth (some say that the loose earth was in a snail's shell), and for tools a five-toed hen and a pigeon.

When Orìṣà-nlá arrived, he threw the loose earth on a suitable spot on the watery waste. Then he let loose the hen and the pigeon; and these immediately began the work of scattering and spreading the loose earth. This they did until a great portion of the waste was covered. When enough of it had been covered, Orìṣà-nlá went back and reported to Olódùmarè that the work had been accomplished. Whereupon, Olódùmarè dispatched the chameleon to go down and inspect what had been done. The chameleon, it must be noted, was chosen on the merit of the extraordinary carefulness and delicacy with which it moves about, and the still more extraordinary way in which it can take in any situation

[1] See below, pp. 27 ff. and Chapters 7, p. 69, and 8, pp. 89 ff.
[2] See Chapter 8, pp. 71 ff.

immediately.[1] From the first visit, the chameleon took back the report that although the earth was indeed wide enough, it was not yet sufficiently dry for any further operation; from the second visit, however, it returned with the cheering report that it was both "wide enough" and sufficiently dry.

The sacred spot where the work began was named Ifẹ̀—"That which is wide", from the Yoruba word fẹ́, meaning "to be wide". And that, according to the tradition, was how Ifẹ̀, the Holy City of the Yoruba, got its name. The prefix Ilé- was added much later on to signify that it was the original home of all and to distinguish it from the other towns called Ifẹ̀[2] which have come into existence as a result of migrations.

The creation of the earth was completed in four days; the fifth day was therefore set apart for the worship of the Deity and for rest.[3] When Olódùmarè was satisfied that the work had indeed been accomplished, He sent Orìṣà-nlá back to equip and embellish the earth. This time, He sent Ọrúnmìlà to accompany him and be his counsellor. To Orìṣà-nlá, Olódùmarè handed the primeval Igi Ọ̀pẹ (Palm Tree). This he was to plant—its juice would give drink, its seed would give oil as well as kernels for food. He gave him also three other trees which were full of sap. These were Irẹ́ (Silk Rubber Tree), Awùn (Whitewood), and Dòdo. These also were to be planted and propagated: their juices would give drink. For as yet, there was no rain upon the earth. The original hen and pigeon which had been used in spreading the loose earth should now increase and multiply and provide meat for the dwellers on earth.

Orìṣà-nlá came down and did as he was told. When all was ready, Ọrẹ̀lúéré,[4] one of the beings who had been prepared beforehand, was commissioned to lead a party of those beings down to the earth. He brought them down as he was instructed and those became the nucleus of the human occupation of the earth.

When the affairs of the earth had been running for some time and its inhabitants were multiplying, it was discovered that there was not enough water for use. Therefore Orìṣà-nlá appealed to Olódùmarè and, as a result, rain began to fall upon the earth.

[1] The chameleon is sacred to the Yoruba; it is variously described as the messenger of Olódùmarè or the messenger of Orìṣà-nlá. It is remarkable for the way it can merge into its surroundings by changing its colour. Its eyes move independently of each other and so can look towards different directions simultaneously.
[2] We have Ijẹ̀bu-Ifẹ̀, for example.   [3] See Chapter 9, p. 112.
[4] See below, pp. 23 ff.

Orìṣà-nlá was assigned another special job. He was made the "creator" of human physical features for the future. It is not clear from the oral traditions when he first began to do the work. However, he got the job; and his allotted duty was thenceforth to mould man's physical form from the dust of the earth. He thus became the sculptor-divinity. But the right to give life Olódùmarè reserved to Himself alone for ever. The instruction given to Orìṣà-nlá, therefore, was that when he had completed his own part in the creation of man, he should lock up the lifeless form in a room and leave the place. Olódùmarè would then come and give breath, thus completing the creation of the human being.

A story is told of how, once, Orìṣà-nlá envied Olódùmarè this right to be the sole Giver of life. He therefore laid a plan to spy on Him. When he had completed his work one day, instead of locking up the completed forms and leaving the place, he locked himself in with them and hid in a corner, awaiting the arrival of Olódùmarè. Olódùmarè, however, by His omniscience[1] knew his crafty design and forestalled him by putting him into a deep slumber from which he awoke only when all the forms in stock had become human beings. Since then, Orìṣà-nlá has contented himself with his own allotted part of the work.

The office of a "creator" gave Orìṣà-nlá the prerogative to make at will human figures perfect or defective, and of whatever colours he wants them to be. The hunchback, the cripple, or the albino, are special marks of his prerogative or, more often than not, displeasure.

Besides Orìṣà-nlá, only one other divinity is said to know the secrets of man's being, and that is Ọrunmìlà. He was with Olódùmarè at the beginning and knew how all the work was begun and completed. He knew the secret of the existence of all the divinities, too. From the very beginning, he has been endowed with extraordinary wisdom and foreknowledge, in which attributes he is next to Olódùmarè Himself.[2] Hence he was sent to be a counsellor to Orìṣà-nlá in all matters pertaining to the world. Since his appointment, and by reason of his attributes, he has been the one major divinity whom everyone, divinities and men, consult as an adviser, guide, and director.[3]

It would seem that when the world began, everyone could travel to heaven and back as he wished[4] and that all could have immediate, direct contact with Olódùmarè. The oral traditions say that heaven was very near to the earth, so near that one could stretch up one's hand and touch it. Whether this is taken literally or interpreted as a metaphor,

[1] See Chapter 5, pp. 41 f.   [2] See Chapter 8, pp. 77 ff.
[3] See Chapter 8, pp. 77 ff.   [4] See Chapter 2, pp. 13 f.

there is no doubt that our people believe that there was a time when there were no limitations at all to communication between heaven and earth. There was a kind of Golden Age, or a Garden-of-Eden period. Then something happened, and a giddy, frustrating, extensive space occurred between heaven and earth. The story of what happened is variously told. One story is that a greedy person helped himself to too much food from heaven; another that a woman with a dirty hand touched the unsoiled face of heaven. The motif is all one—man sinned against the Lord of Heaven and there was immediately raised a barrier which cut him off from the unrestricted bliss of heaven. The privilege of free intercourse, of man taking the bounty of heaven as he liked, disappeared.

Although it is plain that from the beginning the divinities had been ordained to be ministers of Olódùmarè in the theocratic government of the world, a study of the oral traditions suggests, nevertheless, that the "Fall" of man has considerably enhanced their mediatorial status.[1]

To the myth of the creation of the earth, there is a variant which we cannot ignore. We have related above that Orìsà-nlá was the agent of Olódùmarè in the accomplishment of the work. This variant, however, makes another agent whose name was Odùdúwà the one who actually carried out the instruction which Olódùmarè gave to Orìsà-nlá; and that happened in this way. When Orìsà-nlá had got his instructions, he left the presence of Olódùmarè in order to go and do as he was told. On his way, he became very thirsty and drank his fill of a tempting supply of palm-wine which happened to be around. In consequence of that, he became drunk and fell into a deep slumber. We are not told for how long he slept; but the sleep must have been rather protracted. For Olódùmarè became worried about him and had to send Odùdúwà to go and find out why it took him so long to return. Odùdúwà came down, descending by a chain, and found Orìsà-nlá lying helpless. He did not wake him up or pity his sorry plight; he simply collected quietly the material and tools handed to him by Olódùmarè and went to perform the task. Apparently, Odùdúwà's action received the approval of Olódùmarè because, as the myth has it, he thereby supplanted Orìsà-nlá, not only in the honour of being the creator of the solid earth, but also in seniority over all the other divinities.

We have said that this variant could not be ignored because it raises a very significant question which involves the early history as well as the religion of the Yoruba. And the question is "Who is Odùdúwà?"

[1] See Chapter 7.

From what we are able to gather from research work on the early history of the Yoruba, we learn that the personage who has been given the name *Odùdúwà* was the powerful leader under whom the nucleus of a strand of the present Yoruba race migrated into this land from their original home. He was a man of strong repute, capable in leadership, with a personality which dominated the scene. It is not certain what his original name was; but it could not have been Odùdúwà.[1] During the course of history, his figure has become wrapped in legend to the extent that we can now only dimly discern the concrete outlines of the original. There is no doubt, however, that he lived in Ile-Ifẹ̀, the capital city from which he ruled over the land and held sway over a wide area through conquest or by sheer force of an overwhelming influence. Among his followers were distinguished warriors by whose aid he established a Yoruba dynasty. Today, he is acknowledged by the Yoruba as the progenitor of their race; for, as the tradition has it, he begat several children who in due course became the progenitors of the various clans which, taken together, are the Yoruba people.

We learn from the oral traditions that when *Odùdúwà* arrived in Ile-Ifẹ̀ there was already a community of aboriginal people under the headship of Ọrẹ̀lúéré.[2] The tradition persists that when *Odùdúwà* arrived with his colonising party, he at first did not pay any respect to Ọrẹ̀lúéré or recognise his headship. He was haughty and disdainful in his attitude. Ọrẹ̀lúéré at once planned to teach him a lesson. He therefore found a way of poisoning one of his daughters. *Odùdúwà* tried every remedy he could to cure the young woman of her malady but all to no avail. Then he was informed that Ọrẹ̀lúéré was a skilful doctor and that it was only he who could cure the malady. This made him run to Ọrẹ̀lúéré for help; and that gave Ọrẹ̀lúéré the opportunity of reprimanding him for his haughtiness and disrespect. *Odùdúwà* was made to pay fines of sheep and fowls, after which his daughter was cured. By this, *Odùdúwà* placed himself, if only temporarily, under the protection of the original divinity of the land, who was Orìṣà-nlá, the tutelary divinity of Ọrẹ̀lúéré and his people.

For a long time in Ile-Ifẹ̀, Ọrẹ̀lúéré as an "ancestor" was the guardian of domestic morality and preserver of sound family traditions. When he was alive those who broke any *tabu* in connection with these had to go before him, or before his image after his death, to make their confession and undergo the prescribed penance.

It is certain then, that the incursion of *Odùdúwà* and his party, with

[1] See below, pp. 25 f.   [2] See above, p. 20.

his domineering claims, was not unopposed; and while the opposition must have been rather weak in consequence of the superior resources available to *Odùdúwà*, it did not die down altogether for a very long time. Everything points to the fact that it was at this time that the *Ògbóni* cult began.[1] This was a secret cult formed, in all probability, to protect the indigenous institutions of the land from annihilation under the influence of the new regime. It must have been originally an exclusive organisation limited to the original owners of the land. The cult object of the *Ògbóni* is called *Onile*—"The Landlord"—in contradistinction from the "interloper" who was Odùdúwà, the cult object of the new people.[2] The members were bound to secrecy, and membership was by a dreadful initiation: no member should reveal any secret of the cult to the "stranger" or the uninitiated on pain of death.

The cult must have remained an underground movement for a long period while *Odùdúwà* was busy possessing the land and spreading his power over it. *Odùdúwà* settled down and organised steadily and extensively, however, and children were born to him and his party by indigenous women of the land; and so people of mixed blood who would be at home in both worlds of the old and the new began to come into being. Mutual assimilation, in part at least, took place between the new element and the old, with the result that a sympathetic link was forged between the two. There were now people who were without bitterness towards either of the opposing parties.

By the time that *Odùdúwà* died, this sympathetic link had become sufficiently strong to be of considerable influence. After his death, he became an ancestral cult object within the setting of Ancestor-worship; but the memory of his prowess and his influence which persisted in a haunting way soon qualified him for a place in the pantheon. That promotion has produced "a riddle inside an enigma"; for in consequence of it we are now confronted, not only with the question: "Who created the solid earth—Orìṣà-nlá or Odùdúwà?" but also with the question: "Was Odùdúwà a god or a goddess?" This second question we must tackle first.

The factual answer which we have to the question of the sex of Odùdúwà in Yorubaland today is that Odùdúwà is accepted as either a god or a goddess, depending upon the locality. Ile-Ifẹ̀ presents a god under the name; and so also do all the other parts of Yorubaland which

[1] See *Sacred Wood Carvings*, by H. U. Beier (a special "Nigeria Magazine" production, July 1957), the pages of which are not numbered.
[2] See below, p. 26.

derive from Ile-Ifẹ̀ the tradition of a male-divinity Odùdúwà. In Adó, however, we meet a goddess under the name; and so also in places which follow Adó's persuasion in the matter. Throughout Yorubaland, therefore, we have the predominating traditional note that Odùdúwà is a god, while at the same time there is the weaker but sufficiently audible undertone that Odùdúwà is a goddess, both traditions claiming to belong to one and the same character. How do we explain this?

It is no help to dismiss the question with the matter-of-fact statement that one side is right and the other wrong.[1] The theory that the female-divinity tradition is a proof that Yoruba society was at one time based on a matriarchal system,[2] which is indeed plausible, requires more than just this one illustration to substantiate it. In order to get some direct light on the subject, let us try and unravel the problem of the name Odùdúwà itself. What does the name mean?

As the name stands, it contains, in its first part, the word Odù[3] which is its key component. Odù means in this case "the supreme head", "chief", or "one who bears the sceptre". The second part of the name is a contraction of either dá wà—"self-existent" or "existing by oneself (in solitude)", or ti o dá ìwà—an adjectival clause meaning "who created being". The full name, then, means either "The Chief who is self-existent" or "The Chief who created being".[4] The name would thus point to someone who is underived or who is the author of all that is. By forcing a combination of both meanings we have "The Self-existent Chief who created being". That is, Someone who is un-derived and who is at the same time the creator of all that is. It must have been the notion of this possible combination which has led some people to suggest that Odùdúwà is the name of the Deity Himself.[5]

This would be in order if we were to depend only on the possible meanings of the name, and especially if we were to force the combination. In our oral traditions, however, the name is never used for Olódùmarè, although it is strongly suggestive of His attributes. But it is also a name which could not have belonged to any human being. It belonged then to a divinity. In the end, we are left with the only alternative of the

---

1 See Chapter 1, pp. 6 f.

2 See article by H. U. Beier in Odu (January 1955, No. 1).

3 See Chapters 1, pp. 7 f., and 4, pp. 33 f.

4 We omit the idea of "solitude" as it does not occur in our tradition with reference to the Deity or the divinities.

5 See Ifa Amọna Awọn Baba wa, by Rev. D. O. Epega (Ode-Remo, 1956), p. 25.

second possible meaning of the name which designates the bearer as someone who is the author of all that is.

We are strengthened in this because it bears on the real point in dispute, which is the question of who carried out the instructions of Olódùmarè with regard to the creation of the solid earth.

Our conclusion is that the name Odùdúwà belonged originally to a divinity and not to the personage to whom the name was later given. It was this divinity who came into conflict with Orìṣà-nlá. Orìṣà-nlá is the arch-divinity of Yorubaland; and, so far as we know there has never been any civil war in the Yoruba pantheon, although domestic bickerings are not unheard of. But from the traditions of Yoruba religion, we gather that Orìṣà-nlá was in fiery and trying conflict with a certain adversary. Wherever we have the cult of Orìṣà-nlá in full, there is an annual ritual re-enactment of a campaign, an ejection, and a coming back. In the image of him preserved at Idẹta in Ile-Ifẹ he is depicted as carrying in his hands the head of a defeated enemy; and in the one at Ijùgbẹ̀, in the same town, his face is amply decorated with the scarifications of some "foreign" facial marking. The story told in connection with this second image is that the present head is not the Orìṣà's original head: the Orìṣà had been engaged in a fierce warfare with his enemy; each time he was beheaded he had only just to stoop down, pick up the head, and replace it; but the last time he did so, he mistakenly picked up a beheaded foreigner's head, and placed it on his own shoulders, and went on fighting: it was too late when he realised what had happened, and so he has to "put up" with the foreign head!

All this is to say that Orìṣà-nlá was engaged in a fierce battle. Now, Orìṣà-nlá is never a warrior; by nature he is no fighter: he is for peace, order, and clean living. Therefore fighting must have been forced upon him by his enemy; his battle was a battle of necessity.

This enemy, Odùdúwà, was therefore, without doubt, a divinity who belonged to the man *Odùdúwà*. It was he who brought this divinity with her own cult to the land. For a period at least, the conflict went against Orìṣà-nlá and the Ọrẹ̀lúéré party; and that would mean that Odùdúwà had prevailed over the indigenous divinity. As *Odùdúwà* became established in the land, he would of course make people learn their revised article of belief, namely, that his own goddess was strongest and supreme; that it was she, and not Orìṣà-nlá, who created the earth. This must have gone down well with a good section of the people.

Later generations who belonged to both worlds found it not impossible to accept both versions of the story about the agent of creation and make

a conflation of them. This conflation is the one now generally accepted
as the orthodox story in Ile-Ifẹ̀: that it was indeed Orìṣà-nlá who got
the commission from Olódùmarè but, through an accident, he forfeited
the privilege to Odùdúwà who thus became the actual creator of the
solid earth. That this story is accepted without question today by the
priests of Orìṣà-nlá is not strange: they also have the blood of *Odùdúwà*
in their veins.

As a result of the conflation, there has taken place in some localities a
kind of hybridisation between the cult of Orìṣà-nlá and that of Odùdúwà,
which often appears as if one has been superimposed upon the other.
For example, Igbó-ọrà worships Orìṣà-nlá under the very transparent
veneer of Odùdúwà. One can easily discern the foundation cult to be
that of Orìṣà-nlá and that the other one has been thinly spread over it.

Now, why do we maintain that *Odùdúwà*'s divinity was a goddess?
We are led to see this, primarily by the goddess-tradition in the land.
Many things point to the fact that the name belonged to a female
divinity originally. Even in Ile-Ifẹ̀ where the male-divinity tradition is
strongest, there is in the liturgy a hint which strongly indicates that the
divinity was a goddess. In a brief, unemphasised point in the liturgy,
we catch the words *Iye 'malẹ̀ (Iya Imalẹ̀)*—"The mother of the divinities" or "Mother-Divinity". Even though the priest would rather call
this an aberration than a genuine part of the liturgy, it stands there,
whenever it is allowed to, as a witness. In Adó, Odùdúwà is indisputably
a goddess. She is said to be the first of seven divinity-children of whom
Orìṣà-nlá was one. Igbó-ọrà claims to have received her cult from Adó.
But, as we have observed, there is confusion in the cult at Igbó-ọrà, and
this in more ways than one. Part of the liturgy there begins

> *Iyà dákun gbà wá o;*
> *Ki o tọ́ 'ni, tọ́ 'mọ;*
> *Ọ̀gbẹ̀gí l' Adó*

> O mother, we beseech thee to deliver us;
> Look after us, look after (our) children;
> Thou who art established at Adó.

But yet, as the ritual ballad is recited, we hear phrases like "my lord",
"my husband" and such phrases as strongly indicate that a god is being
addressed.

The male conception of Odùdúwà has very likely arisen in this way
then. *Odùdúwà* was the priest of the goddess as well as the head of his

dynasty. At the time of his death he had won the respect of people far and wide, so that it was an easy matter for him to become an Ancestor deserving a cult. Before very long, however, he became identified with his own divinity and entered the pantheon on her attributes. In this way, Ile-Ifẹ̀ began to think, not of a goddess, but of a god Odùdúwà. But, before this identification, there had already been clans which had dispersed with the pure cult of a goddess; these keep on with the tradition. It must be observed here that it is almost in Ile-Ifẹ̀ alone that the male-divinity cult is strong. In most other places the man *Odùdúwà* is regarded only as an ancestor and not as a divinity.

We have the hint of the androgynous nature of Odùdúwà wherever there has been a hybridisation between her cult and that of Orìṣà-nlá, either by superimposition or through a compromise.

Let us summarise.[1] Our first story that Orìṣà-nlá was commissioned by Olódùmarè and that he created the solid earth with the material and tools supplied by Him represents the earlier belief of the Yoruba about the foundation of the earth. The variant came into being in consequence of the incursion of a foreign people which became masters of the land and therefore sought to displace the indigenous cult with their own. It is a conflation of two conflicting traditions by "children" who belonged to both worlds and therefore were making "the best of two worlds".

To these "children" compounded of the once opposing elements, there were not two traditions but two complementary sides of one tradition. By physical and spiritual heritage they were loyal to the two sides in which mutually they were involved, since these were the warp and weft of their racial being. This generation welcomed back Orìṣà-nlá and restored him to his place as the supreme divinity of the land while physically they remained *Ọmọ Odùdúwà*. It is as the irony of things would have it that the very *Ògbóni* movement which was designed to oppose *Odùdúwà* has now adopted the name *Ọmọ Odùdúwà* almost as an exclusive preserve of its own to designate its membership; for during the period of assimilation, the cult became a racial property, raised to the vital status of the major governmental organ for preserving law and order, checking excesses in kings and keeping the citizens law-abiding, and protecting civic rights.

Orìṣà-nlá came into his own again. For, today, the Sceptre of Yorubaland is in his hand; it is through him that authority to be and to rule passes to all Yoruba kings whose sceptres derive from Ile-Ifẹ̀. The

[1] This is not the place for all that can be said on the problem of Odùdúwà, especially as that concerns the history of the Yoruba.

Sceptre was handed to him by Olódùmarè and, according to the belief of the Yoruba, it has remained with him ever since. In spite of the strong compromise which has taken place, the priests of Orìṣà-nlá find it necessary to make the compensatory claim that even though Odùdúwà once supplanted Orìṣà-nlá in the honour of creating the solid earth and therefore in seniority over all the other divinities, he could not maintain the machinery of the world and therefore Olódùmarè had to send Orìṣà-nlá to go and set things right and maintain order.

It is to be observed further that Orìṣà-nlá has always, from the earliest, been the one universally recognised all over Yorubaland as the arch-divinity of the pantheon. He is *Bàbá*—"The Father", *Ba' nlá* —"Great Father", *Ba' t' orìṣà*—"Father of the divinities". Odùdúwà has nothing near this universal cultic recognition. For all Yoruba, Orìṣà-nlá is the supreme divinity.[1]

[1] See Chapter 8, pp. 71 ff.

4

Olódùmarè—The Name

As we focus our attention closer upon the Yoruba concept of the Deity in order to know what they think and believe about His eternal Godhead and attributes, it will be well for us once again to emphasise the fact that God has never left Himself without witness anywhere in His world. This emphasis is necessary because of the misconceptions which in the past and up to the present have attended certain studies on this fundamental issue.

Dr. Edwin W. Smith relates an encounter which he had with the eminent biographer, Emil Ludwig.[1] Ludwig was curious about what was the business of the missionaries in Africa. Whereupon Edwin Smith informed him about Christian work and how the Africans were given the saving knowledge of the "living, present, loving God". Ludwig was plainly puzzled and expressed his perplexity with the question, "How can the untutored African conceive God?" . . . "How can this be? Deity is a philosophical concept which *savages* (italics mine) are incapable of framing."

Ludwig and people who think like him in this matter may be entitled to their opinion that only a trained philosopher can know God. But one is compelled to ask the question, "What is Ludwig's definition of 'Deity'?" If he means by "Deity" an abstract, intellectual concept, a thing to be attained by ratiocination, then it might indeed be that Ludwig's *savages* could not frame it. But since the Deity of religion and human experience is not an abstraction but a Reality, a Being, Ludwig's premise is patently wrong, and his conclusion inevitably doomed to come to grief.

In any case, it would seem that, under the coverage of this high-sounding phraseology, there lies the bare notion that there are peoples somewhere in the world to whom "the high and lofty One that inhabiteth eternity" would not stoop so low as to reveal Himself, peoples who could

[1] *African Ideas of God*, edited by E. W. Smith (London, Edinburgh House 1950), p. 1.

not attain to the knowledge of the living God and the assurance of His being, just because they happen to have been born in some particular geographical location and brought up in their own native cultural atmosphere. One cannot help feeling, when one has heard the presumptuously sweeping things which have been said on this vital issue, that those who think and speak in this way either do not know God sufficiently to appreciate His divine nature as personal, righteous, and loving; or that through a subtle intellectual pride they have arrived at the Pharisaical stage of thinking, "If I were God, I would not have anything to do with those *savages*"!

The whole matter, apart from the definition of "Deity", pivots round the vexed question of whether the revelation of God is restricted to any particular race or creed, or whether indeed "by divers portions and in divers manners" God has spoken from the very beginning to every heart of all the peoples of the earth—all the peoples whom He has made and set in their places on the face of the earth—in the way which each understands; whether all religions in which God is not a mere abstraction but a personal, present, living, active and acting, succouring Reality are not each in its own way a consequence of the divine activity of the loving God Who is seeking man, and of man's responsive soul reaching out (however feebly and uncertainly) for Him, each according to its native capability.[1] This is not a place in which to launch out into an argument on this question. Suffice it to observe that, surely, God is One, not many; and that to the one God belongs the earth and all its fullness. It is this God, therefore, Who reveals Himself to every people on earth and Whom they have apprehended according to the degree of their spiritual perception, expressing their knowledge of Him, if not as trained philosophers or educated theologians, certainly as those who have had some practical experience of Him. It would be looking at facts through the spectacles of cultural pride and affected superiority to deny this; it would be blasphemous to say that while the loving God cared for a particular section of His world, He had nothing in a clear, unmistakable way, to say to, or do with the rest.

However, in the words of Edwin Smith, "First and foremost we must seek a factual answer to the question."[2] There is little point in theorising on a matter on which ample proofs abound, except perhaps that that might be a source of leisurely and comfortable intellectual exercise for

[1] See "Editorial Comments" in *London Quarterly and Holborn Reviews* (London, Epworth Press, January 1959).
[2] Op. cit.

some types of mind. The way to truth in a matter of this nature, as we have observed already,[1] is to let the people say for themselves what they themselves think and believe; and what they reveal to us should be the final answer to the question if we want to be honest. This does not stop us from exercising judgment in sifting evidence and interpreting where necessary, as long as we are true to our material and not working only in the service of our own theory.

We know, of course, that with growth and maturity, a people's idea of God inevitably undergoes modification by way of enrichment and correction, if the growth is in the right direction; or retrogradation, if the growth is in the wrong direction. This is, however, different from saying that God has never spoken or revealed Himself to those people at all.

We shall now begin to look more closely at the ways in which the Yoruba have obtained and interpreted the revelation which has been vouchsafed to them by the Deity Himself.

In the last chapter, one name stands above every other name. That is Olódùmarè,[2] the name of the Deity. In our account of the creation, we have met Him as the Prime Mover of things, by Whom the origin of our inhabited earth was commissioned.

We shall do well to look more closely at Him, first by examining the meaning and implications of His name. Our guiding question is, "What do the Yoruba mean when they pronounce the name Olódùmarè? What idea does the name connote to them?

At this point, it will be very rewarding for us to pause awhile and learn briefly the pregnant significance of Yoruba names in general. That would make a very illuminating study in itself, but we can only mention the subject here by way of introduction to our theme.

---

[1] Chapter 1, pp. 1 ff.
[2] See *Yoruba Heathenism*, by Bishop James Johnson (England, James Townsend, 1899), p. 8.
   The Yoruba-Speaking Peoples, by Sir A. B. Ellis (Chapman and Hall,
   1894) p. 37.
   The Religion of the Yoruba, by Dr. J. O. Lucas (Lagos, C.M.S., 1948)
   p. 48.
Of the explanations offered by the above authors with regard to the name Olódùmarè, that of Bishop James Johnson alone is based on what the Yoruba themselves think and believe; the one by Dr. Lucas is rather far-fetched; while Sir A. B. Ellis is patently in error.

Olódùmarè is used in the Yoruba translation of the Bible for the words "almighty", "omnipotent"; cf. Genesis 17:1, Job 5:17; Psalm 91:1; 2 Cor. 6.18; Rev. 21:22. The name indeed strongly implies "almightiness" and "omnipotence"; but it is not just a descriptive title of the Deity. It is the real Yoruba name for Him.

Every Yoruba name has a character and a significance of its own. No child is given a name without a cause; and that cause is not the bare, inevitable one that a child must be born before it can receive a name! Every one of the names is almost invariably a sentence, or a clause, or an abbreviation of a sentence, which can be broken into component parts. Besides, the name must tell some clear story, whether it be of the circumstances surrounding the child's birth, the state of the parents' or family affairs when it is born, or a remarkable event in the town or the general world into which it is born. Also, with the Yoruba, name represents character and the essence of personality, as among the Hebrews. It is generally believed that if a person's real name is known it will be easy to bless the person, or harm him by magic. Let us take the name Táiwò, for example. That name is, in full, Ẹnití-ó-wá-tọ́-aiyé-wò—"He who came to taste the world". That is the name given to the first child of twins. And this is the story behind it in Yoruba thinking. The second child is the senior one. When the time comes for the two to come into the world, the senior one says to the junior, "You first go into the world, taste it: if it is sweet, give me a shout, and I will come down"! It is believed that if on being born the first child for any reason does not cry, it will be really difficult to get the second one to follow. In general, every Yoruba name should be similarly self-explanatory.

Unfortunately, however, the name Olódùmarè is not as fully self-explanatory as we may have been led to expect: it is only partly so. This is because Olódùmarè is an ancient, unique name, the etymology of the second part of which has been a subject of much guess-work and debate. But it should be clear to us what the significance of the name is, if not fully etymologically, at least theologically and by connotation.

The name is made up of two words, with a prefix, thus: OL-ODÙ-MARÈ. The prefix Ol results from the ellision of the vowel "i" from Oni, which means "owner of", "lord of", or "one who deals in". Oni, in one or other of its modified forms, is a prefix which occurs frequently in Yoruba to denote ownership or one who deals in a trade or profession. For example, we have the words Olóko (Ol-óko) meaning "the owner of the farm", Oníbodè (On'-íbodè): "one who keeps the town's gate", or Onigbánsọ—(on'-igbá-nsọ): "one who mends broken calabashes". This prefix has also other characteristics which may be mentioned: but this is not a book on Yoruba Grammar!

Of the two main components of the name Olódùmarè, the key one is ODU. What word the three letters signify depends on which tone marks are placed upon its vowels. Thus it may be *Odù* which is a sub-stantive meaning "a main heading or chapter" as in the corpus of *Ifá* recitals, "chief head" or "chief" as in the title *Odùgbèdę* which means "The Chief of the smiths", "sceptre", or "authority". Or it may be *Òdù*, also a substantive meaning "very large and deep pot (container)", "the full cell in the board of *ayò*"[1] from the analogy of which it is said of a person *Òdù rę kún*—"His Òdù is full", meaning that "He has blessing in abundance", "Fortune smiles on him". *Òdù* is also used as an adjective with the meaning "very large", "very extensive", "very full", "of superlative quality and worth". Thus we speak, for example, of *òdù òyà*—"a very large grass-cutter", *òdù ayò*—"the full cell in the board of *ayò*", *òdù aṣọ*—"a cloth of superlative quality and worth". Hence *òdù* also means "superlative in greatness, size, or quality and worth."

There is, however, no way of knowing by the tone marks whether the component as it stands in the full name of the Deity is *odù* or *òdù* as there is only one traditional way of pronouncing Olódùmarè, the tone marks on the vowels of which are not affected whichever of the two words it may convey.

Odu taken together with the prefix in either case is therefore *Olódù* and means that the name indicates either someone who is a supreme head, one who possesses the sceptre or authority; or one who "contains" the fullness of excellent attributes, one who is superlative and perfect in greatness, size, quality and worth.

Now we come to the difficult part of our task. The component—*marè* in Olódùmarè confronts us with some etymological difficulty, and we can do no more, at the moment, than look at some explanatory attempts on the matter, and then draw our own conclusion.

The word is said to be a contraction of the phrase-name Olódù-ọmọ-èrè—"Olódù, the offspring of the boa". This suggestion is based upon a myth which derives from the natural phenomenon of the rainbow. The Yoruba believe, generally, that the rainbow is produced by a very large boa: the reptile discharges from its inside the sulphureous matter which sets all its surroundings aglow and causes a reflection, which is the rainbow (*Oṣùmarè*), in the sky. The matter which is so discharged is known as *Imi Oṣùmarè* ("rainbow-excrement") and is considered very

---

[1] *Ayò* is a Yoruba game made up of a board with twelve cells, six on each side, and each cell containing four seed counters to begin with. It is played by two people sitting opposite each other on either side of the board. See *Religion and Art in Ashanti*, by R. S. Rattray (O.U.P., 1927), pp. 382–390.

valuable for making people wealthy and prosperous. It is the Yoruba equivalent of the "philosopher's stone"! Whosoever could lay hold of it would never want for material possessions. It is, however, very rarely obtained, in spite of the fact that it is so much earnestly sought after, one reason being that anyone who approached the spot at the moment when it is on the ground would be consumed forthwith; and another that the reptile itself has the miserly habit of swallowing it all up again when the ritual is over! Rumours abound that some strange individuals do come by bits of it occasionally but such rumours have really never come to anything more than the swindler's bait!

Now, what has this got to do with the Deity? It is this. The myth has it that the name of this personage who is above was originally Olódù. He was the offspring of the large primordial boa, and was a prodigy from birth. Very early he acquired a reputation for prowess and goodness. For some reason, the earth could no longer contain him, and so he went to dwell in heaven. There he exceedingly increased in all good and divine qualities. But before he went up, both he and his parent had entered into a covenant that they would always remember, and from time to time communicate with, each other. The rainbow which occurs in the sky is the sign of that age-long covenant and communion between Olódù and the boa, a sign that the covenant remains for ever.

This myth, by the way, may easily be the Yoruba way of expressing the same conception as the one in the Biblical story which has it that God set the rainbow in the sky as a sign of the covenant which He made with the world.[1] Anyway, it appears to be the Yoruba way of explaining the rainbow rather than explaining Olódùmarè. The real truth enshrined in this is the fact of eternal significance that there is communion between heaven and earth.

Secondly -marè may be really two words which form the imperative Má rè. This imperative means "Do not go", "Do not proceed". The phrase may also be a descriptive adjective meaning "that does not go", "that does not move or wander", "that remains", "that continues". If it combines both senses in Olódù-marè, the implication is that Olódùmarè, the Deity, who possesses superlative qualities has also the added attribute of remaining stable, unchanging, constant, permanent, reliable.

Thirdly, the name may be taken as Ol-odù-m'árè, which written in full, is Ol-Odù-mó-Arè—"One who combines Odù with Arè"—Ol-Odù-cum-Arè. Arè is the symbol of uniqueness fixed on the original crown

[1] Genesis 9:8–17.

35

worn by the first king of Yorubaland and something of which has been
included in the crown worn by each successive Ọ̃ni (king) of Ile-Ifẹ̀
to emphasise his succession to the spiritual headship over the Yoruba
people. No other king of Yorubaland may wear the same kind of crown,
as it is a sign of supreme headship. Olódùmarè thus describes the Deity
as one who possesses, in addition to the sceptre, the unique Crown
which no one else may wear. That is, He is Head and Overlord of all
in heaven and on earth; indisputably, absolutely unique and beyond
comparison in majesty and fullness of attributes.

Fourthly, the name may be originally Ol-odù-kàrì. *Kàrì* is more
often than not used to describe the perfectly full cell in the board of the
ayò game. When we speak of *Odù-kàrì*, we mean that the cell has reached
its perfect fullness; if then any one counter is added to it, the perfectness
is spoilt. Olódù-kàrì, as the name of the Deity, means that He is One who
is absolutely perfect in superlative qualities.

Now, the question is, which of these shall we accept as the explanation
of the name Olódùmarè? Our answer is, all together. We have arrived
at this conclusion, not only by looking at the name alone, but also by a
careful study of the liturgies and the *Odù* corpus in particular, and the
oral traditions in general.[1] What the Yoruba have in mind when they
speak the name Olódùmarè, call upon the Deity in prayers, or approach
Him in worship, is expressed by all the descriptions taken together.
The name Olódùmarè has always carried with it the idea of One with
Whom man may enter into covenant or communion in any place and
at any time, one who is supreme, superlatively great, incomparable and
unsurpassable in majesty, excellent in attributes, stable, unchanging,
constant, reliable.

As we close this chapter, we must mention two other very important
names by which Olódùmarè is known. These are Ọlọ́fin-Ọ̀run and
Ọlọ́run.

Ọlọ́fin-Ọ̀run occurs frequently in the liturgies and in the *Odù* corpus
either as a title added, or as an alternative, to Olódùmarè. It signifies the
high office of Olódùmarè as the Supreme Sovereign Ruler Who is in
heaven. Sometimes, it is used in contrast to Ọlọ́fin-Aiyé—"The supreme
ruler on earth"—which, according to Yoruba belief, was the title of the
first priest-king from whom the title has passed on to the successive Ọ̃ni
of Ile-Ifẹ̀. There is the significant Yoruba saying, *Ohun ti Ọlọ́fin-Aiyĕ
ba wi ni Ọlọ́fin-Ọ̀run ngba*—"Whatever is said by the sovereign ruler
on earth, that the Sovereign Ruler in heaven will accept." This name

[1] See Chapter 1, pp. 6 ff.

36

appears to be as old as Olódùmarè, according to Yoruba liturgies and the *Odù* corpus.

The name Qlǫrun is the one commonly used in popular language. It appears to have gained its predominating currency in consequence of Christian and Moslem impact upon Yoruba thought: it is the name used mostly in evangelistic work and in literature. It occurs also frequently in ejaculatory prayers like *Qlǫrun, gbà mi o!*—"Deliver me, O Qlǫrun!", or in answer to salutations, e.g. *Ẹò ji 're bi? A dúpẹ l' ǫwǫ Qlǫrun*—"Have you risen well (this morning)?" "I (or We) thank Qlǫrun."

Qlǫrun is self-explanatory. It is composed of the prefix *Ol* (*oni*), and *Ǫrun*—"heaven". The name thus means "The Owner or Lord of Heaven". It may also be the shortened form of Olu-Ǫrun—"The Chief or Ruler of Heaven", or a contraction of Qlǫfin-Ǫrun, which may have dropped the suffix *-fin* in Qlǫfin and so become contracted to Qlǫrun.

The three names Olódùmarè, Qlǫfin, and Qlǫrun are sometimes run together in urgent ejaculation: *L'ojú Olódùmarè! L'ojú Qlǫfin! L'ojú Qlǫrun!*—In the presence of Olódùmarè! In the presence of Qlǫfin! In the presence of Qlǫrun!—the one Deity is thus called by a threefold name to express intense emotion or urgent appeal.

5

Olódùmarè—His Attributes

In the last chapter we have considered the etymological significance of the name of the Deity. We have, in that way, learnt that the Yoruba think of Him as One who possesses superlative greatness and fullness of all excellent attributes. By calling Him Olódùmarè, the Yoruba acknowledge Him to be unique in heaven and on earth, supreme over all.

We observed, however, that we cannot depend upon the etymology of the name only for a detailed knowledge of His essential attributes. And, fortunately, we have other sources[1] which give ample confirmation to what we have learnt through the study of the name, and which will give us a great deal more. With these sources, we shall find our feet on surer ground, because they bring us into actual contact with the Yoruba in the business of daily living as they think, worship, and express their beliefs. We shall learn, especially, that the Deity is, after all, not as distant from man's daily life and thought as some would lead us to think.[2] Let us, therefore, hear what those sources have to say on the subject.

A question of first importance is, "Who or what is Olódùmarè?" The Yoruba conception of the nature of the Deity is naturally anthropomorphic. But what worshipping people can wholly divest their thoughts of anthropomorphism in a matter such as this? We know how difficult it becomes in the more "developed" religions, and in Christianity, to make Him comprehensible in abstract terms to the worshipping and praying mind. We note with interest the prayer of the Indian sage Sankara[3]:

O Lord, pardon my three sins.
I have in contemplation clothed in form Thee Who art formless:
I have in praise described Thee Who art ineffable:
And in visiting temples I have ignored Thine omnipresence.

[1] See Chapter 1, pp. 7 ff.   [2] See Chapter 11, pp. 142 f.
[3] *Comparative Religion*, by A. C. Bouquet (Penguin, 1945), p. 19.

But Man really finds little satisfaction except in a Deity who lives, who has a heart, who speaks, who hears. Centuries of metaphysical thinking have not succeeded, and may never succeed, in curing man of anthropomorphism in his private thought about Him. He will ever project something of himself into his thought of Him in order to make the Unknown intelligible by analogy from that which is known.[1]

The Yoruba do little abstract thinking. Their picture of Olódùmarè is, therefore, of a Personage, venerable and majestic, aged but not ageing, with a greyness which commands awe and reverence. He speaks; He commands; He acts; He rules; He judges; He does all that a Person of the highest authority, in whose control everything is, will do. That is what we shall see clearly as we examine the detail of His attributes.

He is the Creator:

In our account of Yoruba theogony and cosmogony,[2] we have learnt that the divinities were brought into being by Olódùmarè and that the work of creating the earth was commissioned by Him. Everything in heaven and on earth owes its origin to Him. In His capacity as Creator He is known as Ẹlẹ́dă—"The Creator", "The Maker". He is the Origin and Giver of life, and in that capacity He is called Ẹlẹ́mì—"The Owner of the spirit", or "The Owner of life".

He made the rain to water the earth and to give drink to all. When the solid earth was created, only the juice of the trees which He first gave was used as water. Soon, more water was needed, and it was to Him that Orìṣà-nlá appealed; he replied by sending rain. This fact is fully acknowledged when we say, Ọlọ́run Ọba ni 'wọn 'fọn eji iwọrọ́-iwọrọ́—"It is Ọlọ́run, the King, who pours down the rain in regular flow".

Times and seasons owe their origin to Him. He is the Author of day and night. Therefore, He is known as Ọlọ́jọ́-òni—"The Owner of this day". We also say in this connection, Òni, ọmọ Ọlọ́fin; òla, ọmọ Ọlọ́fin, ọtúnla, ọmọ Ọlọ́fin; irèni, ọmọ Ọlọ́fin; òrúnní, ọmọ Ọlọ́fin.—"Today is the offspring of Ọlọ́fin; tomorrow is the offspring of Ọlọ́fin; the day after tomorrow is the offspring of Ọlọ́fin; the fourth day hence is the offspring of Ọlọ́fin; the fifth day[3] hence is the offspring of Ọlọ́fin".

The works of Olódùmarè are mighty and wondrous. One hears very frequently the Yoruba saying, Iṣẹ́ Ọlọ́run tóbi—"Ọlọ́run's works are

[1] See Chapter 7, pp. 64 ff.   [2] See Chapter 3.
[3] See Chapters 3, p. 20; and 9, p. 112.

mighty", which is an expression of awe, of wonder, of praise, in consequence of some manifestations of His greatness as the Author of things
and events. *Ọrunmìlà f' ẹ̀hìn tì, o wò títí: o ni, Ẹ̀nyin èrò òkun, ẹnyin èrò
ọsà, njẹ́ ẹnyin ò mọ̀ wipe iṣẹ́ Olódùmarè tobi?*—"Ọrunmìlà leaned back,
and gazed contemplatively: then he said, 'You who travel by sea, and
you who travel by the lagoon, surely you perceive that the works of
Olódùmarè are mighty?'" So, the Yoruba, like the Psalmist, know that
the great waters and the deep declare the glory of the great Creator's
work.[1]

He is King:

To the Yoruba, Olódùmarè is The King with unique and incomparable majesty.[2]

He is over and above all divinities and men.[3] He is the King whose
habitation is in heaven above, and so is called *Ọba-Ọrun*—"The King
Who dwells in the heavens". His majesty, which is unique and surpasses
all others, makes Him, *Ọ̀gá-ògo*—"The Master in resplendence."[4]
His resplendent majesty is of such dimension to the Yoruba that they
equate the whole spread of the sky, which they sometimes describe
also as the mat on which he is sitting, with the extent of His great and
"wide-spread" Being. The permanent canopy of heaven belongs to
Him and manifests Him to the entire world. So He is *Atẹ́rẹrẹ-k'-áiye,
Ẹlẹ́ní à-tẹ́-'ka*—"He Whose Being spreads over the whole extent of the
earth, the Owner of a mat that is never folded up".[5]

As the Great King, He has full prerogative and exercises it over all.
His will is absolute. Thus He is called "*Ọba ti dandan rẹ̀ kì 'sé 'lẹ̀*—
"The King whose behests never return void", *Alábàláṣẹ, Ọba Èdù-
marè*—"The Proposer Who wields the Sceptre, King of Superlative
Attributes".

He is Omnipotent:

The Yoruba believe that Olódùmarè is most powerful in heaven and
on earth. He is able to do all things; He is the Enabler of all who
achieve any ends. Things are possible only when and because they are
ordered by Him; they are impossible when He does not permit them or
give His aid. This is what we mean when we say, *A-dùn-'ṣe bí ohun ti*

---

[1] Cf. Psalm 107: 23 ff.   [2] Chapter 4, pp. 32 ff.   [3] See Chapter 6.
[4] "The Most High" is translated *Ọ̀gá-ògo* in the Yoruba Bible—cf. Psalm 91:1
—and it is quite appropriate.
[5] Cf. Isaiah 40:20.

Olódùmarè ṣe: a-ṣòro-'ṣe bi ohun ti Ọlọ́run kò l' ọwọ́ si—"Easy to do as that which Olódùmarè performs; difficult to do as that which Ọlọ́run enables not".

It is He alone Who can speak and bring His word to pass without any possibility of failure. He is therefore described as *Aléwìlèṣe*—"He who alone can speak and accomplish His words"—absolute fiat belongs to Him.

He is *Ọba A-ṣè-kan-má-kù*—"The King Whose works are done to perfection", because it is He alone who is capable of bringing His works to a perfect finish.

He is the One who set the machinery of the universe in motion. He can bring it, in part or as a whole, to a standstill, and set it going again, if need be. He did that, for example, when the divinities once foolishly questioned the absoluteness of His supremacy.[1]

He is All-wise, All-knowing, All-seeing:

Ọlọ́run nikan l' ó gbọn—"Only Ọlọ́run is wise" is a common Yoruba saying. That is, He Alone is perfect in wisdom and is infallible. The divinities can make mistakes. Men, as a matter of course, never come any-where near to perfection in wisdom. But Olódùmarè can never make mis-takes. It is of His own wisdom that He gives to both divinities and men.

Olódùmarè knows all things. No secrets are hid from Him. He knows all things because He sees all. The Yoruba call the extensive sky *Ojú-Ọlọ́run*—"The face (implying the eyes) of Ọlọ́run".[2] When it lightens, they often say, *Ọlọ́run nṣẹ'ju*—"Ọlọ́run is winking". He is called *Ar'inu-r'ode, Olùmọ̀ ọkàn*—"He Who sees both the inside and outside (of man), the Discerner of hearts". Nothing passes unobserved by Him. When Orìṣà-nlá planned to spy on Him at His secret work of putting life into man, He knew his crafty design and forestalled him.[3] However much a person may try to conceal his deeds, it is all known to Him. We say therefore, *A-m'-ōkùn ṣ' olè, bi ojú òba aiye kò ri i, ti Ọba Ọrun nwò o*—"He who steals under concealment, even though the eyes of the earthly ruler do not see him, those of the King of Heaven are looking at him". A line of a popular song which gives expression to this same conception runs thus: *Kil' ẹ nṣe ni bẹkùlù t' ojú Ọlọ́run ò to?*—"Whatever do you do in concealment that Ọlọ́run's eyes do not reach?" People often hand an offender over to Him for judgment by saying *Ọlọ́run rí i* or *Ọlọ́run rí ọ*—"Ọlọ́run sees him!" or "Ọlọ́run sees you!"

[1] Chapter 6, pp. 54 f.   [2] But see Chapter 9, p. 127.
[3] Chapter 3, pp. 21 f.

He is Judge:

In the Yoruba conception of "The Last Things",[1] Olódùmarè is the final Disposer of all things. He is the Judge. He controls man's destiny, and each will receive from Him as he deserves. But here on earth, judgment has already begun for every man according to his character. It is believed that the divinities punish men for any breach of *tabu* or for ritual offences; but it is Olódùmarè who judges man's character.[2]

He is Judge over all. In the myths, the divinities are often represented as bringing their disputes before Him for judgment or settlement. For example, Ọrunmìlà was once brought before him on an accusation by all the other divinities. Olódùmarè is portrayed as sitting in judgment: the divinities as plaintiff stated their case; Ọrunmìlà defended himself; Olódùmarè heard both sides; then He pronounced His verdict, by which Ọrunmìlà was acquitted.

The work and deeds of each divinity are under regular inspection, and reports are made to Him from time to time. To this end was Èṣù[3] appointed the Inspector-general. Therefore all divinities walk circumspectly in fear of Èṣù, and of the judgment of Olódùmarè.

The judgment of man's character is in His hand. The knowledge of this is one of the important facts which makes Him a concrete reality to the Yoruba. Because he is All-wise, All-knowing since He is All-seeing, His judgment is impartial. We often hear the expression *Ọlọrun mu u*— "He is under the judgment of Ọlọrun", or *O wà l' abẹ́ pàṣán Olódùmarè* —"He is under the lashes of Olódùmarè", when a misfortune befalls a person who is known to be a moral offender. Olódùmarè is often called *Ọba, Adákẹ́-dá-'jọ́*—"The king Who dwells above, Who executes judgment in silence". This refers to His judgment upon the deeds of men here on earth; although He does not arraign evil-doers before a visible judgment-seat, His judgment is nevertheless sure and inescapable.

He is Immortal:

Immortality is an attribute which stands out very prominently in the Yoruba conception of the Deity. This is emphasised in every way possible. In a sense, this is a comfort and encouragement to the worshipping soul. It is necessary to know that the Deity is alive for evermore, that He is unchanging in the midst of all the changes and decay which have

---

[1] See Chapter 14, pp. 197 ff. [2] See Chapter 12, pp. 148 f.
[3] Chapter 8, pp. 80 ff.

been the constant experience of man, if religion and life are to have any ultimate meaning. However much Olódùmarè might *appear* to be remote in consequence of His many agents who fill a large space between Him and man, it is certain that the Yoruba could not think of anything remaining if He ceased to be. The bottom would drop out of all things. Thus we find the fact of His "ever-living-ness" very dominant in their thoughts of Him. This they express in myths, songs, epigrams, and by several other media.

Olódùmarè is called *Òyígíyigì, Ọta Àìkú*—"The Mighty, Immovable Rock that never dies". This appellation makes a strong, threefold concept of the ideas of His superlative greatness, His steadfastness, and His "ever-living-ness". The figure used is of a large, very extensive mountain of very hard rock which cannot be spanned or measured by any conceivable means. And, of course, to move such a mountain is beyond the wildest probability; where it is, there it remains for ever.

A popular song says, *Fẹrẹkúfe, a kí 'gbọ 'kú Olódùmarè*—"*Fẹrẹkúfe,*[1] one never hears of the death of Olódùmarè". It is a thing which never happens.

Let us now look at three *Odù* recitals[2] which speak in support of the fact:

    (a) Ogbè Yẹkǔ:
    Kòròfo, Awo Àjà-Ilẹ,
    L' ó d' ifá fun Olódùmarè,
    T' o sọ wipe nwọn ò ni 'gbọ́ ikú rẹ̀ laílaí.

    Kòròfo, the Cult of Underground,
    Is the one which consulted the oracle about Olódùmarè
    And declared that His death would never be heard of.

The "Cult of Underground" was, apparently, a school of divination. It is not clear why the consultation was made in this case. It appears that a question arose concerning the duration of Olódùmarè's life. People wanted to know in order to make sure; and a sure way of doing that was to refer the matter to this important Cult. In our verse, the Cult is quoted as a trusted authority in support of the doctrine of the immortality of Olódùmarè.

    (b) Ogbè Yẹkǔ:
    Olódùmarè sà 'yẹ̀, ě kú mọ́;
    Gbogbo orí nfun puru-pùrù-puru.

---

[1] This is onomatopeia for the sound of a flute.   [2] Chapter I, pp. 7 f.

Olódùmarè has rubbed His head with bar-wood dust (*iyè-iròsùn*), He never will die;
(His) whole head is become exceedingly hoary.

In the myth connected with this verse, it is Olódùmarè Himself who is represented as desiring immortality and seeking the guidance of the oracle. The oracle declared that what He sought was attainable; but He must offer a sacrifice and perform a certain rite. The main part of the rite was that He should rub His head with bar-wood dust. He did that; His head became exceedingly white and He became immortal.

Here, partly, we find the Yoruba speaking in symbolic terms; white hair is the glory of old age and commands respect and something akin to awe in everyone. Olódùmarè, as the Everlasting Oldest, is pictured, therefore, as wearing the mark and glory of old age. But more about this myth below.

    (c) Ǫkànràn-Ǫsǎ:

       Ǫdǫmǫdé ki 'gbǫ́ 'kú aṣǫ:
         Yéyéyé l' aṣǫ 'gbó;
       Agbàlágbà ki 'gbǫ́ 'ku aṣǫ:
         Yéyéyé l' aṣǫ 'gbó;
       Ǫdǫmǫdé ki 'gbǫ́ 'ku Olódùmarè:
         Yéyéyé l' aṣǫ 'gbó;
       Agbàlágbà ki 'gbǫ́ 'ku Olódùmarè:
         Yéyéyé l' aṣǫ 'gbó.

    The Young never hear that cloth is dead:
      Cloth only wears old to shreds;
    The old never hear that cloth is dead:
      Cloth only wears old to shreds;
    The Young never hear that Olódùmarè is dead:
      Cloth only wears old to shreds;
    The old never hear that Olódùmarè is dead:
      Cloth only wears old to shreds.

The myth connected with this verse also has it that it was Olódùmarè Himself who sought the means of immortality. In consequence, He was told to make some sacrifice and to provide Himself with a large piece of white cloth. When the necessary rites had been performed, the white cloth was spread over Him so that He was completely covered. From that time, He became immortal. He also became invisible. People can only hear of Him, and of His greatness and majesty. Thus, naturally, He came to be held in honour, awe, and reverence.

Because Olódùmarè adds the attribute of invisibility to His immortality, He is known to the Yoruba as Ọba Àìrí—"The King Invisible": Ọba Awamaridi—"The King who cannot be found out by searching".

It must have become evident that in the last two myths in this section, there are a few things mixed up; and that therefore the myths raise one or two important questions for religion. The questions are, first, did Olódùmarè become immortal and invisible, or has He always been so? And, secondly, if those rites were performed and the sacrifices offered, to whom were they offered, and who performed the rites for Him? In answer, we can only repeat in summary here a little of what we have said on the oral traditions in general.[1]

First, we need to remember that the myths do not set out to be logical accounts of things. Like most illustrations, they are not to be pressed on all points. The main teaching of the myths, in this case, is that Olódùmarè is immortal and invisible. The Yoruba know and accept this as a given fact. But their exploring minds would, nevertheless, find some supporting explanation for the existence of an accepted fact, and hence such myths.

Secondly, we need also to remember that while these Odù myths enshrine the theological and philosophical thoughts of the Yoruba, their primary purpose is to answer the questions of the devout enquirers and suppliants who go before the oracle.

For example: if a person goes to a Baba'láwo in quest of longevity, the diviner takes his tools of divination and manipulates them until he gets the suitable Odù.[2] Under this head, he selects a verse which will be appropriate to the occasion. Attached to this verse, as we have observed, will be a story telling of an original or some prominent character— usually a divinity or the Deity Himself—who once had desires similar to those of the present suppliant and was successful in his quest by virtue of a certain prescribed rite which he fulfilled. He then instructs the suppliant to do exactly what was done by that character in the story, as then he was sure to gain his end. We can see how impressive a myth in which the name of Olódùmarè occurs would be. It is an indisputable fact that Olódùmarè has a permanent longevity; he is very "old", yet immortal. The client will certainly want to do what the oracle, through the diviner, prescribes in that way.

And so we conclude that the real points of our two myths are, first,

---

[1] Chapter 1, pp. 6 f.   [2] Chapter 1, pp. 7 ff.

an emphasised statement of the fact that Olódùmarè is both Immortal and Invisible; and, secondly, a belief in, and practice of, "sympathetic magic" as seen in the sacrifices and the white cloth to be spread over the suppliant so that the evil eye or the eye of death may not catch him!

This is a suitable place to look at the question of the Eternity of the Deity. In Yoruba theology, this is a conception which is not clearly stated. We can only derive what we know of it largely from the teaching on His immortality. It is certainly clear that He has been before all things as they came into being because He made them or commanded them to be made.[1] It is also clearly stated that no one knows His antecedent or beginning. A story gives the warning example of one Tèlà-Iròkò who made the futile attempt to investigate and prove His antecedent. This character was branded as a heretic and a liar to all generations. About him came this *Odù* under *Òyèkŭ-l'-Ogbè*:

" Èò mọ iyă,
  K' ẹnyin ó ma tŭn súré purọ́ mọ́;
Èò mọ Bàbă,
  K' ẹnyin o ma tún súré ṣ' èkẹ́ mọ́;
Èò mọ iyă, ẹò mọ bàbă Olódùmarè."
  Èyi l'o d' ifá fùn Tèlà-Iròkò
T' o sọ wipe on nrè 'ki Olódùmarè,
  Ọba a-t'-ẹni-tan f' orí gb' eji.

"You do not know the mother,
  Stop your impetuous lying;
You do not know the father;
  Stop your impetuous lying;
You do not know the mother, you do not know the father of Olódùmarè."
This is the oracle's verdict against Tèlà-Ìròkò
Who proposed to name the origin of Olódùmarè,
  The King Who spreads the mat, but yet exposes His head to the rains.[2]

He is Holy:
Here we must go warily. What can be gathered from our sources about the holiness of Olódùmarè is only by inference. The idea of

[1] Chapter 3.
[2] The Yoruba picture Him as sitting on top of the spread sky, while he is exposed to the elements in an unsheltered position.

holiness in the sense of "separate-ness" is already implied in the emphasised uniqueness of his essential qualities. He is transcendent; so transcendent is He that the fact of His immanence has received little emphasis except, of course, in the implicit understanding that He is there all the time, in control of the whole course of nature, and available to man whenever or wherever He is called upon. But the clear idea of "The Holy" in the sense of the active, swift, consuming "numinous"[1] is lacking in the Yoruba conception of the Deity Himself. This has been transferred to some of the divinities, particularly *Jàkúta*, the thunder divinity, and *Ṣọ̀pọ̀nà*, the smallpox divinity.[2] These two are prominent among the divinities as the agents of "The Wrath". In thinking of Olódùmarè Himself, the Yoruba emphasise His benevolence, the "goodness" rather than the "severity" of His character.

There is no doubt, however, that the Yoruba think of Him as both ritually and ethically holy. They have never thought of Him except as absolutely clean and pure. He is never spoken of as being involved in anything immoral. Therefore He is known as *Ọba Mimọ*—"The Pure King", *Ọba ti kò l' ẹ̀ri*—"The King Who is without blemish", *Alàlàfun-fun-òkè*—"The One clothed in White Robes, Who dwells above", *Àlà-ti-kò-l'ọnà, ikin-n' ifin*—"Whiteness without patterns (absolutely white), essentially white object."

We have already seen Him in this chapter as the Judge of man's character. We shall meet Him later on[3] as the Disposer Supreme of man's final destiny. And all these because He is transcendent, essentially pure, and righteous.

---

[1] *The Idea of The Holy*, by Rudolf Otto (London, Oxford University Press, 1943).
[2] Chapter 8, pp. 89 ff.　　　[3] Chapter 14, pp. 197 ff.

6

Olódùmarè—His Status

Hitherto, so much has been revealed to us about Olódùmarè that we
should be able to infer easily what the Yoruba believe and think with
regard to His relationship to the divinities in particular, and the universe
in general. Our sources, however, encourage us to search further,
dangling before our eyes the concrete, irresistible promise of a wealth
of material which will put the matter beyond dispute.

There have been a few things written on this theme,[1] all of which
agree in making Him of little account in the religious life of the Yoruba.
But, as we develop this thesis, we shall soon discover that the authors of
this conception of Him have erred; and they have erred in that way
because they have been ignorant of that which forms the real core of the
religion which they endeavour to study. Appearance has been sufficient
for them as the criterion of judgment.

Truly, to the cursory observer, the "gods many and lords many"
which form the Yoruba pantheon are, to all intents and purposes, sufficient for the needs of the people: to these the Yoruba address their
worship and prayers as a general rule. It seems, therefore, that Olódùmarè is a remote Deity who could be thought of or called upon very
occasionally. But we have to agree that the truth in a matter of this
nature consists not in what the outside observer thinks, but in what the
Yoruba themselves think and believe about the Deity.

In order to see clearly how the conception of the Yoruba with regard
to the status of the Deity stands, we shall do well to consider one or two
illustrations. First let us take an earthly governmental system. Think in
particular of a government which is a Monarchy. In such a state, the
function of the government is portioned out to a hierarchy of officials
at the head of which is the King. The citizens know that they have a
King; but each of them contents himself with the particular section of
the government, and the head of the department in that section, which
answers his immediate needs. As a matter of fact, he probably does not

[1] See Chapter 11, pp. 140 f.

48

bother to think, except when need be, of the supreme head of the kingdom, so long as he feels that his needs are answered. Very often, a head of a department within the government may arrogate to himself an "almightiness", by which he becomes overbearing, which makes people fear and regard him as one having a power of life and death over them. And, indeed, there are heads of departments of the government who are charged with such authority as permits them to take far-reaching, executive action with reference to the affairs of the citizens. But there occur also occasions when a citizen feels compelled to think that the head of the department, who to all intents and purposes is "almighty", is himself, after all, a man under authority. Those are, for example, occasions when he feels that he must make an appeal against an action on the part of this head of department, or when the head of department for some reason comes under discipline. As long as things go on smoothly to the satisfaction or acquiescence of all concerned, the ordinary citizen does not seem bothered as to what actual part the King is playing in the government of the kingdom. It will be wrong, however, to think, for that reason, that he is not alive to the fact that he has a King. As a matter of fact, it is his very alive-ness to the fact that he has a King that gives him the comfort and confidence of citizenship. The King to him must be a symbol of order, of provision for his well-being, and of national cohesion.

We shall go further and make a reference to the pattern of society among the Yoruba. Here the hierarchical pattern is very pronounced. In each department of life, religious or civil, communal or family, both custom and convention place each person in his own grade and lay down what should be the manner of approach between one grade and another.[1]

It is in the light of the above explanatory illustrations that we can the better understand the "attitude" of the Yoruba towards the Deity. We shall have more to say on this when we come to the chapter on the Cult of Olódùmarè.[2] Let it suffice here to say that the Yoruba are quite convinced that the world and all that is in it owe their existence to Him. They believe, nevertheless, that He has portioned out the theocratic administration of the world among the divinities whom He brought into being and ordained to their several offices. By the functions of these divinities, and the authority conferred upon them, they are "almighty" within certain limits. But their "almightiness" is limited and entirely subject to the absolute authority of the Creator Himself. There is a

[1] Chapter 11.   [2] Op. cit.

great number of them; and the prominent part which they play in the daily life of the Yoruba gives the impression that they have absolutely displaced Olódùmarè as a factor to be seriously taken into account in the devotional life of the people. For example, it is strongly believed by the Yoruba, and the belief affects their religious attitude, that Orìṣà-nlá[1] is capable of making man of whatever shape or colour he wills; that Èṣù[2] is capable of promoting good or evil with what appears to be unrestrained licence. All these are to be expected where these divinities are believed to have been charged with gigantic executive powers in their administration of the world, perhaps without having to refer the matter to the Deity Himself each time.

We shall now go on to show that the Yoruba knows, in spite of all this heavy structure of theocratic, governmental arrangements, that at the head of all, and controlling all is Olódùmarè, and that there is no time, really, when He is far away from them, or when they keep Him absolutely out of their minds. They may appear to live their lives in absolute devotion to the divinities, but underneath all their acts of worship is the deep consciousness that Olódùmarè is above all and ultimately controls all issues.

In Yoruba theology, Olódùmarè has always been placed first and far above the divinities, and all else. He is over all. In the following lyric He is being sung as One whose authority is asserted once and for all on earth:

> *Ilẹ̀ njà on Ọlọ́run:*
> *Ọlọ́run l' On l' àgbà;*
> *Ilẹ̀ l' on l' ẹgbọ́n;*
> *N'torí eku ẹmọ́ kan,*
> *Ojò kọ̀ kò rò mọ́,*
> *Iṣu p' ẹyin kò ta,*
> *Agbàdo ta 'pẹ̀ kò gbó,*
> *Gbogbo ẹiye kú tán l' oko;*
> *Igún ngb' ẹbọ r' ọ̀run.*

Earth has a contention with Ọlọ́run:
Ọlọ́run claims to be senior;
Earth claims to be older;
On account of one *ẹmọ́* (brown) rat,
Rain ceases and falls no more,

---

[1] Chapter 8, pp. 71 ff.   [2] Chapter 8, pp. 80 ff.

Yams sprout but do not develop,
The ears of corn fill, but do not ripen,
All birds in the forest are perishing;
Vulture is carrying sacrifices to heaven.

The lyric issues from a myth: Olódùmarè and Earth went out to hunt. Between them, they caught only one rat. On their return, they arrived at the parting of the ways where they were faced with the problem of what to do with the one rat. Olódùmarè claimed it as His right because He was senior; but Earth protested and claimed to be older, and that therefore she it was who must take the rat away. Olódùmarè thereupon let Earth have the rat but went back to heaven determined to show Earth how much she was mistaken. The upshot was that when He arrived in heaven, He immediately "switched off" things, with the result that all the benefits which Earth used to receive from heaven were no longer obtainable: there were no more rains; the crops failed on the farms; and all living things were perishing. Earth became worried. She took counsel of the oracle, and was advised to send the rat with apologies to Olódùmarè. The way to do that was to make a sacrifice of it. She made the sacrifice; but at first she could find no one to take it up to Olódùmarè. In the end, however, the vulture volunteered. When Olódùmarè had received the propitiation, He gave a small gourd to the vulture and told him to smash it on reaching earth's gates. The vulture, overcome by curiosity, smashed the gourd too soon after he left the presence of Olódùmarè. The result was that it immediately began to rain in torrents on earth. Every living creature took shelter and barred the entrance. The vulture could find nowhere for shelter because he was dripping wet— at each attempt to enter any shelter, he was severely pecked on the head. So he had to content himself with staying out in the open till the rain had stopped. Hence the baldness of the vulture's head, and his permanent shabby appearance!

The main point of this myth is to emphasise the supremacy of Olódùmarè; He is the One Who has the first right to, and the final say about, all things.

Olódùmarè is the Head. The *Odù* corpus repeatedly portrays Him as the Head Chief to whom all matters are referred for sanction, judgment, or settlement. The divinities very often go to Him for the judgment or settlement of their disputes. In the pure Yoruba pattern of society, anyone in this position is the head or chief of his people. Constantly in the myths, we have a picture of Olódùmarè as the One before whom final appeals go. Here is an illustrative verse under *Èjì-Ogbè*.

Àfìntí ni 'p' ẹrú,
Èpè ni 'p' olè
Ilẹ̀ dídà ni 'p' ọ̀rẹ̀
Alájọbí ni 'pa 'yèkan.

. . . .

O dá fun ọ̀kàn-le-n'-irinwo Irúnmalẹ̀
Ni 'jọ́ ti nwọn njà 're ọdọ Olódùmarè.

It is tale-bearing that kills the slave;
It is curses that kill the thief;
It is covenant-breaking that kills the friend;
It is consanguinity that kills the maternal-relative.

. . . .

This is the oracle's response to the one thousand seven hundred divinities.
On the day they were going to Olódùmarè in consequence of a quarrel.

Olódùmarè is the Disposer Supreme to whom belongs the ultimate sanction of anything proposed, the acceptance of any act of worship, the blessing of any enterprise, and the credit for the success of any priest's mediation or performance. Hence the saying, *Nwọ́n yin baba-'láwo, baba'láwo yin 'fá, Ifá yin Olódùmarè*—"People praise the *baba-'láwo*, the *baba'láwo* gives the praise to *Ifá*,[1] and *Ifá* gives the praise to Olódùmarè". After each act of worship before any one of the divinities, people conclude by saying *Ki Olódùmarè gbà a o*—"May Olódùmarè accept it"; or *Olódùmarè a gbà a o*—"Olódùmarè will accept it"; or *Olódùmarè a rán rere si i o*—"May Olódùmarè send blessing upon it". This means that all is in vain unless they meet his approval and acceptance. This is something of which every priest is aware and which every worshipper knows. It is one important reason why Èṣù,[2] Olódùmarè's inspector-general, is greatly to be feared by both divinities and men. It is believed that Èṣù inspects the details of every act of worship and makes due reports regularly to Him, and that no act of worship has achieved its end until He has given His sanction to it. Therefore, it is in the consciousness of every worshipper that *Àṣẹ d' ọwọ́ Olódùmarè, àṣẹ d' ọwọ̃ Baba*—"Sanction belongs to Olódùmarè, sanction is in the hands of the Father". That is why at the end of

---

[1] Chapter 8, pp. 77 f.   [2] Chapter 8, pp. 80 ff.

52

each petition or blessing, when people answer *Àṣẹ*—"May it be sanctioned", or "So let it be", they have in mind the complete phrase, *Àṣẹ o, Olódùmarè*—"May it be sanctioned, O Olódùmarè", or "So let it be, O Olódùmarè". Olódùmarè is thus known as *Alábàláṣẹ, Ọba Èdùmàrè*—"The Proposer Who wields the Sceptre, King of Superlative Attributes".

Olódùmarè is the Fountain of all benefits. He is the Author and Giver of all the good things that man can possess—children, wealth, possessions, good living, good character, everything that exists for the benefit of man. It is a strong belief of the Yoruba that both divinities and men draw from His inexhaustible providence. There are several illustrative myths on this point. It will be sufficient for us to quote just one from the *Odù* corpus: When the earth had been established and its trappings arranged, a personage called Àgànrara came down to visit it, and was not satisfied with the condition of the inhabitants. There was poverty; there was suffering; there was no happiness. He returned and told Olódùmarè about it, appealing to Him that something should be done to improve conditions. In reply to his appeal, Olódùmarè gave him *Igbá Ìwà*—"The Casket of Well-being". Out of this, he was instructed to distribute to people according to their needs. Thus Àgànrara became a minister of Olódùmarè for the distribution of things which would make for men's well-being. Hence the saying in *Ọwọ́nrín Méjì*:

Njẹ́ owó ti a ní ni 'ò tó ni?
Àgànrara, iwọ l' awo ilé Olódùmarè;
Njẹ́ ọmọ ti a bí ni 'ò tó ni
Àgànrara, iwọ l' awo ilé Olódùmarè.

Is it the money we have that is not enough?
Àgànrara, thou art the minister of Olódùmarè's abode;
Is it the children we have that are not enough?
Àgànrara, thou art the minister of Olódùmarè's abode.

Olódùmarè is the Author and Disposer of man's destiny.[1] Man's life is in His control; he lives and moves because He permits it. He is known as *Ẹlẹ́mì*—"The Owner of spirit or life". When the Yoruba make a promise or arrangements for the future, it is usual for them to impose the condition, *Bí Ẹlẹ́mì kò ba gbà a*—"If the Owner of life does not withdraw it"; that is, "If by the permission of the Owner of my life, I am still alive". The Yoruba believe that every act of man

---

[1] Chapter 13, pp. 197 ff.

53

is as Olódùmarè ordains. An *Odù* myth speaks of one *Alágemoteré̩-kangè̩* who came into the world to settle and work. But he met with opposition and persecution. So he pleaded with his persecutors, *E̩ jé̩' mi jisè̩ ti Olódùmarè rán mi*—"Let me fulfil the mission which Olódùmarè committed to me." This echoes the belief that Olódùmarè is the One who commits to each person the mission which he comes to fulfil on earth.

Olódùmarè controls the seasons and the course of events. He is therefore known as *O̩lójó̩ òni*—"The Owner of this day", that is, each day owes its being to Him.

He is supreme over all in an absolute sense; and His authority cannot be questioned by any one of the divinities, or by all of them together. He is in full control of all issues; and the divinities have executive powers only in so far as He permits them. Here again, the oral traditions give us abundant material out of which we can draw illustrations: An *Odù* recital called *Ìròsùn O̩s̩ó* tells of how the divinities—one thousand seven hundred[1] strong—once conspired against Olódùmarè. The matter in dispute concerned the absoluteness of His authority and control over all. They coveted His status and questioned His right to it; and so they went to Him and demanded that He should retire from His high office. He should do that at least for sixteen years in the first instance, while they would take full, uncontrolled charge of the affairs of the earth. Olódùmarè knew their folly, but told them that He agreed to their proposal; only, He would permit them to try first an easier experiment. What if they took charge of the earth as they proposed for a trial period of sixteen days? To this they all readily agreed; so sure were they of their collective ability. Cheerfully, they left the presence of Olódùmarè to address themselves to their new responsibility. No sooner had they left, however, than He switched off the machinery of the universe and brought everything to a standstill. Before eight days had passed, the divinities found themselves in trouble, and were faced with utter confusion. They devised every means they could think of to keep things going but made no headway; they adopted all the tactics they knew but failed; the heaven withheld its rains, rivers ceased to flow; rivulets became glutted with dead leaves; yams sprouted but did not develop; the ears of corn filled but did not ripen; the juice of trees was being licked to quench thirst; O̩runmìlà[2] was consulted but his oracle was dumb and the appliances of divination refused to work; the daily feasting in the houses of the divinities stopped; the whole earth was

[1] See Chapter 7, pp. 67 f.   [2] Chapter 7, pp. 75 ff.

1. Ọ̀pǎ Ọrǎnyàn, Ile-Ifẹ̀

2. Ọrẹ̀lúéré, Ile-Ifẹ̀

3a. An image from the shrine of Odùdúwà, Igbó-Ọrà

3b & c. Prominent images in the shrine of Odùdúwà, Igbó-Ọrà

4. An Ayò game

certainly going to perish! The divinities thus found themselves at their wits' end. There was nothing else they could do but go back to Olódù-marè. And so, in shame, and with drooping heads, they went back to Him and confessed their folly, acknowledging His absolute sover-eignty and supremacy over all, and pleading for mercy. The Benevolent Father laughed at their foolishness and forgave them. Then He switched on again the machinery of the universe and it immediately resumed normal running. The divinities went away singing:

> *Njé à bá f' ẽgun 'lé ṣe 'gbèje,*
> *K' á f' orìṣà ojà ṣ' ẹgbẹ̀fà,*
> *Orìṣà bi Olódùmarè kò sí mọ́:*
> *Olódùmarè mà l' ọba pàtàkì*
> *Njé ẹjọ́ a wí isẹ̀yí,*
> *Èdùmàrè l' o jàre o,*
> *Èdùmàrè.*

Be there one thousand four hundred divinities of the home;
Be there one thousand two hundred divinities of the market-place,
Yet there is not one divinity to compare with Olódùmarè:
Olódùmarè is the King Unique.
In our recent dispute,
Èdùmàrè[1] it is who won,
Yes, Èdùmàrè.

As the Head over all, Olódùmarè must be accorded His due. It is believed that the one thousand seven hundred divinities render to Him annual tributes of their substance in acknowledgment of His Lordship over them. This is certainly a sufficient proof of His supremacy. In the *Odù* corpus we have many sayings to support this. Here is one from *Ìròsùn Ọsá*:

> *Olórí l' a 'f' orí fún:*
> *L' o dá fún ẹ̀rúnlójọ orìṣà*
> *Nigbàti nwọn nkó ẹsin ọdún re ọ̀dọ̀ Olódùmarè.*

"The Head should be accorded His due":
This is the oracle's charge to the one thousand seven hundred divinities
Who must render annual tributes to Olódùmarè.

---

[1] Èdùmàrè is the usual abbreviation of Olódùmarè.

Yoruba theology emphasises the unique status of Olódùmarè. He is supreme over all on earth and in heaven, acknowledged by all the divinities as the Head to whom all authority belongs and all allegiance is due. He is not one among many; not even "Olódùmarè-in-council". His status of Supremacy is absolute. Things happen when He approves; things do not come to pass if He disapproves. In worship, the Yoruba holds Him ultimately First and Last; in man's daily life, he has the ultimate pre-eminence.

7

The Ministers of Olódùmarè

In the earlier chapters, we have referred to certain beings whom we designated as divinities. These, according to the indigenous belief of the Yoruba, serve the will of Olódùmarè in the creation and theocratic government of the world. We shall now give a closer attention to them and consider their functions in some detail.

The problem with which we are to deal here is a delicate one. It is that of resolving the age-long riddle with regard to "gods many and lords many" in religion. The subject appears to be perennial, inasmuch as it belongs to the very existence of man in his dealings with a world which, at best, he can only see darkly—rather darkly, as in a mirror, while he remains in his "native sphere".

But, that the problem arises so persistently and demands to be examined so constantly is a proof that it is real. It presents itself under several questions—Have the gods come into being in consequence of the "retreat" of the Deity from the day-to-day life of man ? Are the gods after all nothing more than a result of the intellectual fragmentation of the one Deity ? Or, are they indeed celestial overlords among whom the universe has been partitioned ? To a few aspects of this problem we shall give more attention below. Let us look now at some of the attempts which have been made to deal with it.

John Oman[1] summarises the well-known opinion of Andrew Lang on the topic. To Lang, the sorry situation had been caused mainly by the advance of culture: the moral pre-eminence of a God who could not be bribed proved too much a handicap in competition with the ravenous but serviceable ghosts or ghost-gods, and shades of ancestors; add to that the rise of autocratic institutions, and you have arrived at the reason why "the old supreme Being was obscured or superannuated or at best enthroned as Emperor-God". In dealing with this question, John Oman himself said, "Polytheism is far from being the simplest

[1] The Natural and the Supernatural (Cambridge University Press, 1931), pp. 485 f.

of all stages of religion to understand. Why did man thus break up what he must always have known to be in some sense one experience? And this is the greater difficulty that, however we explain it, at least Polytheism Proper has always gone with great progress in material civilization and with very remarkable advance in mental culture."[1]

In 1942, the Cambridge expert in Comparative Religion, Dr. A. C. Bouquet, made a concise and admirable survey of the whole field of religion and gave due place to this question. In his book, *Comparative Religion* (Pelican),[2] he is of the opinion that there is something inherent in human nature which makes pluralism more satisfying to him than a unitary conception of Reality. This, he says, is not necessarily a matter of race but of traditional culture. Among his illustrations he quotes not only African or Sumerian worshippers, but also many Roman Catholics "who prefer to address their devotions to a variety of saints and to erect in their churches a multiplicity of altars, rather than to adopt the centralised simplicity of Protestant Reformation". He sees pluralism partly as the product of the rich diversity of life, coming especially with the development of the communities.

William James approaches the matter in a practical way when he was grappling with the problem of the existence of evil in the world. He observed that ". . . practical polytheism . . . has ever been more or less frankly pluralistic . . . and shown itself well satisfied with a universe composed of many original principles, provided we be allowed to believe that the divine principle remains supreme, and that others are subordinate.[3]

Almost simultaneously, in 1946 to be precise, Atkinson Lee found "aesthetic impulse" in the forefront of the impelling motives to polytheism, adding to this the secondary motive of "a certain fascination to most minds about mere numbers of things".[4]

We have quoted these few representative thinkers to show how the problem has all along exercised man's mind. We need to point out here that "polytheism", especially "proper polytheism", does not apply to the Religion of the Yoruba as we shall amply prove in this chapter and elsewhere in this book.[5]

It will be best for us now to concentrate on the facts as revealed by our field of study and infer from them the real purpose of the divinities. After all, "facts are not to be answered by arguments".

[1] Op. cit., p. 369.   [2] See Chapter 5.
[3] *The Varieties of Religious Experience* (London, Longmans, 1945), p. 129.
[4] *Groundwork of the Philosophy of Religion* (London, Duckworth), p. 215.
[5] See especially Chapters 11 and 15.

The Yoruba designate the divinities by the generic name of *Orìṣà*. This is a name the etymology of which is rather obscure. There have been attempts, of course, to find out how it is derived,[1] and it is among such attempts that we must class the following myth.

As the myth has it, the name *Orìṣà* was first used in designating the arch-divinity of Yorubaland. The arch-divinity and Ọ̀runmìlà had descended into the world to fulfil the functions allotted to them by Olódùmarè,[2] and the affairs of the world had been running smoothly for some time when, for some reason, the arch-divinity decided that he wanted a slave. He therefore went to the slave-market at Emùré and bought himself one. The name of that slave was Àtọwọ́dá (That-which-one-brings-upon-one's-own-head). Àtọwọ́dá proved very serviceable at the beginning and so gave his master much satisfaction. On the third day after he was bought, he asked if his master would kindly let him have a piece of land for cultivation. To this request the arch-divinity readily gave his consent and allocated to him a piece of land on the side of a hill situated not far from his home. In two days, Àtọwọ́dá had cleared the land, made a farm, and built a hut. This impressed his master the more, so much so that he reposed every confidence in his apparently good slave. But Àtọwọ́dá was not good at heart; for he somehow developed the desire to murder his master. He was only biding his time, thinking of the best ways and means of carrying out his purpose. He soon found a way. There were large stones embedded in the soil of his farm, and he discovered that by loosening the soil under one of those stones, he could easily set it rolling downhill to crush his unwary master any time the latter was climbing up the hill to pay one of his wonted visits to the farm. Therefore, he carefully selected his stone and set to work immediately. Soon he was able to get it ready: there it lay precariously, waiting for the little push that would send it careering downhill on its errand of murder. One or two mornings later, the arch-divinity started on his way to visit the farm. From the top of the hill, Àtọwọ́dá watched him—his habitual white clothing[3] marked him out clearly. When Àtọwọ́dá was sure that there could be no escape for him, he suddenly gave the stone a push; the stone made straight for the arch-divinity; the arch-divinity, paralysed with astonishment and terror, could not escape; he was crushed to bits and scattered.

---

[1] See *Faith, Fancies and Fetich*, by S. S. Farrow (London, S.P.C.K., 1926), pp. 34 f.
The Religion of the Yorubas, by J. Olumide Lucas (Lagos, C.M.S. Bookshop, 1948), pp. 58 ff.
[2] See Chapter 3.   [3] See Chapter 8, p. 73.

The report of the disaster soon reached Ọrunmìlà who went to the scene immediately. After a short time spent in lamenting the fate of his poor leader, he performed a certain rite which made it possible for him to find all the scattered pieces. These he collected in a calabash and carried to Irànje, the city of the arch-divinity. There he deposited a portion of the pieces and then distributed the rest "all over the world" as *Ohun-ti-a-ri-ṣà*—"What was found and gathered" of the arch-divinity. Hence the name *Orìṣà*, which is a contraction of *Ohun-ti-a-ri-ṣà*. Thus began the cult of the arch-divinity "all over the world".

When the other divinities derived this name from the arch-divinity, then it became necessary to qualify the name as applied to him. So, he got the modified name of Orìṣà-nlá—"The arch-, or great, divinity". It is said that it was the arch-divinity who gave the name *Orìṣà* to his "children"—the divinities.

The significance of this myth lies in its suggestion that *Orìṣà* was originally a unity; that this is the Yoruba way of giving recognition to the process of "fragmentation" which comes as a result of giving concrete shapes in the mind to certain outstanding attributes of the Deity, or of that renaming, due to circumstances, by which one and the same divinity becomes apparently several divinities. It does not really answer the question about the meaning and derivation of the name *Orìṣà*. Therefore, we have to look elsewhere for its real derivation. I am very inclined to the view that the name *Orìṣà* is a corruption of an original name *Orìṣè* (*Ori-ṣè*)—"Head-Source". Orí is "head". It is the name for man's physical head. It means also, however (and, I think, primarily), the essence of personality, the ego.[1] *Ṣè* in Yoruba is a verb meaning "to originate", "to begin", "to derive or spring (from)". The name *Orí-ṣè* then would be an ellipsis of *Ibiti-orí-ti-ṣè*—"The Origin or Source of Orí". Now, what is this Origin, or "Head-Source"? It is the Deity Himself, the Great *Orí* from whom all *orí* derive, inasmuch as He is the Source and Giver of each of them.

I am strengthened in this view of the derivation of the name by the analogy of the Igbo *Chi*. In a general sense, *chi* is the essence of personality, or the personality-soul. The generic name for the divinities is also *chi*. All *chi*, man's or the *chi* which is the divinity, derive from Chi-Uku, the Great *Chi* which is the Deity. So that either the Yoruba *orí* or the Igbo *chi* means, in the general sense, that essence which derive from the Head-Source, the Great Source of all life and being, the Source from which all take their origin.

[1] Chapter 13, pp. 170 f.

In Yoruba, the name *Orìṣè* (the original form), then, refers originally to Olódùmarè. This is borne out by the fact that the name *Orìṣà* is applied to Him in some parts of Yorubaland, even though He is indisputably *not* one among the *divinities*.[1] The original Orìṣè is His common name in Ọ̀wọ̀ and district, and among the Itsekiri and Western Ijaw. We must take account also of the fact that Orìṣè-nlá and some of the earlier divinities are often spoken of as the offspring of Olódùmarè, in the sense that they all derived from Him. That, in fact, is why they are entitled to the generic name of divinities. Thus, the divinities would be the small *orìṣè*, taking their name as their origin from Orìṣè, Olódùmarè Himself. *Orìṣà* is only a corruption of *orìṣè*.

The name *orìṣà* is used exclusively for the divinities, and never for any ordinary spirits. When it is applied to man—usually a king—it carries the connotation that he derives his authority to rule from the divinities and ultimately from the Deity, and that he is a visible, concrete symbol of the theocratic government of the world. More often than not, however, the title used for man is *Ibìkejì Orìṣà*—"Deputy *Orìṣà*".

By connotation, *orìṣà* brings to the mind the image of beings with personal, if not physical, certainly anthropomorphous, qualities which make them individual realities to their worshippers and qualify them for their functions in the world of men. The conception of their anthropomorphous qualities is well substantiated in some of the myths which represent a good many of them as culpably too much like human beings in waywardness!

There are a few other generic names by which the Yoruba designate the divinities. A common one, next to *orìṣà*, is *Imalè*. This is less frequent than *orìṣà*, although it is now as universally employed and has its place in the oral traditions. It is also interchangeable with *orìṣà* as, for practical purposes, the two have become synonymous. We are again in difficulty when we come to the derivation of *Imalè*. It would seem that, earlier on, the name was used in a restricted sense of divinities or spirits which were connected in a specific way with the earth. In consequence of my discussion on the subject with some elders and friends, I have adopted the tentative conclusion that the name is a contraction of *Ẹ̀mọ̀-tí-mbẹ-n' ilẹ̀*—"The supernormal beings of the earth". The name would thus connote divinities who were of a different supernormal order from the *orìṣà*. It suggests awesomeness, eeriness, the *mysterium tremendum*,[2] whereas *orìṣà* is somewhat prosaic and homely. Therefore, it

[1] See below, p. 62.
[2] *The Idea of the Holy*, by Rudolf Otto (London, Oxford University Press, 1943).

would seem that while *orìṣà* was originally used for the divinities who were in a way "familiar" and were an essential part of man's life, *imalè* was the designation for the dreadful ones whose habitations were the thick, dark groves and unusual places; those who walk the world of men at night and prowl the place at noonday; the very thought of whom was hair-raising; to pass by whose groves was blood-curdling; with whom man feels compelled to make terms for his own safety; more propitiated out of fear than worshipped in reverence.

Since *imalè* has become more loosely used, however, it has lost something of its connotation of dread.

According to Yoruba theology, the *orìṣà* were brought forth by Olódùmarè. We do not know by what method they were produced; but the strong suggestion of our oral traditions is that they were either engendered by Him or that they emanated from Him.[1] Orìṣà-nlá, who is the oldest among the divinities and from whose "scattered pieces" a number of them are believed to have been constituted, is definitely called His offspring in the sense that he derived directly from Him. Anyway, they are beings of a higher order than man in consequence of their nature and functions. They have been employed, from the very beginning, in duties connected with the earth and its fullness.[2] Thus, they are the ministers of Olódùmarè, looking after the affairs of His universe and acting as intermediaries between Him and the world of men. To each of them is assigned a department over which he is ruler and governor.

All together, the *orìṣà* form the Yoruba pantheon. Olódùmarè is *not* one among them. He is "wholly other" than they. But they are under His constant vigilance and control, and to Him they owe absolute fealty.[3]

Arising out of the question, "Who are the divinities?" is another delicate question from which we must not run away. It is this: "Are these divinities objectively real? or Are they no more than vivid conceptualisations of some outstanding attributes and the power of Olódùmarè as manifested in natural phenomena or discerned by experience? Could it not be that it is imagination that

> . . . bodies forth
> The forms of things unknown . . .
> . . . and gives to airy nothing
> A local habitation and a name"?

[1] See above, p. 60 f.   [2] See Chapter 3.
[3] See Chapters 5 and 6 for a detailed study of the relationship between Olódùmarè and the divinities.

In answering this question, it will be relevant first to quote a dialogue which Richard Garnett[1] put into the mouths of the Olympian Prometheus and the Greek girl Elenko:

"Is Man, then, the Maker of the Deity?" she asked. "Can the source of his being originate in himself?" asked Prometheus. "To assert this were self-contradiction, and pride inflated to madness. But of the more exalted beings who have like him emanated from the common principle of all existence, Man, since his advent on the earth, though not the creator, is the preserver or the destroyer. He looks up to them, and they are; he outgrows them, and they are not. . . ."

This, in part, is very much like the saying of our elders that *Ibiti enià kò sí, kò sí imalè*—"Where there is no man, there is no divinity". We must have seen, however, that these two quotations are only attempts to answer a subtle metaphysical question about which it is not easy to be positive. What we must appreciate here is that with this question before us, we are on the frontier of a spiritual province into which we cannot *really* enter unless we carry the requisite passports of experience. We must accept as indisputable the fact that to the believing, worshipping minds, the divinities are *real*; as *real* as are those ministering angels who all down the ages have been constant sources of spiritual comfort to those who believe in their existence. The divinities are, in fact, so *real* to the worshippers that they have, for practical purposes, almost become ends in themselves, instead of the means to an end which, technically, they are according to Yoruba theology. This is a fact of experience which is not to be answered by psychological arguments.

So much then can be said in answer to the question: We admit that the supersensible world is beyond us: our natural vision is too limited to penetrate its secrets; nevertheless, we have the notion that there are among the divinities those who can be no more than conceptualisations of some attributes of Olódùmarè or varied characterisations[2] of some of the few principal divinities; to those who worship the divinities and derive succour from belief in their existence, to such they are real: but to those who have outgrown them, all reality is concentrated in the Deity.

It will be proper, at this point, to discuss the emblems of Yoruba divinities. Each one of them has his own emblems according to people's conception of him.[3] To an outsider, these emblems would appear

---

[1] *The Twilight of The Gods* (Penguin Books, 1947), p. 12.
[2] See above, pp. 59 ff. and below pp. 68 ff.   [3] See Chapter 8.

crude, meaningless, or absurd. Not a few investigators have tripped up here, because they have been struck by the conspicuous place assigned to the emblems in the religion of the Yoruba and impulsively arrived at the conclusion that the Yoruba are worshippers of "wood and stone". For quite a while every one of those investigators believed firmly that

> In vain with lavish kindness
> The gifts of God are strewn;
> The heathen in his blindness
> Bows down to wood and stone.

As a result, the terms *fetichism* and *juju* were brought into being as adequately descriptive of the religion of the Yoruba.

By now, it is becoming accepted in some quarters, as we have observed, that these terms were, in fact, born of errors of judgment. The Yoruba divinities are not "things made" by hand, nor are they "toys".[1] Though the Yoruba bow down *before* the emblems of their divinities, which may be "things made", things of wood and stone, yet they do not bow down *to* wood and stone.

In the history of religion, symbolic representations have played a very important part. It is a way of making the spiritual perceptible through the material. But it is a misinterpretation not to see beyond the symbol to its meaning. By the accumulated evidence which has come down to us, the method of symbolising the unseen began with some rough-and-ready objects—a stone, a plant, or a piece of wood—to mark out sacred spots or to set places apart as evidences of the presence of the Deity. Following this was the period of plastic art when man had begun to think of his divinities as beings endowed with living characteristics in consequence of which he gave them the shapes of creatures in worked stone or graven images of wood or metal.[2] The purpose thus served is to present visible and tangible evidence of the invisible, intangible, and spiritual entity. They are only means to an end, therefore; a means which, for the nonce, man finds necessary and adequate for the apprehension of things which are supersensible.

For some reason which we cannot yet fully comprehend, the supersensible world in which we are encompassed claims to be understood, and that in a way which is irresistibly compulsive yet somewhat elusive

[1] Chapter i, p. 2
[2] See *Religion of Ancient Greece* by Jane Ellen Harrison (London, A. Constable & Co. Ltd.), pp. 35 f.

and almost tantalising. For, notwithstanding the compulsive pressure which it places upon us, we continue to find that the supersensible world is beyond our ken; that our natural faculty is too poor an instrument to search what lies within it. We therefore can do no more than take that which is "revealed" to our feeble, too-often-erring, vision. *Each With His Own Brush* is the title of a collection of works of art[1] in which are represented the way in which each nation of the Christian world has apprehended some salient truths of Christianity. As it is with this collection, so it has always been with the more general and broader field of the apprehension of spiritual things. It is to each according to his own ability. To the reflective, contemplative or speculative, the method of abstraction may lead to the goal of spiritual satisfaction. But they are a minority. To the remaining majority, fundamental truths can only be grasped when they are presented in descriptive patterns—in pictures; in something concrete, at least palpable—in the form of a modelled figure maybe, or the conception of a ladder which reaches up to heaven, with the angels of God ascending and descending by it.[2] For the two classes there is a common ground, however: each in its own way is laying claim to

> O world invisible, we view thee,
> O world intangible, we touch thee,
> O world unknowable, we know thee,
> Inapprehensible, we clutch thee!

This is the basic motif of Yoruba cultic art; for that is why they say that the home of the divinity is in heaven; and that is the relevance of invocation at the beginning of worship.

There has, of course, been a grave risk attending the use of images and symbols in worship. What is designed to be a means to an end could easily become an end in itself. We know too well how these emblems can become heavy weights tied to the wings of the soul, thus making earth-bound a thing meant for heaven. This is where idolatry comes in; and anyone who describes a religion which has become idolatry as *fetichism* is fully justified. For it is quite possible and does happen, that men can become "fools" who *actually* exchange the glory of the living God for the images of mortal man, who *actually* bow down to wood and stone. This is a sin which in its crude or refined form constantly besets religion at every stage of its development. It is in the

1 By Daniel J. Fleming (Friendship, 1952).
2 Genesis 28: 12; cf. John 1:51.

light of this that we should understand why the Old Testament prophets called idols "vanity" or "nonentity", and roundly condemned idolatry. It happened some time ago that when the arch-priest of a principal divinity in Ile-Ifẹ̀ was asked the question, "May I see the emblem of Orìṣà-nlá ?" he turned to his assistant and said in a matter-of-fact way, "This is one of our sons; he wishes *to see our father*." The emblems themselves are usually referred to loosely as *orìṣà*. As a rule, the Yoruba does not go into the analytical trouble of saying, "These are the 'emblems' or 'images' of my *orìṣà*." He only says in a sweeping way, "This is my *orìṣà*," although if the question is put to him whether the emblems were in reality the *orìṣà*, his prompt answer will be "No, these are only images—*ère*—of the *orìṣà*." The risk of taking the means for the end materialises more easily where some statues are believed to be the actual physical "body" of an ancestor who instead of dying in the normal way had metamorphosed himself into stone.[1]

When all this has been said and admitted, there is still the primary question of interpretation: we have to make the correct judgment and call things by their proper names. Whatever may be the momentary attitude of the Yoruba to the emblems of their divinities, if the question is put to them whether those were in reality the divinities or not, their answer will be an emphatic negative, because "the home of the divinity is in heaven". The fact that, in the final analysis, these emblems are no more than images or symbols is proved by the fact that they can be abandoned and replaced, if need be, without any sense of loss. Some time ago, an old statue representing a famous tutelary Èṣù[2] in Ilàrẹ́ ward of Ile-Ifẹ̀ was replaced by a new one. Upon enquiry, it was revealed that the old, "venerable" one, had crumbled away (it was a thing of wood!) and had therefore been replaced by a new one.

There can be no doubt that as man advances in knowledge and attains clearer spiritual vision, he *could* grow above this kind of material aid to his beliefs. Among the Yoruba, the *crude* or *absurd* emblems will certainly pass away with the passage of time. Already, cultural development is making even some of the best images of the land museum pieces, to the horror of our conservative elders who appear to be looking forward with sanguine hope and sadistic anticipation to the severe vengeance of heaven upon all those who are parties to the sacrilegious exposure of sacred things. Nevertheless, it will be a pity indeed if the apprehension of reality and beauty which is expressed in plastic art in religion should also pass away.

[1] See Chapter 2, p. 13.   [2] Chapter 8, pp. 80 ff.

But it seems that Man can look after himself in this matter. In spite of all changes in the external world, he will often sneak back, in the practical business of daily living, into some easier way of making contact with the unseen through that which can be seen or touched: his mind is a queer instrument and has the almost incorrigible habit of reverting to type. No one knows why Garnett so strongly suspects that Plotinus was keeping a very repulsive serpent which he called his tutelary daemon[1]; but it is certain that one could depend upon the spiritual ingenuity of Man to find some form of medium or prop to sustain his faith. We can look through the set-up in some churches, if we like. Try as it may, iconoclasm has often succeeded, by some miscarriage of purpose, only in clearing the house for new, perhaps more subtle or more absurd, images. This state of things can only be set to rights when there takes place in every heart an "expulsive power" of the spirit of God, by Whose aid only things spiritual can be spiritually discerned.

Now, to our second question—"How many are the divinities?" This is another difficult question. I have been variously informed by Yoruba elders and priests on the matter. In Ile-Ifẹ̀, we are told that there were originally two hundred and one of them represented in the palace of the Ọ̃ni, the Ọ̃ni himself being the two-hundred-and-first! The *Odù* corpus gives a confusing impression of the census of the pantheon: sometimes they speak of *Ẹ̀rúnlójọ orìṣà*—"One thousand seven hundred divinities"; often they speak of *Ọ̀kàn-lé-n'-irínwó imalẹ̀* —"Four hundred and one divinities". We are told also that there are *Igba-'malẹ̀ ojùkọ̀tún, igba-'malẹ̀ ojùkòsì*—"Two hundred divinities of the right hand, and two hundred divinities of the left hand", making four hundred. During invocations we sometimes hear

> *Ibà irun-'malẹ ojùkọ̀tún;*
> *Ibà igba-'malẹ̀ ojùkòsì;*
> *Ibà ọ̀tà-lé-n'-irún Irún-'malẹ̀*
> *Ti ó já àtàrí ọ̀nà ọ̀run gbangba.*

Worship to the four hundred divinities of the right hand;
Worship to the two hundred divinities of the left hand;
Worship to the four hundred and sixty divinities
Who actually line up the very road of heaven.

---

[1] *The Twilight of The Gods* (Penguin Books, 1947), p. 69. Garnett makes Plotinus say at the appearance of the serpent in his room "My guardian, my tutelary daemon, ... visible manifestation of Aesculapius. Then I am not forsaken by the immortal gods."

Here we have a suggestion that there are one thousand and sixty. There are still *Òjì-lé-l'égbèje irúnmalè ti nwón nlu edan fún, ti nwón nlu ìwo fún*— "The one thousand four hundred and forty divinities for whom metal rods are sounded, for whom horns are beaten". In ejaculatory utterances we gather the impression that there are six hundred of them. We often hear *Irun-'malè! Igba-'malè!* "O four hundred divinities! O two hundred divinities!" . . .

Now, what do we make of these figures? It is only this: we know that the name of the *orìsà* is legion, for they are many. The exact census of the pantheon no one is now able to tell. Whatever the original significance of the figures, therefore, they have now come to be no more than symbolic at the same time of the plurality of the *orìsà* and the indefiniteness of their numbers. So, to quote any of the figures is now only "a manner of speaking".

Having said that, we still have to face the question whether the Yoruba pantheon has always been as crowded as it now appears to be. To that our answer is that in earlier times, the divinities were much fewer. Yoruba theogony shows that, to begin with, there were only a few of them. Therefore their present number must be due to certain processes which later set in and caused them to increase and multiply.

One important factor which made for such increase was the fusion of clans. Wherever that happened, it usually resulted in the fusion of cultures as well. The cults which each party brought into the fusion would also be involved. As a result, adjustments would take place through syncretism or hybridisation. But in spite of such adjustments, there would be divinities who stubbornly maintained their identities and so counted as separate individuals, thus making additions in the existing pantheon. There would be other divinities, too, who became duplicated through adoption by other clans. Such divinities, on being adopted, did not retain their original names but took on new or modified names which were suggested by their new environments and circumstances, in consequence of which they are accepted as different from what they were in their earlier homes. So that, in Yorubaland today, one and the same divinity is worshipped under several names and (because people have either forgotten or do not know his history and circumstances) the several names have become several individual divinities. This is so, even in spite of the fact that the details of the cultus of the several individual divinities may be practically the same. In Ile-Ifè, for example, Orìsà-nlá is worshipped under three different names and, in consequence of this, three distinctive divinities have come into being out of the one: he is Orìṣà Idẹ̀ta, Orìṣà Akirè, Orìṣà Ijùgbẹ̀, according to the quarter or household which has custody of the cultus. The interesting thing about this is that there are three separate orders of priesthood and separate cultus, even though the rituals and *tabu* are practically identical. The same change of environments and circumstances was responsible for the emergence of the Yoruba conception of "the Wrath" of Olódùmarè as more than one divinity: we have Jàkŭta who was the original Yoruba thunder divinity, Ṣàngŏ who attracted the attributes of Jàkŭta and entered the pantheon on that strength, and Ọ̀ràmfẹ̀ which is the Ifẹ̀ name for the same conceptualisation.[1]

The priests must have contributed a great deal to the establishment of not a few divinities. The stronger the character of the priest, the more influential he was in the community; the more subtle he could be, the easier it would be for him to capture the minds of simple folk and lead them to accept certain beliefs. Where the priest could win the co-operation of people of the same persuasion as himself, his work is made the more effective. Some of our elders, in their usual honesty, will not hesitate to say that some of the trappings of the religion of the Yoruba were first "invented" to serve certain emergencies; but since they were found useful and good for religion, prudence has decreed that they should be allowed to stay on, and there they are today.

Hero-worship is one more important factor which certainly worked for increase in the number of the divinities. Naturally, the ancestors who live in the After-Life[2] are increasing daily. As a rule, the Yoruba make a careful distinction between the divinities and the ancestors. Strictly, the divinities are essentially "of the heavens"; but certain ancestors have found their way into the pantheon, usually by becoming identified with some earlier divinities. In this category, we have Odùdúwà[3] and Ṣàngŏ for example. Some have got there through excessive veneration by the people. Here we may take Ọbàlùfọ̀n[4] as our example. It is in consequence of these instances that some investigators have concluded that the religion of the Yoruba is all ancestor-worship.[5]

We cannot close this chapter without looking at yet one more question: "Which are the principal divinities and in what order do they come?" Here, again, we have to be careful. While a number of the divinities certainly have recognition all over Yorubaland in consequence of their

[1] Chapter 8, pp. 89 ff.   [2] See Chapter 14, pp. 196 f.
[3] See Chapter 3, pp. 22 f.
[4] Ọbàlùfọ̀n is one of the divinities worshipped in Ile-Ifẹ̀ and all over Yorubaland. But he began by being an ancestor.
[5] Cf. *Nigerian Studies*, by R. E. Dennett (Macmillan, 1910), p. 58.

places in the pantheon, there is no doubt that each of them has particular localities in which he is *the* chief divinity while in others he may be, for all practical purposes, of rather secondary status. Not a few of them belong to villages or hamlets beyond which little thought is given to them. The question cannot be settled, therefore, by the mere external appearance of things.

But our difficulty is considerably minimised when we turn to the oral traditions. These sources reveal which divinities belong to the earliest times and were closest to Olódùmarè from the beginning in creative and executive functions. From the study of our sources, therefore, we can fix the status and order of these principal divinities with regard to their relationship to Olódùmarè. Thus we find that Orìṣà-nlá, Ọrúnmìlà, Ògún, Èṣù, Ṣàngó (Ọràmfẹ̀, Jàkúta), Ṣọpọ̀ná, will satisfy our question.[1] These are prominent divinities, believed to be charged with vital functions, universally recognised and worshipped by the Yoruba.

We shall now proceed to look at these representative divinities more closely. There is yet one more: Ẹ̀là is his name. His place is not very clearly defined in the system; but he is of vital importance nevertheless. It is really his elusive yet compelling character that catches our attention. In Ẹ̀là, it appears that we may discern a spiritual principle, the full appreciation of which should revolutionise the understanding of the religion of the Yoruba.

[1] But cf. *Faith, Fancies, and Fetich*, by S. S. Farrow (S.P.C.K., 1926), p. 94.
    The Peoples of Southern Nigeria, by P. A. Talbot (Oxford University Press, 1926), pp. 30 f.
    The Religion of the Yorubas, by J. Olumide Lucas (Lagos, C.M.S. Bookshop, 1948), pp. 49–115.

5. The Head Baba'láwo of Ifàkì standing by his shrine of Ọ̀runmìlà

NOTICE (a) The vessel containing his tools of divination, which is at the same time the emblem of Ọ̀runmìlà

         (b) The statuette of Èṣù sitting in close proximity to Ifá

6a. The image of Orìṣà-nlá in his principal shrine at Idẹ̀ta, Ile-Ifẹ̀. Here Orìṣà-nlá holds the head of a beheaded enemy

6b. Orìṣà-nlá and his Consort, Yemòwǒ, Ile-Ifẹ̀ →

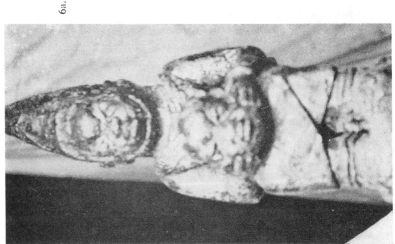

8

The Ministers of Olódùmarè
continued

ORÌṢÀ-NLÁ

Orìṣà-nlá is the supreme divinity of Yorubaland. As his name implies, he is the great or arch-divinity. It is sometimes said that he is the father of all the *orìṣà* of Yorubaland and that it was he who gave each one of them the name *orìṣà*, thus naming them after himself. Thus, the title "father" here denotes his relationship to the other divinities as well as suggests that he was the original divinity from whom at least a number of them derived. He is automatically the senior and head of them all. He is also called Ọbàtálá, the name which has been variously interpreted as *Ọba-ti-ó-nla*—"The king who is great"; or *Ọba-ti-àlà*— "King in white clothing".

According to our oral traditions, Orìṣà-nlá is very ancient. He was the very first to receive a definite characterisation,[1] and that will explain why he is described by some of our elders as the image or symbol of Olódùmarè on earth. Yoruba theology also calls him the off-spring of Olódùmarè in the sense that he derived immediately from him and that the attributes of Olódùmarè are revealed through him. The oral traditions give much emphasis to the teaching that he takes after Olódùmarè in many essential attributes: he is called by some of Olódù- marè's very significant appellations. For example, he is known as *A-tẹ́-rẹrẹ-k'-áiye*—"He who spreads over the whole extent of the earth"; he is called *ẹlẹ́dà*—"maker", since Olódùmarè has committed to him the creation of the physical part of man, as also the creation of earth and the arrangement of its trappings.[2] He is the sculptor-divinity who has been given the prerogative to create as he chooses, so that he makes man of shapely or deformed features. The hunchback, the cripple, the albino, are regarded to be special marks of his prerogative, either signifying his displeasure at the breach of some *tabu*, or to show that he

---

[1] See Chapter 7, pp. 59 f.   [2] See Chapter 3, pp. 19 ff.

could do as he likes. The "defective" in this category are called *Ẹni Orìṣà*—"The votaries of the *Orìṣà*", and should observe certain restrictions in respect of food and drink. The albinos are in a more special way *Ẹni Orìṣà* and have the heavier burden of *tabu* to bear. Constitutionally they will easily break out in disgusting spots, it is believed, if they are not careful about what they eat or drink! Orìṣà-nlá is called *Alámọ̀ rere*—"The one who deals in choice clay"—the clay with which he moulds man. We have the saying: *Ki 'ṣe ẹjọ́ eléyín gan-n-gan; Orìṣà l'ó ṣe e, ti kò fi awọ bò o*—"The person with prominent teeth is not to blame: it is the *Orìṣà* who made them and did not provide sufficient covering for them". And when a woman is pregnant, it is often the customary prayer in some parts of Yorubaland to say: *Ki Orìṣà ya 'nà 're ko ni o*—"May the *Orìṣà* fashion for us a good work of art". It is believed that when Orìṣà-nlá has finished the moulding of man's body and Olódùmarè has put into him the vital principle, he takes charge again and sends man on his way into the world, still keeping an eye on him and guiding him as he fulfils his destiny. So the Yoruba sing:

Ẹni ṣ'ojú, ṣe 'mú:
Orìṣà ni ma sìn;
A-dá-'ni b' ó ti rí:
Orìṣà ni ma sìn;
Ẹni rán mi wá:
Orìṣà ni ma sìn;

He who makes eyes, makes nose:
It is the *Orìṣà* I will serve;
He who creates as he chooses:
It is the *Orìṣà* I will serve;
He who sends me here:
It is the *Orìṣà* I will serve.

The *Orìṣà* is also called *Alábàláṣẹ*—"The proposer who wields the sceptre". This title belongs to Olódùmarè. But our oral traditions say that when Orìṣà-nlá was coming down to the world, Olódùmarè invested him with something of this attribute in order to fit him for his work of creation and ordering of the earth's trappings. What he gave him is called *Odù*.[1] In this case it means an endowed attribute of supreme authority to speak and act and be implicitly obeyed. This *odù* involves *àṣẹ*—"The sceptre". Therefore, the Õni of Ile-Ifẹ̀, at his installation,

[1] See above, p. 34.

72

ORÌ ṢÀ-NLÁ

must go before Orìṣà-nlá to receive the sceptre of office, thus derivatively
becoming a divine ruler.

He is called and known as *Ibìkejì Èdùmàrè*—"Deputy Olódùmarè".
Yoruba theogony, besides emphasising that Orìṣà-nlá is the offspring of
Olódùmarè, claims also that he is Olódùmarè's vicegerent here on earth.

Orìṣà-nlá represents to the Yoruba the idea of ritual and ethical
purity, and therefore the demands and sanctions of high morality.
Immaculate whiteness is often associated with him—this symbolises
"holiness" and purity. He is often pictured as an ancient clothed in
white and bedecked with white ornaments. His temple, especially on
the inside, is washed white; his emblems are to be kept in white containers and consist among other things of white chalk and white beads;
his priests and priestesses are robed in white and wear white ornaments.
For his sacrificial meals, the normal thing is the bloodless snail cooked
in shea-butter, although the priests take care that fowls and even
animals are not infrequent among the offerings! The water in his shrine
should be changed daily with the cleanest, clearest, water drawn very
early in the morning from a spring. The person who draws the water
must do so before anyone else has been there to disturb the spring. In
the old days, the water-bearer must be either a virgin of unimpeach-
able virtue or a woman who has passed the age of child-bearing and has
therefore ceased from sexual habits, and is of excellent reputation. All
the way to and from the spring, the water-bearer must keep ringing a
bell, to show that she is on a sacred errand and must not speak or be
spoken to. It is enjoined upon the worshippers of Orìṣà-nlá that they
must be upright and true: they must be clear in their hearts and
behaviour like water drawn early in the morning from a spring that has
not been previously disturbed. Thus their lives would be as clear as such
water—*Aiyé wọn a tòrò bí omi á-f-' òrò-pọn*—"Their lives will be clear
and pure like water drawn early in the morning".

Orìṣà-nlá enjoins monogamy. As our oral traditions have it, he himself is a monogamist. Once it was brought to his notice that the world
was in a bad state because men were not getting on well with their work
and there was general unhappiness. Upon enquiry, he found out that
the reason for that state of affairs was the noises and quarrels of the
men's several wives. So he pronounced: *A ò lè gbé ãrín òjì enìà k' ẹni ó
má ṣì wí. Orìṣà-nlá rí on' igba aiya n' lẹ k' ó tõ f' ọwọ mú Yemòwó nìkan; a
ò lè gbe aiye Olú'fẹ k' ọrùn k' áiya jẹk' ọná gún*—"It is sheer impossibility
to live among forty persons (wives) and avoid saying the wrong things.
Orìṣà-nlá sees the possibility of marrying two hundred wives and yet

73

cleaves to Yemòwǒ alone; one who bears the responsibility of rulership over the civic life of Ifẹ̀ cannot expect to succeed if at the same time he has to cope with a multiplicity of wives.

In consequence of his creative power and the *odù* with which he was invested, he has the power to make his worshippers great, to prosper them by making them increase and multiply, and by conferring material blessing upon them. Hence he is called *Adìmúlà*—"One who is held for safety". It is therefore said of him *O gbe ọmọ rẹ̀, ó sọ ọ́ d' ajé; ó ni kí nwọn r' ẹ̀rìn, nwọn r' ẹ̀rìn*—"He stands by his children and makes them materially prosperous; he gives them cause for laughter, and they laugh". On account of that also, people pray to him saying:

> *Ikú ti 'bá 'ni gbé 'lé tí 'f' ọlá ran ni!*
> *Aláṣẹ!*
> *Ò-sọ-ẹnìkan-ṣoṣo-d'-igba-ènià!*
> *Sọ mí d' irun,*
> *Sọ mí d' igba,*
> *Sọ mí d' ọ̀tà-lé-l'-égbèje ènià.*

> O Death,[1] You who domicile with a person and imbue him with nobility!
> O Sceptre-Wielder!
> O You who multiply only one into two hundred persons!
> Multiply me into four hundred,
> Multiply me into two hundred,
> Multiply me into one thousand four hundred and sixty persons.

The Yoruba think of him as a very ancient person of very venerable aspect in whom greatness combines with splendour; kindly, but holy and authoritative.

> *Orìṣà! Ẹtì! Ẹni ọlá!*
> *A-fi-ọjọ́-gbogbo-tóbi;*
> *O tóbi, kò ṣe 'gbé;*
>
> .   .   .   .   .
>
> *Bàntà-banta n'nu àlà!*
> *O sùn n'nu àlà,*
> *O jí n'nu àlà,*
> *O t' inú àlà dìde.*

.   .   .   .   .

[1] Ikú—"Death"—is a designation often used for a being or person of high authority who is believed to have the power of life and death.

Ba' nlá! ọkọ Yemòwó!
Orìṣà wù mí ni 'bùdó;
Ibi 're l' Orìṣà ka 'lẹ̀.

Orìṣà! The Immovable! The Noble One!
He-who-lives-daily-in-gorgeous-greatness;
He is so mighty that he cannot be lifted;

. . . . .

Immense in white robes!
He sleeps in white clothes,
He wakes in white clothes,
He rises in white clothes.

. . . . .

Venerable Father! Yemowo's consort!
Orìṣà delights me as he is in state;
It is a delectable place where Orìṣà is enthroned.

Tradition fixes the original earthly home of Orìṣà-nlá at Igbò. He is described as *Ẹnití nwọn bi l' óde Igbò ti o rè 'j' ọba l' óde Irànje*—"He who was born in Igbò town and went to be king at Irànje". He is *Orìṣà-nlá, Ọṣẹ̀rẹ̀ màgbò*—"Orìṣà-nlá, divinity of Igbò". His worship certainly became firmly established at Irànje which is called his city, and at the same time spread all over Yorubaland where he is known and worshipped universally under one name or another. There are many places which claim him as their special tutelary divinity.[1] In Ile-Ifẹ̀ alone, he is worshipped under at least three names.[2] At Ifọ́n, where one tradition says that his mother was born, he is known as Olúfọ́n; at Ijàyè, he is Orìṣà Ijàyè; at Owu, he is Orìṣà-ròwu; at Ọ̀bà (near Akúrẹ́), he is called Orìṣà-Ọlọ́bà[3]: and so one could go on!

ỌRUNMÌLÀ

It is the belief of the Yoruba that while Orìṣà-nlá is the deputy of Olódùmarè on earth in his creative and executive functions, Ọrunmìlà is His deputy in matters pertaining to omniscience and wisdom. The name Ọrunmìlà is a contraction either of *Ọrun-l'-o-mọ-à-ti-là*—"Only Heaven knows the means of salvation" or *Ọrun-mọ-ōlà*—"Only Heaven can effect deliverance".

[1] See Chapter 7, pp. 68 f.   [2] Op. cit., p. 69.
[3] See Chapter 2, pp. 15 ff.

Ọrunmìlà is the oracle divinity. According to our oral traditions, he first came into this world when he was sent by Olódùmarè to accompany and advise Orìṣà-nlá in the matter of arranging the earth's trappings.[1] We have evidence in the oral traditions that he was one of the earliest products of Olódùmarè and that it was his special privilege to know about the beginnings of most things, including the origins of most of the divinities and, of course, man. There are still other myths of his origin: We are told that he had parents who were in heaven and never visited this earth—his father's name being Òrokò, and his mother's Alájèrù. Ile-Ifẹ̀, on the whole, is of the opinion that his father actually lived in Ile-Ifẹ̀, at Oke-Igẹti,[2] and that the father's name was Agbọn-nìrègún.[3] It is also said that the actual occasion of his coming into the world was when he was sent by Olódùmarè to go and set a disordered world right and supervise matters in respect of pregnancy, births, child-bearing, child-rearing, sicknesses, the use of herbs, and the general run of things. According to the *Odù* sources, when he left heaven, his first stopping place was Uṣì in Èkìtìland; he decided, however, not to make Uṣì his permanent abode on earth, in spite of pressing invitation from the inhabitants that he should abide with them. He only established his cult there and moved on. Next, he stopped at Adó and with exactly the same result. The third place was Ijẹ̀sà-Obòkun (Ileṣà) where yet he would not abide permanently and again only repeated what he did in the first and second stopping places. But when he arrived at Ile-Ifẹ̀, he was satisfied that he had found a home: there he settled; but not until he had made it known that he belonged to "the whole world" and would at all times and in all places be available if he was wanted or called upon. By the way he is saluted, he appeared to be intimately connected also with Ọwọ̀ as well as Benin: he is called Ara Uṣì; Ara Adó; Ara Ijẹ̀sà-Obòkun; Ara Ọwọ̀; Ara Ibíní—Indigene of Uṣì; Indigene of Adó; Indigene of Ijẹ̀sà-Obòkun; Indigene of Ọwọ̀; Indigene of Benin.

There is no doubt that Ọrunmìlà is universally worshipped in Yoruba-land. His cult is found everywhere. Therefore his priests would claim that he is a universal king. The substance of this claim is that the Yoruba have implicit faith in Ọrunmìlà as the oracle divinity. Traditionally, the Yoruba believe that Olódùmarè has endowed Ọrunmìlà

[1] See Chapter 3, p. 20.

[2] Oke-Igẹti is the name of a ward in Ile-Ifẹ̀. The name is also used to designate the heaven to which a good devotee of Ọrunmìlà goes after death.

[3] The name Agbọnnìrègún is often used as an additional name of Ọrunmìlà himself.

with special wisdom and foreknowledge to the end that he may be His accredited representative on earth in matters relating to man's destiny.[1] In support of this belief, there is a story which has it that Olódùmarè Himself was once perplexed over a very important matter. All the other divinities tried but failed to tell Him the reason for His perplexity; only Ọrunmìlà succeeded in putting his finger on the source of the trouble: and that is, Olódùmarè needed on earth someone who should act as his deputy—to whom the divinities and men could turn for counsel and guidance. There and then, Olódùmarè appointed Ọrunmìlà to be the deputy; and since then he has been the great "consultant" for all on earth. Obviously, this is a story formulated to enhance the importance of Ọrunmìlà without any realisation that it might detract from Olódùmarè's attribute of "all-wise-ness".

The oral traditions emphasise the part played by Ọrunmìlà in guiding the destinies both of the divinities and of men. One reason given for his intimate knowledge of matters affecting man's destiny is that he is present when man is created and his destiny sealed. Therefore he knows all the secrets of man's being. Thus he can predict what is coming to pass or prescribe remedies against any eventuality. He is called Ẹ̀lẹ́rì ìpín—"The witness, or advocate, of destiny or lot". This refers to the two-fold conception of him as witness of all the secrets connected with man's being and as one who is in a position to plead with Olódùmarè on behalf of man so that unhappy issues may be averted or rectified. In fact, the reason why a man should adopt Ọrunmìlà as his divinity is either to make sure that his happy lot is preserved or in order that an unhappy lot may be rectified. One of his appellations is Òkìtíbìrì, a-pa-ọjọ́-iku-dà— "The great changer, who alters the date of death".

Connected with the cult of Ọrunmìlà is the geomantic form of divination known as Ifá.[2] Ifá is very popular in Yorubaland. The Yoruba are rather impatiently curious about the future or what the outcome of an enterprise may be; and they regard Ifá as a sure and unfailing source of comfort: their faith in it is complete. The reason for this is that the Yoruba believe that Ọrunmìlà as the oracle-divinity is the one who through the priest receives the questions and petitions of devout enquirers and suppliants and vouchsafes the revelations which the priest declares. It seems absolutely impossible for a Yoruba whose soul is still fettered to his traditional belief to attempt anything at all without consulting the oracle by Ifá. It has always been throughout the history of the Yoruba a *sine qua non* to life. Before a betrothal, before a marriage,

---

[1] See Chapter 13, pp. 176 ff.   [2] See Chapter 1, pp. 7 ff.

77

before a child is born, at the birth of a child, at successive stages in man's life, before a king is appointed, before a chief is made, before anyone is appointed to a civic office, before a journey is made, in times of crisis, in times of sickness, at any and all times, *Ifá* is consulted for guidance and assurance. As the saying goes, *Òní l' a rí, a ò r' ọla, on ni baba'láwo ṣe nd' Ifá l' ọrọrún*—"It is today we see, we do not see tomorrow, hence the *baba'láwo*[2] consults the oracle every fifth day".[1]

Ọrunmìlà is said to be a linguist and to understand every language spoken on earth. So it is easy for him to understand and give counsel to all. The corpus of oral recitals connected with *Ifá* contains the stories of most, if not all, of the divinities; hence it is said that there is nothing that Ọrunmìlà does not know about them. Besides, the corpus contains also much historical matter which is awaiting careful sifting.

Ọrunmìlà is believed to be "almighty" to promote success and happiness. Blessed is the one who is favoured by Ọrunmìlà. An *Iwòrì-Mejì* recital says, in part:

Ifá tẹ 'jú mọ́ mi ki o wò mí 're:
Bi o bá tẹ 'jú mọ́ 'ni là 'l' owo l' ọwọ:
Bi o bá tẹ 'ju mọ́ 'ni là 'ri 're.

Ifá, fix your eyes upon me and look at me well:
It is when you fix your eyes upon a person that he is rich;
It is when you fix your eyes upon a person that he prospers.

He is reputed to be a great doctor. Therefore, every qualified *baba-'láwo* must know, not only how to practise divination, but also the elaborate set of herbal remedies connected with the *Odù* corpus. The *baba'láwo* claim that Ọsányìn, the doctor's divinity, is his younger brother, over whom he is senior by one thousand four hundred and sixty years!

The oral traditions show that there is a close relationship between Orìṣà-nlá and Ọrunmìlà. Orìṣà-nlá is his senior and leader. We have heard that he was sent to help and advise Orìṣà-nlá about the earth's trappings; we have also been told what he did when Àtọwọ́dá crushed Orìṣà-nlá with a stone![2] One oral tradition tells us that even though Ọrunmìlà was very fond of palm-wine, he would refrain from it to please Orìṣà-nlá. This tradition has it that once during a festival Orìṣà-nlá paid Ọrunmìlà a visit. On this occasion, Ọrunmìlà wanted to drink palm-wine, as the custom was, so he had to buy two new drinking

[1] See Chapters 3, p. 20, and 9, p. 112.   [2] Chapter 7, pp. 59 ff.

calabashes, one for Orìṣà-nlá to use for drinking his wonted water, while
the other one he himself used for palm-wine. The fact is, this oral
tradition emphasises, Ọrunmìlà could not refrain from palm-wine for
too long, because he was brought up on palm-wine, which was the milk
of his mother's breast.[1] Said he in this connection,

> *Nwọn ò bi iyâ mi ni 'lé Ifọn;*[2]
> *Nwọn ò bi bàbâ mi ni Èrìngbọ̀n;*
> *N'nu ọpẹ ni mo jẹ, n'nu ọpẹ ni mo mu,*
> *Màrìwò ọpẹ ni mo ti rìn gbọnran-gbọnran wá 'nu aiye;*
> *Ānú ba' nla, ba' t' orìṣà, ni mo ṣe*
> *Ti mi ò mu ẹmu.*

My mother was not born at Ifọn;
My father was not born at Èrìngbọ̀n;
Of the palm-tree do I eat, of the palm-tree do I drink,
Palm-fronds formed the direct path through which I walked into
the world;
It is out of compassion for the venerable father, the father of
divinities,
That I refrained from drinking palm-wine.

As Orìṣà-nlá enjoins monogamy on his "children", so also is it
required of a *baba'láwo* that he should be a husband of one wife. An
Odù recital says that it was laid upon Ọrunmìlà that he should be a
monogamist. But, by the look of things, he could not live up to the
ideal!

In Ọrunmìlà, we meet again another element of the demands and
sanctions of morality in the religion of the Yoruba. It is laid down that a
baba'láwo must not abuse his office in any way: if he does, he will never
be received into heaven. Therefore no *baba'láwo* should use his position
to enrich himself in any way; he must not refuse anybody his service on
account of money—if any person is too poor to pay the customary pit-
tance for divination, the *baba'láwo* must divine for him free of charge;
or if the person cannot afford the prescribed sacrifice, the *baba'láwo* must
take whatever he can afford and translate the will for the deed. It seems,
in fact, that the *baba'láwo* is under a vow of poverty, to spend himself
in the service of the community, making just enough to keep himself,

[1] The palm-tree is connected with the cult of Ọrunmìlà because palm-kernels
are used as the instruments of divination.
[2] Ifọn is an important centre of the cult of Orìṣà-nlá.

his real reward being in the service of Ọrunmìlà. Now that materialism is the order of the day, however, this sacred injunction is largely disregarded, and there are many who appear not to know it at all. Charlatans abound.

The shrine of Ọrunmìlà is usually in the house. The emblems, which consist mainly of palm-kernels (sixteen at least) held in a bowl or dish with a lid, some graven pieces of elephant's tusk, and some cowries, are placed upon an elevation either in a corner or in the centre of the room. The *baba'láwo* should wear strings of special beads round his wrists and hold an animal's switch in one hand and a divining rod made of elephant's tusk in another as the insignia of his office. For the ceremony of receiving a suppliant as a devotee of Ọrunmìlà, a grove is used.

ÈṢÙ

In Yoruba theology, Èṣù is depicted as so versatile a character that one must be wary of what one says about him. He has often been sweepingly called either the "Devil" or "Satan".[1] He is certainly not the Devil of our New Testament acquaintance, who is an out and out evil power in opposition to the plan of God's salvation of man. On the whole, it would be near the truth to parallel him with Satan in the Book of Job,[2] where the Satan is one of the ministers of God and has the office of trying men's sincerity and putting their religion to the proof.

What we gather from our sources is that Èṣù is primarily a "special relations officer" between heaven and earth, the inspector-general who reports regularly to Olódùmarè on the deeds of the divinities and men, and checks and makes reports on the correctness of worship in general and sacrifices in particular.

The *baba'láwo* usually hold the view that Èṣù was created to be the right-hand divinity to Ọrunmìlà. It is his duty to run errands for Ọrunmìlà; he must be always in attendance upon him and act under his orders. To Ọrunmìlà is assigned the duty of hearing the voice of Olódùmarè and declaring His will to the world; but wherever Ọrunmìlà's declaration is not heeded, it is the duty of Èṣù to bring some calamity by way of punishment upon the recalcitrant. In return for the service which Èṣù gives to Ọrunmìlà, Ọrunmìlà feeds him. But whenever he is not satisfied with the feeding, he takes it upon himself to spoil the works of Ọrunmìlà.

[1] This is the name used in the Bible to translate these two words into Yoruba.
[2] Job 1:6 ff.

By what we gather of the character of Èṣù from the oral traditions, however, it is difficult to accept as correct the status into which the *baba'láwo* are trying to place him. He is certainly such as cannot accept a subordinate position to any divinity in that way, especially that of an obedient boy to Ọ̀runmìlà. There is no doubt at all that the traditions show that there is a very close link between Èṣù and Ọ̀runmìlà; even though a misunderstanding of the relations may easily lead to an error of judgment in favour of one or the other. They are linked together in consequence of the connection which there is between their respective functions. Èṣù is ubiquitous because he must always be about his business of inspection. His portfolio includes, among other things, the inspection of worship and sacrifices. Ọ̀runmìlà also belongs everywhere and is the great "consultant"; his functions include the prescription of sacrifices or ritual acts. It is also believed that between Ọ̀runmìlà and Death[1] there is a pact which was brought about because Èṣù once overcame Death in a combat and deprived him of his club and it was Ọ̀runmìlà who helped Death to get his club back.

Whenever anybody gets into trouble through the agency of Èṣù, Ọ̀runmìlà can always be relied upon to show the way out of the difficulty. That is why it usually happens that wherever there is a cult of Ọ̀runmìlà, that of Èṣù is set up also, on however small a scale. The two of them often work in collaboration. Èṣù as the approver and bearer of sacrifices to heaven is known to the *baba'láwo* as Ọ̀ṣẹ́tùrá. On the whole it appears that it is Ọ̀runmìlà who is always placed under obligation to Èṣù rather than the other way round. It is an acknowledged belief that Èṣù can spoil the works of Ọ̀runmìlà whenever he finds cause to do so. He also helps him out of difficulty on occasion. Once when all the other divinities conspired against Ọ̀runmìlà and took him in accusation before Olódùmarè, it was Èṣù who defended him and whose submission Olódùmarè accepted.

The attitude of the Yoruba to Èṣù is generally one of dread. It is believed that he is held in constant dread also by the other divinities. This is because, by virtue of his office, he holds the power of life and death over them as prosperity or calamity for them depends upon what reports he carries to Olódùmarè. Everybody seeks therefore to be on good terms with him. We hear the warning, *Bí á bá rúbọ, kí á mú t' Èṣù kuro*—"When sacrifices are offered, the portion which belongs to Èṣù should be set aside for him". He is feared also because, incidentally, he is malicious and a mischief-maker, quite capable of causing confusion,

[1] See Chapter 14, pp. 188 f.

bringing about complicated situations or promoting malice among people. By his guile he would make enemies of very close friends, cause husband and wife to quarrel, and make antagonists of father and children.

There are several myths which illustrate him as the trickster or the mischief-maker. Here is one. There was a man who had two wives, both of whom he loved equally and who were on the best of terms. So peaceful was the house in which they lived that they became to their neighbours models of conjugal harmony, and people thought that nothing could disturb the happy relations which existed among them all. Èṣù knew about this and did not like it. So he laid a trap for them in one of his usual, crafty ways. He made a very beautiful cap, turned himself to a trader, and went and displayed it for sale in the market. But he took care not to sell it to anyone else until one of the two wives came to the market and was attracted by it so much that she immediately bought it. Joyfully she took it home and presented it to her husband. The husband was so pleasantly surprised that he unwittingly showed his appreciation and gratitude in a way which made the other wife suspicious and jealous. But she said nothing. She awaited with mounting uneasiness the next market day; when the day arrived, she went very early to the market in search of a gift—a much better one at all costs—for her husband. Èṣù was ready with another cap compared with which the first one paled into insignificance. Triumphantly, the second wife bought this new cap and carried it home for her husband. The effect was magical. The second wife became the favourite for the time being. And so the stage was set for keen rivalry between the two wives, each striving to out-do the other in the dangerous game of winning the husband's love, Èṣù coming to the aid of each one in her turn of the game, and the husband's mood wavering to the right or left with the arrival of each still-more-beautiful gift. When Èṣù was satisfied that the mines had been sufficiently laid and that the disastrous explosion would inevitably take place, he abruptly ceased going to the market. The next wife to visit the market was frustrated: she returned home in a great rage. Things then just needed a little touching-off and the domestic catastrophe towards which Èṣù had been working ensued.

Our oral traditions emphasise that Èṣù certainly is also dreaded by the divinities: he seems to possess a power which none except Olódùmarè can curb. It was said that once Ṣàngò[1] was making a boast that there was no *orìṣà* whom he could not subdue. Èṣù promptly challenged him,

[1] See below, pp. 89 ff.

"Does that include me?" To which Ṣàngǒ immediately replied apologetically, "But why, surely, you could not have been included?" It was said that Ọ̀runmìlà once bought a slave without first of all consulting Èṣù about it. Èṣù became offended; and one night, he strangled the slave! We often hear the expression, Èṣù, ọ̀tá orìṣà—"Èṣù, the adversary of the divinities"—an expression born of his mischievous dealings with them.

There is an unmistakable element of evil in Èṣù and for that reason he has been predominantly associated with things evil. There are those who say that the primary function of Èṣù in this world is to spoil things. But even so, we cannot call him the Devil—not in the New Testament sense of that name.[1] What element of "evil" there is in Èṣù can be found also to some degree in most of the other divinities. The most that we can gather from the evidences of our oral traditions is that he takes mischief-making as his "hobby", just as any person corrupted by power which seems uncontrolled may find sadistic relish in throwing his weight about in unsympathetic, callous ways. He is not the personal embodiment of evil standing in opposition to goodness.

But when all this has been admitted, it is quite clear still that the Yoruba put almost every evil tendency and practice in man down to his agency. When a person commits any deed which results in unpleasantness or harm to himself or his neighbour, the Yoruba immediately say, Èṣù l' o ti i—"It is Èṣù who stirred him". The unruly, the headstrong, the one given to evildoing or wickedness, are all Ọmọ Èṣù in the sense of the Bibilical "Sons of Belial".[2] It is usually said of any such, Èṣù l' o nṣe é—"It is Èṣù who is moving him". And people often pray pro-pitiatingly, Ki a má ṣe ri 'jà Èṣù—"That we may not experience the battle of Èṣù"; or Èṣù, má ṣe mí, ọmọ ẹlòmî ni kí o ṣe—"Èṣù, do not move me; it is another person's child you should move".

There is also a strong belief that Èṣù could be employed against an enemy. One ritual method of employing him in that way is as follows: The supplicant goes before the emblem of Èṣù, taking with him palm-oil and palm-kernel oil. It is said that Èṣù delights in drinking palm-oil, while palm-kernel oil is tabu to him. The supplicant therefore pours the palm-oil on the emblem saying, "This is palm-oil, O Èṣù: I know that

[1] See above, p. 80.
[2] Cf. Judges 19:22. "Sons of Belial" in the historical books of the Old Testament is a term frequently used for "disreputable characters". In the post-biblical Jewish literature Belial often occurs as the name for Satan. See I and II Samuel (The Century Bible, edited by A. R. A. Kennedy), p. 40.

it is your food, and so I have come to give it to you. Grant me your favour and protection." Then he takes the palm-kernel oil and says, "O Èṣù, this is palm-kernel oil; I know that it is not your food and I dare not give it to you. But so-and-so (here he names the enemy) has asked me to give it to you even though he knows that it is not your food, and here (he pours the palm-kernel oil on the emblem) I give it to you in his name. Go now and avenge yourself." It is believed that immediately after the ritual is completed, Èṣù will rush off to deal the enemy a blow, or stir him to some action which will bring upon him a calamitous consequence. The suppliant must observe certain precautions, however. He must not go to sleep until he has made sure that Èṣù has completed his errand. There are two ways of making sure of that. He must prepare a "tip" ready for when Èṣù returns from his errand. This he will know by a certain sign. It is when Èṣù has returned and received his "tip" that he as the suppliant is free to give his attention to anything else. But supposing the enemy is stronger and has protected himself against the suppliant's probable designs with some magic which may ward off Èṣù, or some propitiatory remedy which may change the wrath of Èṣù into favour towards him? Then, since the cudgel of Èṣù once raised must not be lowered unused, Èṣù will return to demand why the suppliant had sent him out on a fruitless pursuit, and that means that the blow will now be dealt at him. The suppliant therefore should anticipate the probability of this happening and prepare an acceptable substitutionary victim—a fowl or an animal—ready in a suitable place for the blow. Again, he must learn to know by some sign when it is all over! When Èṣù is employed in this way, he is called Ṣìgìdì or Ẹlẹ́gbára.

Nevertheless, Èṣù is worshipped also because the Yoruba have faith in his protective and benevolent capabilities. In fact, to his worshippers, he occupies a tutelary position. It is in this capacity that he is represented by his emblem which stands in the centre of the town, village, or compound. Such an emblem is often inside the house. People address him worshipfully but also with a note which indicates father–children relations. He is called Bàbá—"Father". There are people called Èṣúbíyì—"Scion of Èṣù", Èṣúgbàyi—"One who is claimed by Èṣù". There are places where annual festivals are held in his name. In Ilẹ̀-Olújì, for example, the festival comes in February, and it is to mark the beginning of the annual cultivation of the land. The festival is primarily to ask for the blessing of Èṣù on farming, and incidentally of course, to propitiate him that all may be well with the farmer's work throughout the year.

It would seem, on the whole, that what Èṣù does depends largely on how much man can be on the right side of him. And that is the real difficulty. From all accounts he is not only a bewilderingly versatile character but also extremely capricious. It is believed that Èṣù has two hundred names, by which it is meant that he is an elusive, slippery character whom it is not easy to fix. He is called *Lógẹmọ ọ̀run; A-nla-ká'lú; Pǎpǎ-wàrà; A-túká-ma-ṣe-'ṣa*—"The indulgent child of heaven; He whose greatness is manifested all over the place; the hurrying, sudden one; He who breaks into fragments and cannot be gathered together!"

From the oral traditions, it seems that his earliest home in Yorubaland was Ọ̀fà (the original Ọfà[1]) although it is sometimes suggested that it was Kétu. His worship predominates today in Ẹ̀rìn, near Ilobù. But he is undoubtedly one of the principal Yoruba divinities. There is not a place where he is not worshipped and propitiated. His shrine can be anywhere—in the centre of the town or village, compound or household; cross-roads or a grove; the entrances to a house, a compound, a village, or a town. Èṣù's emblems are various. It can be a piece of laterite or rock: this is usually stuck in the ground or on a mound of earth; it can be a graven image of clay or wood: this may be with or without a knife in one hand and a club in the other; it can be an earthenware pot turned upside down, with a hole in its middle; or it can be a piece of hard rock in an earthenware dish; this has oil poured regularly upon it.

ÒGÙN

Indisputably, Ògùn is another one who ranks high in status among the divinities of Yorubaland. He is universally acknowledged in the indigenous belief of the Yoruba as a most indispensable divinity, inasmuch as all iron and steel belong to him.

According to the oral traditions, he is one of the earliest divinities. He was a hunter; and before the earth was founded, he used to descend by a spider's thread upon the primordial marshy waste for the purpose of hunting.[2] When the earth had been founded and its furniture arranged, he and a number of other divinities set out to possess the earth and take up their allotted offices. But they had to come to a halt at a place of "no-road". Orìṣà-nlá tried to cut a way through, but his machete bent because it was of lead. Of all the divinities it was only Ògùn who

---

[1] This is called Ọ̀fà-Ilé, and was the original home from which the present aborigines of Ọ̀fà moved.
[2] See Chapter 3, p. 19.

possessed the implement which was adequate for the task. Ògǔn therefore undertook to make a way, but not before he had made the other
divinities promise him a worthy reward when the task had been accomplished. This the divinities did. In no time, Ògǔn had cut a way
by which the divinities arrived on earth. When they arrived at Ile-Ifè,
which was the "headquarters", they rewarded Ògǔn with the only
crown they brought with them. So Ògǔn received the title of Ọ̀ṣìn-
Imalè—"Chief among the divinities". There are priests of Ògǔn who
maintain that by virtue of the power and status of Ògǔn, he should
have been the "head" of all the divinities, but for the fact that he did
not care for the post.

However, Ògǔn, being a very ferocious being who was addicted to the
savage sports of hunting and carnage, did not find it easy to adjust himself to community life; and so he had to go and live in solitude at a place
called Orí-Òkè—"The Top of the Hill". Thence he went about hunting
and to his wars and conquests, whether on behalf of the divinities or to
gratify his own innate propensity.

After a while, however, he became tired of his seclusion and so sought
the settled life which he had once rejected. At first, his fierce and for-
bidding appearance made it impossible for him to find a home in any
community. Ọjọ́ ti Ògǔn nti Orí-Òkè bọ̀, aṣọ iná l' o mú bo 'ra, èwù èjè
l' o wọ̀—"The day Ògǔn was descending from Orí-Òkè, he was clothed
in fire and wore a garment of blood." He therefore went and borrowed
clothes from the palm-tree! Attired now in fresh palm-fronds,[1] he
entered Irè and was immediately proclaimed king. Since then, he has
become Ògǔn, On'Irè—"Ògǔn, the Lord of Irè".

It is a strong belief of the Yoruba that Ògǔn is the pioneer divinity—
pioneer in the literal sense of one who goes in advance to prepare the
road for others. It is believed that it has been his main function from
the beginning to prepare the way for the other divinities. This carries
also a metaphorical meaning because it is believed also that Ògǔn
makes the way smooth for the divinities in their spiritual encounters
with the world of men and that he also opens the way of material and
spiritual prosperity for his worshippers. He is called Ògǔn Aládǎ mejì:
o nfi ọ̀kan ṣá 'ko, o nfi ọ̀kan yè 'na—"Ògǔn, the possessor of two
machetes: with one he prepares the farm, and with the other he clears
the road". Hence at the approach to the grove or temple of every principal divinity in Ile-Ifè and in other places where this belief is suffi-

---

[1] Palm-fronds are sacred to several divinities and are used to decorate their
shrines. They are called "the clothes of Ògǔn."

ciently strong, there is stationed an emblem of Ògŭn in conspicuous
and loud proclamation of the belief that without Ògŭn, there is no
"way" for or to the divinity.

He is also praised as *Ògŭn, on' ilé owó, ọlọ́nà ọlà, on' ilé kángunkàngun ti mbẹ l' ọ́run*—"Ògŭn, the owner of the house of money, the
owner of the house of riches, the owner of the innumerable houses of
heaven".[1] He is also *A-wọ́n-l'-ẹ̀yin-'jú, ẹgbè l' ẹhin ọmọ òrùnkàn, on' ile
kàngun-kángun ti mbẹ l' ọ́run*—"One whose eye-balls-are-rare (to
behold),[2] support behind the orphan, the owner of the innumerable
houses of heaven".

Ògŭn is believed to be the divinity to whom belong iron and steel
and therefore any implements and tools made from them. All who make
use of these tools and implements therefore depend upon him and
owe him some tribute, be that in form of becoming his regular worshippers or making offerings to him as occasion demands. In this, the
divinities are not excepted. It is said that *Orìṣà ti o wipe t' Ògŭn kò tó
nkan, a f' ọwọ́ jẹ 'ṣu 'ẹ̀ n' igbà aìmoye*—"Whichever divinity regards
Ògŭn as of no consequence will eat his yams with hands (without a
knife) times without number".

As the master-artist, it is Ògŭn who gives the finishing touch to the
creative work of Orìṣà-nlá. When Orìṣà-nlá has finished the moulding
of the physical man, it is left to Ògŭn to take charge of the work of cir-
cumcision, tribal marking, tattooing, or any surgical operations that
may be necessary to keep man in good health. This conception stems
from the belief that all iron and steel tools belong to Ògŭn and all who
use them do so under his authority and control.

It is in consequence of this belief in his lordship over iron and steel
that he is acknowledged as the divinity of war and warriors; of hunters
and the chase; of all artisans—smiths, engineers, mechanics, all engine
drivers and machine minders; and, in fact, all who deal in anything made
of iron or steel. Such people are said to be under obligation to worship
or propitiate him, especially before undertaking any new work like
the opening of a smithy or a hunting expedition; or in thanksgiving after
an escape from such a disaster as a motor or gun accident.

Because Ògŭn is ubiquitous and has his hand in every pie, he is
regarded as a presiding divinity over oaths and covenant-making or
the cementing of pacts. In our courts, people who are neither Christians nor Moslems take their oaths to "speak the truth and nothing

[1] This is strongly similar to John 14:2.
[2] This attribute is because his eyes are said to be like flames of fire.

but the truth" by kissing a piece of iron—a machete usually. The pact or convenant made before Ògùn is considered most binding. Two rival wives, when suspected of evil intentions against each other, are usually made to swear before Ògùn in order to prevent them from harming each other in body, mind, or estate. Two friends, or a number of people, who want to enter into a covenant on a serious matter will also go before Ògùn to do so. There are various methods of swearing or making a pact in this way. One method is to put a valve of kola-nut on a piece of iron and when each person has made the requisite under- taking in a prescribed statement, one takes the valve of kola-nut and bites off and eats a portion of it, then replaces it on the emblem of Ògùn; the other person takes the remainder and eats it. For several people there may be several valves of kola-nuts. Or, the covenant-makers may par- take of the water into which a red-hot iron from the smithy fire has been dropped, or one in which an emblem of Ògùn has been washed. It is believed that anyone who swears falsely by Ògùn, or breaks an oath or covenant made before Ògùn, will come under his severe judgment: he will die or be mutilated or deformed through a gun-shot, a machete, or an engine or machine accident. The Yoruba are often reminded, *Bi ọmọdé ba da-'lẹ̀, ki o má da Ògùn, ọ̀rọ̀ Ògùn l' ẹ̀wọ̀*—"If one breaks covenant at all, it must not be with Ògùn, the matter is strictly *tabu* where Ògùn is concerned."

Ògùn is more especially known as Ògùn *On'Irè* because he is believed to be the "Lord of Irè". Iléṣà, Ondǒ, and Ilákǒkó also call for special mention as places where his cult is in special prominence. But, as we have observed, he is known and worshipped all over Yorubaland. A Yoruba ballad gives the suggestion that Ògùn has seven designations, according to the places where he is the prominent divinity, or some functions connected with him, or some celebrated priests of his. In this setting, we are told the foodstuffs on which he feeds.

> *Ògùn méje l' Ògùn mi:*
> *Ògùn Alárá ni 'gb' ajá;*
> *Ògùn Onirè a gb' àgbò;*
> *Ògùn Ikọ̀là a gbà 'gbǐn;*
> *T' Ẹlẹ́mọnà ni 'gb' ẹsun-'ṣu.*
> *Ògùn Akírìn a gba iwo àgbò;*
> *Ògùn gbẹ́nà-gbẹ́nà, ẹran ahun l' o mã jẹ.*
> *Ògùn Mákindé ti Ògùn l' ẹhìn odi—*
> > *Bi on kò bá gba Tápà, a gb' Àbókí.*
> > *A gba Úkù-úkù, a gba Kémbéri.*

There are seven Ògŭn who belong to me:[1]
Ògŭn of Alárá it is who takes dog;
Ògŭn of Onirè habitually takes ram;
Ògŭn of surgery habitually takes snail;
That of Ẹlẹ̀mọnà it is who takes roasted yam.
Ògŭn of Akírìn habitually takes ram's horn (=ram);
Ògŭn of the artisans, it is the flesh of tortoise that he eats.
Ògŭn of Mákindé, which is Ògŭn outside the city wall—
    He either takes a Tápà, or takes an Àbókí,
    Or takes an Úkù-úkù, or takes a Kémbéri[2]

In pranks and mischief-making, Ògŭn is next to Èṣù.[3] But while Èṣù merely derives sadistic pleasure in wickedness and "superfluity of naughtiness", Ògŭn is by nature hard, fierce, and terrible. His true nature is depicted in the saying

Níbo l' a ti pàdé rẹ̀?
A pàdé rẹ̀ n' ibi ìjà;
A pàdé rẹ̀ n' ibi ìta;
A pàdé rẹ̀ n' ibi ògbàrá èjè
Gbé ndá 'ni l' ọrun bi omi ăgo.

Where does one meet him?
One meets him in the place of battle;
One meets him in the place of wrangling;
One meets him in the place where torrents of blood
Fills with longing as a cup of water does the thirsty.

Yet evil is not associated with him; rather, it is strongly believed that he demands justice, fair play, and rectitude.

The emblems of Ògŭn are various. They may be metal—scraps, wrought, or graven; a plant called *pèrègún—Dracaena Fragraves*; a rock or a piece of rock; the tusk or tail of an elephant.

ṢÀNGŎ

We have been led by sheer force of circumstances to choose the name of Ṣàngŏ for the Yoruba conception of the manifestation of "The Wrath" of Olódùmarè.

[1] That is, he has seven designations.
[2] These are designations which the Yoruba give to some clans of N. Nigeria. But they mean nothing more here than that human beings are offered to him. See Chapter 9, pp. 119 ff.   [3] See pp. 80 ff.

Ṣàngǒ was the name of an historical figure, one who was indisputably
a man among men. Samuel Johnson tells us that he was the fourth
Aláfin of Ọ̀yọ́.[1] He was a man, quite distinct from the divinities who are
"of the heavens".

The interesting story of his apotheosis can only be reconstructed from
various legendary versions. He was a strong man; a powerful hunter;
both of which mean primarily that he was versed in various magical
arts. But he was also self-willed, cruel and tyrannical, and passionately
devoted to carnage. As a king of Ọ̀yọ́, he ruled with a rod of iron and
sought to keep everybody under his thumb. In the end, however, people
became tired of his tyranny: his authority was challenged and his purpose thwarted by two of his courtiers. When these two courtiers were
becoming too much for him, he craftily set them one against the other
and one of them was killed as a result. But the surviving one set after
him, and the only way left for him to "play the man" was to commit
suicide. This he did by hanging himself on an àyàn tree. His opponents
then taunted his followers that their king had hanged himself. This led
his followers to seek the means of saving their faces: they went to Ibàrìbǎ
and procured some preparation by which lightning could be attracted.
They set to work with this, with the result that lightning became frequent in and around Ọ̀yọ́: the compounds and houses were often in
conflagrations, and there were losses of lives and property. People
became panic-stricken and so were prepared for the next move by the
followers of Ṣàngǒ who then came out with the story that Ṣàngǒ did not
hang himself; he only ascended to heaven; the lightning and the resulting calamities were the vengeance which Ṣàngǒ sent upon those who
slandered him by saying that he had hanged himself; let all from now
confess that Ṣàngǒ did not hang himself and worship him; the article of
faith to be repeated henceforth should be Ọba kò so—"The king did not
hang himself". Thus began the worship of Ṣàngǒ in Ọ̀yọ́. It began
with this act of confession and submission, and the payment by the
enemies of propitiatory fines in the form of oxen, rams, sheep, fowls,
kola-nuts, and palm-oil. Then a shrine, and later on a temple, came into
being for his worship on the traditional spot where he was said to have
hanged himself, which was renamed Kòso ("He-did-not-hang"). From
there his cult spread all over Yorubaland.

The story as reconstructed above will not be acceptable to the priestly
house of Kòso in Ọ̀yọ́. There the orthodox story is mainly as follows:
two of Ṣàngǒ's wives were very quarrelsome; and there were also a few

[1] The History of the Yorubas (Lagos, C.M.S., 1937), p. 43.

complaints from the subjects of Ṣàngŏ concerning his tyranny. Ṣàngŏ became angry with everybody, mounted his horse, and went into the forest. For a long time he was expected back, but in vain. When he did not return, people feared that he had gone in a fit of temper to hang himself. So they went in search of him; he was not found, but his horse was. The searchers therefore called out, "Where are you, O king? Have you hanged yourself?" To which he replied from a long distance, "No, I have not hanged myself!" "Then, come back to us, we want you," they called back. But he replied, "No, since there has been so much trouble in the compound and so many complaints against me from you all, I will not come back to you; I will now rule you unseen." So he ascended to heaven by a chain which sprang from an *àyàn* tree. From heaven he has since then manifested his kingship by lightning and thunder.

One can understand why the priestly house of Kòso sticks to this "orthodox" version of the account of the apotheosis of Ṣàngŏ! Whatever version of the story is told, the important thing is that people became convinced that Ṣàngŏ ascended to heaven; and that he became thereby the author of lightning and thunder. In the apt words of Leo Frobenius, he became "The Hurler of thunderbolts, the Lord of the Storm, the God who burns down compounds and cities, the Render of trees and slayer of men; cruel and savage. . . ."[1]

Ṣàngŏ evidently has "a help meet for him" in his wife, the goddess Ọya. She is described as a fierce, bearded Amazon who is absolutely indispensable to her husband in every way. It is said that without Ọya, there is nothing that Ṣàngŏ can accomplish. Ọya is *Obìrin t' o t' orí ogun dá 'rùngbòn sí*—"The woman who grows a beard on account of war"; *Èfùfùlèlè ti 'dá 'gi l' okè-l'-okè*—"The rushing wind that tears down trees from the top"; *A-ṣu-'jò ma rò*—"One who causes a heavy, dark cloud but brings no rain". Her face is so terrible that none dare behold it, her wrath so devastating that it must be absolutely avoided.

Nevertheless, she is tall, comely, and can be graceful. In fact, there were sixteen rival goddesses who were competing to have Ṣàngŏ for a husband: Ọya won the husband from them all through her charm of personality, her grace and elegance of movement—*Orìṣà mẹ-'n-di-l'-ogún ni mbẹ́ l' ọdọ Ṣàngŏ, ni 'bi k' s ṣán 'pá, ni 'bi k' a yan, l' Ọya fi gb' ọkọ l' ọwọ́ wọn.*

Whenever any house or property is damaged by lightning, the priests

[1] *The Voice of Africa* (London, Hutchinson, 1913), Vol. i, p. 205.

of Ṣàngǒ make for the place, saying that they are going to find the thunderbolt: and they invariably bring out from the place a celt which they claim to have found. With the finding of the "bolt" goes much ritualistic plunder in the name of Ṣàngǒ. The body of a lightning victim is claimed by the priests, and, traditionally, it is only they who perform the burial offices at a tremendous cost to the relatives; and for a victim only yet struck unconscious, the priests have to make up their minds quickly between completing the work which Ṣàngǒ has so imperfectly done, or accepting a high ransom in the name of a propitiatory service.

Leo Frobenius has raised a very important point about Ṣàngǒ. He thinks that there were two Ṣàngǒ, one from Nupe and the other from Borgu. That, he claims, is responsible for the command to do good as connected with Ṣàngǒ, which command, he wrongly asserts, is "unnegro".[1]

Frobenius is confused at this point; but his confusion is understandable. There is no doubt that there are elements in the moral application of the doctrine connected with Ṣàngǒ which certainly could not have received their origin from the life of the man Ṣàngǒ. We may have some light on the subject if we look at it in this way. The oral traditions tell us that Ṣàngǒ was a son of Ọrǎnyàn—the powerful warrior son of Odùdúwà,[2] who led an expedition as far as Nupeland and the North of the River Niger. In the course of the expedition, he met and married the Nupe woman who became the mother of Ṣàngǒ. Thus, Ṣàngǒ would be of Ifẹ̀ and Nupe parentage. But the man who became known as Odùdúwà was himself not originally of this land; so also was the legendary Ọrǎnyàn probably not his son but one of his able lieutenants. Thus, it is not unlikely that Ṣàngǒ's relationship could be traced as far as Northern Nigeria, or even beyond. Our people still say that it was Ọya, the wife of Ṣàngǒ, who became the river which is now known as the Niger; and that emphasises still that Ṣàngǒ must be related to that part of Nigeria. And if this is so, the name of Ṣàngǒ, who has become a popular hero and a cult object, would not be unknown and unrevered in those parts which could proudly establish some blood relationship with him.

But the real point of Frobenius's confusion is not even in this historical probability. It is rather in this: there are attributes which are claimed for, or affixed to, Ṣàngǒ today which originally did not belong to him. He is said to forbid lying, stealing, and poisoning, which offences

[1] Op. cit., p. 210.   [2] See Chapters 2, pp. 15 f., 18 ff., and 3, pp. 22 ff.

are against prominent commandments in the Yoruba ethical system.[1] By all that we know of the man Ṣàngǒ, he had no claim to such a high standard of morality. He was outstandingly guilty of infractions of all such commandments. And it was the difficulty of reconciling the personal character of Ṣàngǒ with the high moral attributes which are assigned to him that led Frobenius astray.

The truth is, there has been an earlier Yoruba solar divinity, to whom lightning and thunder have been attributed. His name is Jàkǔta, which means "One who fights with stones", or "One who hurls stones". In most of Yorubaland today, people are not quite sure whether to say that it was Jàkǔta who was the father of Ṣàngǒ or to put it the other way round. So much have people become confused by this forceful intrusion which is Ṣàngǒ. There is the fact, however, that it cannot be said, as it can be said in the case of Ṣàngǒ, that Jàkǔta has ever been a human being. And the commandments against stealing, falsehood, and poisoning belong originally to Jàkǔta. Jàkǔta was the Yoruba way of conceptualising "The Wrath" of Olódùmarè against all forms of wickedness. In

> The flashing of the lightning free
> The whirling wind's tempestuous shocks,

the Yoruba see the revelation of "The Wrath"; they experience in a palpable way the "numinous awe" in religion. But this "Wrath" they cannot reconcile with the nature of Olódùmarè Himself as He is known to them; so they transfer it to Jàkǔta and one or two others of the divinities. The Yoruba have a keen sense of "The Wrath", so that when it lightens or thunders, people—especially those who are not sure of their characters—tremble. They salute "The Wrath" as Ògírígirì, Ẹkùn a-ṣ-'èké—"The terrible, rumbling One, the Leopard that devours the liar". It is said when it lightens On'-imu nṣ' imu, èké nsá—"The owner of the nose turns up the nose, the liar trembles".

This is all to say that "The Wrath" is ever-present and ready to manifest itself upon the children of disobedience. Jàkǔta has represented it from the early times; and it was by a clever stroke that the identification between Jàkǔta and Ṣàngǒ was registered in such a way that Ṣàngǒ practically usurped the place of Jàkǔta in the pantheon. Some priests of strong, imposing character, perhaps someone who found a chance of replacing an indigenous divinity with an imperialistic one,

---

[1] Chapter 12.

must have been working upon the credulity of the people. Today, the sacred day of Jàkǔta is still observed regularly by the priests of Ṣàngǒ in Ọ̀yọ́, although this is done in connection with the worship of Ṣàngǒ. The priests only know that they must worship Jàkǔta *for* Ṣàngǒ. Why they do it, they do not seem to know. But it is certain that if this subtle hybridisation had not happened, Ṣàngǒ would have been no more than an ancestor in the same category as the other ancestral kings, perhaps a little more propitiated because of his strong character. At best, he would have remained a little domestic divinity of Ọ̀yọ́. Even now, the priests of Ṣàngǒ are mostly Ọ̀yọ́ or of Ọ̀yọ́ origin.

We still must go a little further and consider, in this connection, Ọ̀ràmfẹ̀ of Ile-Ifẹ̀. He is the accepted solar divinity among the Ifẹ̀, and it was the Ifẹ̀ who gave him to the Ondǒ. The name probably contracted from *Ẹniti-ó-ra-Ifẹ̀-ka'-lẹ̀*—"He who redeemed the Ifẹ̀", as some elders say; although we must not forget that there are those who think that it has reference to an Egyptian divinity from which this one derives.[1] This is one of the divinities who are "of the heavens" because the Ifẹ̀ will say emphatically that he neither came to live on earth nor has any images here. The occasion of his first visit to this earth was a dangerous quarrel which broke out between Orìṣà-nlá and Odùdúwà over some question of authority. The quarrel was going to spell catastrophe for the world as, for a frightful moment, it appeared that all was going to be lost in the burning wrath of two implacable divinities. Upstairs in heaven, however, notice of the situation had been received and Ọ̀ràmfẹ̀ was despatched to go and effect a settlement. This he began to do with a roaring, tempestuous voice which at once won the attention of everybody and called the combatants to order. Then he gave his instructions as from one who must be obeyed, told them how things must be arranged, and so ended the quarrel.

It is thought that Jàkǔta and Ọ̀ràmfẹ̀ are distinct one from another. But undoubtedly they represent one and the same conception—"The Wrath". Our sources disclose that they both have practically the same cultus, particularly with regard to rituals—a circle of ashes in the open, "bitter kola" (orogbo), and an act of worship directed towards heaven[2] are the essentials. Both have no images on earth, that is, they are not represented in graven images; and in their praise-names, the identity can be seen quite convincingly.

[1] *The Religion of the Yorubas*, by J. Olumide Lucas (Lagos, C.M.S. Bookshop, 1948), *passim*, for any word with "*ra*" in it.
[2] See Chapter 11, pp. 142 f.

The following are among the praise-names of Ọ̀ràmfẹ̀, and show that fundamentally he and Jàkǔta (Ṣàngǒ) are one:

On'-ilé ina!

.   .   .   .   .

A dá 'ni ní 'jì!

.   .   .   .   .

Inà ọ̀sǎn!
Inà gun orí ilé fẹ́ 'jú!
Ẹ̀bìtì ré fìrì ṣe gbì!

The Lord of the house of fire!

.   .   .   .   .

One who causes sudden dread!

.   .   .   .   .

Noonday fire!
Fire that mounts the roof and becomes glaring flame!
The murderous weight that strikes the ground with a resounding
force!

ṢỌPỌNÁ

Ṣọ̀pọ̀nà is a dreadful reality to the Yoruba. In Ile-Ifẹ̀, it is believed that he is one of the four divinities whom Olódùmarè invested with *Odù*.[1] His own domain seems to be "earth". He bears in a way which appears exclusive the name Olùw'aiyè (Olùwa Aiyé) or Olùwa—"Lord of the Earth" or "Lord"; Oba-'lu'aiye—"King who is Lord of the earth"; Olóde—"The Lord of the Open". The Earth, which comprises the ground on which man treads, builds, and which he cultivates, the open spaces, is his jurisdiction where it is believed that he holds absolute sway. Whether as "King" he is head of a pantheon of his own, our oral traditions do not state; nor do we have anything to tell us whether or not the other divinities pay him tribute in any form in consequence of their use of the earth. There is a vague indication in certain sayings and ritual acts of a general character that his lordship of earth is acknowledged. For example, when the Yoruba throw out water from inside the house, they usually say, *Agò o, Olóde*—"Excuse me, O Olóde". Or,

[1] See Chapters 3, pp. 25 ff., and 8, pp. 72 f.

often, when people gather together in the open for a ceremony or a musical entertainment, it is the custom first to pay respect to *Olóde* and make sure of his hospitality. Those who play *agbè*[1] begin by singing:

Ẹ jẹ' ng b' on'-ilẹ̀ lêrè,
Bi ó jẹ́ a jó;
Ẹ jẹ' ng b' on'-ilẹ̀ lêrè,
Bi ó jẹ́ a jó.

Let me obtain the landlord's permission,
If he will permit us to dance;
Let me obtain the landlord's permission,
If he will permit us to dance.

or this:

Olóko a yọ̀ ṣẹ̀ṣẹ̀,
Olóko a yọ̀ ṣẹ̀ṣẹ̀;
Òwú 'ì 'là
K' inú ó b' ólóko o:
Olóko a yọ̀ ṣẹ̀ṣẹ̀;
Àwa 'ì 'lù,
K' inú ó b' Ólóde o
Olóde a yọ̀ ṣẹ̀ṣẹ̀.

The farmer should be exceedingly pleased,
The farmer should be exceedingly pleased;
The cotton does not burst
And displease the farmer:
The farmer should be exceedingly pleased;
We do not play the instruments
And displease Olóde:
Olóde should be exceedingly pleased.

Ṣọ̀pọ̀ná is, in the belief of the Yoruba, "the destruction that wasteth at noonday". He is known as the divinity whose main scourge is smallpox. But smallpox (or chickenpox), dreadful as it is, appears to be no more than the most objective symptom of the fact that the "wrath" of the divinity is upon the victim, or upon the community, more often. Any high temperature in a patient, especially when that is accompanied by restlessness or delirium, is put down at once to the

---

[1] *Agbè* is a set of musical instruments consisting mainly of calabash drums of graded sizes, some of which are strung with cowries or seeds, and a few gongs.

divinity; a carbuncle, a particularly troublesome boil, malignant rash, are all regarded as marks of the wrath of Ṣọpọ̀ná. When people have reason to think that Ṣọpọ̀ná is "fighting" in any of these ways, he is more often than not described as *Ilẹ̀'gbóná*—"Hot-earth". That is, the earth on which people tread becomes so "hot" that it affects them adversely.[1] Because Ṣọpọ̀ná is called *Ilẹ̀'gbóná*, the Yoruba traditionally do not say *Ilẹ̀ gbóná*—"The ground is hot" when the ground is indeed hot. They employ a euphemism and say exactly the opposite of what they mean—*Ilẹ̀ tutù*—"The ground is cold". When a person has smallpox or suffers any of the afflictions believed to be caused by Ṣọpọ̀ná, the Yoruba describe the situation in terms of deep respect for the divinity. They say, *Ó nsin ọba*—"He is under bondage to the king"; *Ilẹ̀'gbóná mú u* or *Ilẹ̀'gbóná nbá a jà*—"Hot-earth has laid hand on him" or "Hot-earth is afflicting him"; *O gb' ọfà*, or *Ọfà bà a*—"He falls a victim to the arrow-shot", or "He is struck by the arrow". Ṣọpọ̀ná is described therefore also as *Alápó*—"One who bears the quiver". And when a person dies as a result of any of the afflictions, it is usually said of him not *Ó kú*—"He dies" or "He is dead" in the normal way, but that *Ọba mú u lọ*—"The king has removed him"; or *Ilẹ̀'gbóná gbé e lọ*—"Hot-earth has carried him away".

The Yoruba believe that Ṣọpọ̀ná is the "king" whose will, whatever the issue may be, must be accepted, not only with resignation but with manifest pleasure and gratitude. For example, the relatives of a deceased smallpox victim must not mourn or show in any way that they regret the death. Rather, they must put on a festive and cheerful appearance and show that they are happily thankful for what the "king" has done for them! If not, they are asking for more of the "king's" scourge! So, Ṣọpọ̀ná is known as *Alápa-dúpẹ́*—"One who kills and is thanked for it".

Ṣọpọ̀ná is an awful dread to the Yoruba: rather than call him by that name, they would employ one of his adulatory appellations. He is often depicted as prowling about when the sun is hot, robed in scarlet. People are therefore usually warned not to go about wearing red or anything with a "loud" colour or pattern lest they should appear to be insulting him with their mimicry, the consequence of which could be serious. Care must be taken, especially during the dry season, not to do anything that would offend him. And this is understandable because smallpox spreads more easily and is usually prevalent during the hot, dry season. Because he is believed to be particularly active during the

[1] See *Dahomey*, by M. J. Herskovits (New York, J. J. Augustin, 1938), Vol. II, pp. 136 ff.

dry season, he is called *A-ṣòro-'pè-l'ẹ̀rùn*—"One whose name it is not propitious to call during the dry season". He is considered fierce and almost implacable; so the whole office of his worship tends mainly to the propitiation of him so that he may leave people alone. The remedy used to heal smallpox or any ailments which are calculated to be due to his agency is called *Ẹ̀rò*—"That which softens (Ṣọ̀pọ̀ná) or eases (the restless agony of the sufferer)"; or "That which soothes (the furious nature of Ṣọ̀pọ̀ná)"; it is also called *Ẹ̀bẹ̀*—"That which propitiates or appeases".

As anyone who dies of smallpox is considered taken away by the "king", his body is not buried in the house in the customary way; it is buried in the bush. And the funeral offices are the responsibility of the priests of Ṣọ̀pọ̀ná or any special undertaker whose qualification is his possession of the requisite preventive and propitiatory medicine. As a result of the funeral offices, the undertakers claim all the articles used by the patient before he died, and sometimes even all his belongings, plus a high fee from the relatives. There is no doubt that the exclusive right of special undertakers to such funeral offices, and the removal especially of all articles used by the patient before his death, are a result of the early experience of the Yoruba about the die-hard nature of the germs of the disease. Part of what is done by those undertakers, therefore, is to take hygienic measures to prevent the spread of the disease. That the germs of smallpox belong to the class of germs which do not as a rule die with the death of the victim, the Yoruba have learnt by experience.

This knowledge of the die-hard nature of the disease germs has often been exploited with disastrous consequences by unscrupulous people. When the priests or devotees of Ṣọ̀pọ̀ná threaten to "fight" anybody or any community, what they mean is that they possess the means of spreading the disease and will do so if provoked to the point. And when they actually put up the "fight", this is what happens: they usually have in their possession some virulent preparations made up of powdered scabs or parts of the skin of a smallpox victim, or it may be fluid which they obtain through the action of the weather and putrefaction from the corpse of a victim. Either of these they throw out in an open place or at the doorstep of a house, or even in a house. By the action of the wind, or various other agencies, the germs are carried about and the disease spread.

In one town some years ago, there was an epidemic of smallpox which began in a very small way but spread quickly and threatened to be never-ending, claiming many lives and much property. There was a very proficient undertaker who was in great and urgent demand all over the place. After the epidemic had raged for some frightful time and there was no sign of its abatement, the elders knew by experience that there must be some sinister explanation for the whole situation. So there began a secret enquiry which soon revealed that the wicked, inhuman agent of the continuous epidemic was the very undertaker who had hitherto shown himself as the benefactor of his people. And how did he achieve his diabolic end? It was in this way. Most of the bodies he claimed to have buried and for which he had received very high fees had, in fact, not been buried but tied by the neck to the branches of trees in the forest, with the whole body hanging. Under each body he placed a large pot for the purpose of collecting the fluid which the weather and putrefaction caused to issue from it. This fluid he threw, in the middle of the night, all over the town. And the result was that the disease spread inexorably. The man was caught and exiled; but that was not before much irreparable havoc had been done.[1]

There are a few facts for which we have no adequate explanation yet about Ṣọpọná. He is called *A-ru-'mọ-l'-ōgùn-ikà-dànù*—"One who causes to be thrown away medicines designed for wicked ends". This is because it is believed that such are *tabu* to him, and if he "enters" any house (by way of affliction) and there is found any medicine of that nature, then the place must be cleared of it at once, or the whole house or community will pay a severe penalty for it. But he himself is depicted as armed with a quiver of poisonous arrows and numberless small gourds. The Yoruba use this type of small gourd as containers for either curative or preventive medicine as well as for poison. Could one imagine that the gourds in possession of Ṣọpọná contain only good medicine? Or does he forbid the "bad" medicine because he could not brook any rival in that field? The latter reason appears to be more probable. But when we realise that he represents "the Wrath" to the Yoruba, we see that the real reason for this conception of him is their basic belief that he frowns upon wickedness and punishes the wicked severely.

Some elders say also that Ṣọpọná and Ṣàngó are brothers, born of the same parents, and that the former is the younger. So strong is this belief that the worshippers of Ṣàngó count themselves immune from molestation by Ṣọpọná, and *vice versa*. The saying which expresses the

---

[1] See *The Religion of the Yorubas*, by J. Olumide Lucas (Lagos, C.M.S. Bookshop, 1948), pp. 131 f., for the revelation made by the late Dr. Oguntọla Ṣapara.

belief is, *Kò sí ohun ti ègbón mà fi ọmọ àbúrò ṣe*—"There is no harm that the senior brother will inflict upon the children of his junior". What is the point of this connection? Truly, according to the oral traditions, the two are not unfamiliar to each other; so familiar are they that Ṣòpọ̀ná often makes fun of Ṣàngǒ. He thinks that Ṣàngǒ likes to show off by his dazzling, rumbling, and clapping fussiness; when he is going to kill only one person, he proclaims it flashingly and loudly to the whole universe, whereas he (Ṣòpọ̀ná) will kill hundreds and people will know about it only after he has laid his hand upon his victims. Our elders often say that Ṣòpọ̀ná is to be feared more than Ṣàngǒ.

The real basis of the connection appears, however, to be their suggested common relationship to the North. We have a strong impression of that from the oral traditions, especially from the epics in which their praises are sung.

Ṣòpọ̀ná is described as *Bàbǎ mi, Gàmbàrǐ, ọmọ kò-gb'-edè*—"My father, Gàmbàrǐ, who issued from the barbarians (literally, those who do not understand the language—Yoruba)"; or *Gàmbàrǐ, Úkù-úkù, Ará Aláúsá, Ará Tapà*—"Gàmbàrǐ, Úkù-úkù,[1] indigene of Hausaland, indigene of Nupeland. He is also designed *Elémpe*—"The owner or king of Nupeland".

We have referred to the parentage of Ṣàngǒ as partly Nupe at least.[2] He is also called *Èrò Afọ̀njá*—"Immigrant from Abuja".[3]

Ṣòpọ̀ná is connected with Islam, so is Ṣàngǒ.[4] When a child is declared by the oracle on the third day after its birth to belong to Ṣòpọ̀ná, it is usually named according to the Moslem rite and any victim slaughtered during the ceremony is slaughtered by a Moslem; and the child may later be either a votary of Ṣòpọ̀ná or a Moslem. Ṣòpọ̀ná is called *On'-Imàle, Ọba n' Mọ́ṣáláṣí*—"The Moslem, king of the Mosque". He is also described as *Alágbádá*[5]—"One who wears the voluminous garment", and as one given to Moslem ablutions.

Ṣàngǒ has the appellations of *A-k'ewú-gb'-ẹrú; A-k'-éwú-gb'-ẹṣín, A-ṣ'-alùwàlá n' ibi ọfà gbé nrọ̀ 'jò.*—"One so versed in Arabic reading

---

[1] *Gàmbàrǐ* or *Úkù-úkù* are generic terms used to describe most of the Northern peoples.

[2] See above, p. 92.

[3] *Afọ̀njá* appears to be a Yoruba corruption of Abuja; as, otherwise, it is a person's name.

[4] But this may signify no more than that they are related to the North. To our people, there is the strong illusion that all Northerners are Moslems.

[5] The voluminous, flowing garment is usually connected with Islam in such a case.

as to win slaves by it; One so versed in Arabic reading as to win horses by it; One who performs ablutions under a rain of arrows!"

In Yorubaland, the Nupe immigrants are the custodians of the Gunnu cult,[1] and are notorious for being capable of starting and spreading an epidemic of smallpox, the scourge of Ṣọpọná.

Here, then, it appears that we have a link between the culture and religion of the Yoruba and that of the North, a matter which calls for more accurate investigation.

On the whole, people would prefer the shrine of Ṣọpọná to be outside the house or community, somewhere in the bush, although it could be in houses or within the village or town. Would this be so because of the fierce nature of the "King" or would it be because since there is already a human head appointed for the community, this "King"-at-large could not brook any form of rivalry and would rather stay away from the community? The former is the reason generally accepted by our people.[2] For "Who can approach consuming flame"?

ẸLÀ

There is something tantalisingly elusive about this "character" called Ẹlà. The oral traditions give the feeling that he is the "near-incarnation" of a spiritual principle which was struggling for expression but did not quite succeed in doing so before it was overwhelmed by the increasing numbers of the "gods many and lords many" of Yorubaland. The result is that his entity is not clearly defined.

It is no wonder, then, that Ẹlà has been seen in a confused light. There are those who would not hesitate to say that the name "is one of the many attributive names by which Ifá (Ọrunmìlà) is described, and a principal one among them".[3] But it is doubtful if a really knowledgeable Yoruba priest would say this. Rather, he would concede that Ẹlà is an individual entity. The baffling question is "How individual is he?" To this the oral traditions say that he is a beloved son of Ọrunmìlà—Ẹlà ọmọ-bíbí inú Àgbọnnìrègún—"Ẹlà, the very offspring of Àgbọnnìrègún"; that he is a trusted servant of Ọrunmìlà; or that he is his bosom friend. Some go further and identify him as the son of Olúorogbo.[4]

[1] Nupe Religion, by S. F. Nadel (Routledge & Kegan Paul, 1954), p. 77 ff.
[2] But see Dahomey, ibid.
[3] Yoruba Heathenism, by Bishop James Johnson (England, James Townsend, 1899), p. 29.
[4] See below, pp. 105 f.

Èlà is mentioned frequently in the *Odù* corpus. There appears to be indeed some close relationship between him and Ọ̀rúnmìlà. Ọ̀rúnmìlà has some ritual connection with the palm-tree; so does Èlà. At the annual festival of Èlà, the ritual is performed at the foot of a palm-tree sixteen days prior to the annual festival of Ọ̀rúnmìlà. Thus the festival of Èlà ushers in that of Ọ̀rúnmìlà, takes precedence of it (though the latter is much louder and more elaborate), and appears to be a vital pre-requisite to it. They are also both divinities of divination; but where palm-kernels are employed as a tool of divination when Ọ̀rúnmìlà is consulted, pieces of ivory are used in case of Èlà. Nevertheless, the two sets of tools are often kept together in the same receptacle. It has been remarked that Ọ̀rúnmìlà was sent into the world for the purpose of setting things right. Èlà is called *Alátúnṣe Aiyé*—"One who sets the world right".

From the conception of this close relationship between the two, could it be concluded that one of them is a development from the other? And if so, which is older? This is a difficult question. Our sources, on the whole, would tend to the view that Ọ̀rúnmìlà is the older of the two; if that is accepted, and if one has developed from the other, then it must be Èlà who has taken his origin from Ọ̀rúnmìlà. But no one who has made a very close and critical study of our oral traditions will be comfortable with that conclusion, however inviting it may be as a line of least resistance. We are strongly of the opinion, therefore, that Èlà as the spiritual principle is certainly older than Ọ̀rúnmìlà; and that Ọ̀rúnmìlà is a "materialised" development of Èlà. We are supported in this by the fact that there are strong traditions which say that Ọ̀rúnmìlà had parents and was born by physical generation, while the eternity of Èlà as one who is the offspring of Olódùmarè is unquestioned. But we are working here on the assumption that one of them developed from the other, which matter is little more than a weak hypothesis.

Shall we now proceed to look at Èlà as he stands by himself? The first thing of importance about him is that he is called *Èlà, ọmọ Ọṣìn*—"Èlà, the offspring of Ọṣìn". Who is Ọṣìn? In Yoruba, the word Ọṣìn is either a person's name, or a title. As a title it means "ruler" or "chief". Our sources leave us in no doubt that Ọṣìn here refers to the Ruler of rulers and Chief of chiefs, Olódùmarè: and since this is so, Èlà sprang from Olódùmarè; and it is interesting to know that he is the only one so specifically designated among the divinities.

He is described as "eternal" or, to be precise, "evergreen". There is an evergreen herb which is called Èlà and about which it is said *Èlà ki 'bd ewé oko 'rọ*—"Èlà does not wither when other plants in the forest do". This herb is used frequently for curative medicine or preventive charms; it is often planted in gardens or on the roofs of houses because it is believed to have a homoeopathic property.

While, according to our oral traditions, it was Ọrunmìlà who came down with Orìṣà-nlá to arrange earth's trappings, we have also the explicit statement that it was Èlà who organised earth's affairs and set things in their proper places. He is even described as the one who made all things, in the sense that it was through his agency that all things have their being. To him is credited the main functions of peace-making and of reconciliation wherever there is discord, and the restoration of order wherever there is chaos.

Èlà is described as one who regenerates. It is said that he rectifies unhappy destinies. *On li ó ntún orí ti kò sunwọ̀n ṣe*—"It is he who remedies unhappy lots".[1]

He is depicted as a deliverer. He delivers from Èṣù, from evil machinations, and from unfavourable issues. We remember that Ọrunmìlà is also a deliverer in that he prescribes sacrifices and shows people what to do in critical situations, present or to come. Ọrunmìlà even collaborates with Èṣù or lives in liaison with him. But Èlà is definitely opposed to the evil works of Èṣù and engages himself in obstructing him or undoing his evil deeds in the way a superior would. In this setting, Èlà appears as the one who has power over Èṣù and is able to overcome or subdue him. Èlà delivers whole communities from impending calamities.

According to *Èdi Ìwòrì* in the *Odù* corpus, Èlà is the spirit of truth, rightness, and amicable living, working on earth to create and promote order, happiness, and understanding among the inhabitants of the earth. Hence in this *Odù* we have the recital,

> Èlà Iwòrì[2] ni kì 'jẹ́kí aiyé ra 'jú;
> Nigbàtí aiyé Ọba-'lufẹ̀ dàrǔ,
> Èlà Iwòrì l' o bá a tún aiyé rẹ̀ ṣe;
> Nigbàtí awọn ọ-dà-'lẹ̀ ìlú Akìlà ba aiyé ìlu wọn jẹ́,
> Èlà Iwòrì l' o ba wọn tún u ṣe;
> Nigbàtí ọsán d' òru ni ilù Ọkẹrẹkẹ̀sẹ̀,[3]

---

[1] See above, p. 77, and Chapter 13, pp. 176 ff.
[2] *Iwòrì* is one of the main headings in the divisions of the *Odù* corpus. Èlà is frequently mentioned in the recitals under this heading.
[3] There is a suggestion that Ọkẹrẹkẹ̀sẹ̀ means Egypt and that the reference here is to the Egyptian Darkness connected with the story of the Exodus in the Bible.

Ti aiyé ìlú nã di rúdurùdu,
Ti awọn awo ibẹ̀ bà a tì,
Ẹ̀là Iwòrì l' o ba Olúyọrí ọba ibẹ̀ tún u ṣe:
Nigbàtí Ẹlẹ́gbára¹ bá nfẹ́ s' orí aiyé k' odò,
Ẹ̀là Iwòrì ní 'ma dùbú ọ̀nà rẹ̀;
Ẹ̀là Iwòrì kì 'gb' owó,
Ẹ̀là Iwòrì kì 'gb' obì,
On l' ó sì ntún orì ti kò sunwọ̀n ṣe.²

Ẹ̀là Iwòrì it is who saves the world from ruin:
When the world of Ọba'lufẹ̀ became confused,
Ẹ̀là Iwòrì it was who restored order into it;
When the covenant-breakers of Akilà spoilt the town,
Ẹ̀là Iwòrì it was who put things right for the people;
When day turned into night in the town of Ọ̀kẹ̀rẹ̀kẹ̀ṣẹ̀,
And the sages of the place were baffled,
Ẹ̀là Iwòrì it was who came to the aid of Olúyọrí, its king, with a
    remedy;
Whenever Ẹlẹ́gbára plans to turn the world upside down,
Ẹ̀là Iwòrì it is who obstructs him;
Ẹ̀là Iwòrì receives no money (as remuneration),
Ẹ̀là Iwòrì receives no kola-nuts,
Yet he it is who rectifies unhappy destinies.

Ẹ̀là is frequently invoked during worship to come and bless offerings
and make them acceptable. He is also addressed as the spirit which
inspires acceptable sacrifice as well as the life-giving sacrifice. Thus he
is the spirit which inspires correct worship; and is one whose life has
been offered. The oral traditions tell us that Ẹ̀là came into this world
and was full of good works, labouring selflessly and asking for no
reward; but he became too much for the inhabitants of the world by
reason of his goodness: he was therefore maligned and treacherously
accused of hindering the smooth running of the world. He became
offended and ascended to heaven by means of a rope. It was only then
that the inhabitants of the world found out that it is impossible really
to live without Ẹ̀là; and so since then they have been praying that he
should descend and bless them. Thus we have it further in *Èdi Ìwòrì* that

¹ Ẹlẹ́gbára is another name for Èṣù.
² *Iṣẹ̀dalẹ̀ Yoruba*, by E. A. Kẹnyọ (Lagos, 1953), p. 26.

Ẹlà ṣ' ogbó, ṣ' ogbó,
Ẹlà ṣ' atọ́, ṣ' atọ́,
O f' ọdúndún ṣ' ọba ewé,
O f' Ìròsùn ṣ' Ọṣọrun rẹ̀;
O f' Òkun ṣ' ọba omi
O f' Ọsà ṣ' Ọṣọrun rẹ̀;
A-s'-ẹ̀hìn-wa, a-s'-ẹ̀hìn-bọ̀,
Nwọn ní Ẹlà kò ṣ' aiyé 're;
Ẹlà b' inu, o ta 'kùn, o r' ọrun;
Ọmọ ar'-áiyé tún wá nkígbe:
Ẹlà dẹ̀dẹ̀rẹ̀ l' ó mã sọkalẹ̀ wa gb' ùre,
Ẹlà dẹ̀dẹ̀rẹ̀.[1]

Ẹlà indeed made old age;
Ẹlà indeed made long life;
He made Ọdúndún[2] king of leaves,
He made Ìròsùn his priest;
He made the Ocean king of waters,
He made the Lagoon his priest;
After all, and in the end,
They pronounced that Ẹlà had not conducted the world in the
    right way;
Ẹlà was offended; he stretched out a rope and ascended into
    heaven;
The inhabitants of the world changed tune and have since been
    calling out:
Ẹlà, descending, must come back to bless,
Ẹlà, descending.

Ẹlà is sometimes called Ọmọ Olúorogbo[3]—"The offspring of Olúorogbo", while there are those who would identify him with Olúorogbo.[4]
Here again we must go carefully. Olúorogbo appears to be a late arrival
among the divinities of Yorubaland, and it is quite possible that he
attracted some of the attributes of Ẹlà. Most of the deeds and functions

[1] *Isedale Yoruba*, by E. A. Kenyo (Lagos, 1953).
[2] R. C. Abraham, in *Dictionary of Modern Yoruba*, finds for Ọdúndún the
botanical name of *Kalanchoe* (*Crassulaceae*) and for Ìròsùn *Baphia Nitida*
(*Papilonaceae*).
[3] See Chapter 15, pp. 204 ff for further discussion on Olúorogbo.
[4] *The History of the Yorubas*, by Samuel Johnson (Lagos, C.M.S., 1937),
p. 147.

attributed to both of them are identical. The oral traditions have it that Olúorogbo was the son of Mọrèmi, the great heroine of Ifẹ̀ who offered him as a sacrifice in payment of a vow; but they give also the clear statement which suggests that Olúorogbo was the one who took the initiative in delivering the world from disaster and catastrophe:

O kú gégẹ́, kù gẹ̀gẹ̀, ki aiyé ó bàjẹ́,
Ni Olúorogbo wá tún aiyé ṣe.

It was but a step and a catastrophe would have befallen the world; Then Olúorogbo came and rectified the world.

In this connection, it is interesting that in Ile-Ifẹ̀, the festival of Olúorogbo is independent of that of Mọrèmi. In fact Olúorogbo and Mọrèmi have no cultic connection.

When we compare the above quotation with the first verse already quoted about Ẹ̀là, we see that they both refer to the same event or, at least, identical events. Ẹ̀là is called *Iríjú Olódùmarè; Alátŭnṣe Aiyé*— "The Prime Minister of Olódùmarè"; "One whose function it is to set the world right". Olúorogbo is also called the First Minister of Olódùmarè and the Saviour of the world. Ẹ̀là is believed to be in heaven, but directing the business of the world, being instrumental especially in the matter of spiritual contact between Olódùmarè and the world. Olúorogbo is called *Ikọ̀ Ajàláiyé Ikọ̀ Ajàlọ̀run*—"The Chief Messenger-Link between the king of earth and the King of heaven".

Ẹ̀là is thus a "character" about which we must not reach a conclusion in a hurry, especially as for many years past the Yoruba, with the full support of Ifẹ̀ priests, have made identification between Olúorogbo and Jesus Christ.[1]

The high spiritual quality and attributes of Ẹ̀là are certainly a matter for more research work and careful thought. The name Ẹ̀là means "Safety" or "One who keeps in safety"; "Preservation" or "Preserver"; "Salvation" or "Saviour".

[1] See Chapter 15, pp. 204 ff.

9

The Cult of the Divinities

WORSHIP

To the casual observer, the objective phenomena in the religion of the Yoruba are the divinities and the cults attached to them. It will be worthwhile, therefore, to give attention to these cults; and to do that, we shall begin with the fundamental subject of worship.

Worship is an imperative urge in man. Its beginning may be traced back to the basic "instinct" which was evoked in man by the very fact of his confrontation with the "numinous".[1] Man perceived that there was a Power other and greater than himself, a Power which dominated and controlled the unseen world in which he felt himself enveloped; a Power which he therefore made out by intuition to be the "ultimate Determiner of Destiny".[2] "Ye worship that which ye *know* not" may be predicated of man's ritual acts in the beginning. What happened to him was that the urgent, awesome immanence of the "wholly other" impressed itself upon him in such a compulsive way that he reacted without pausing to think why. Thus worship in its rudimentary form originated in the spontaneous and extempore expression of man's reaction as he found himself confronted with the revelation which evoked in him an active response.

With the growth of spiritual perception, belief gradually became formulated; that formulation resulted in some patterns of worship which, with the passage of time, evolved into set orders. At this stage, worship had attained a social status wherein the force of habit born of frequent repetitions resulted in a demand for conformity to approved cults. Such, roughly, was the basic process which produced all the forms of worship which we have today.

In the life of the Yoruba, worship as an imperative factor stands out prominently. As a deeply religious people, worship for them begins,

[1] Cf. Genesis 28:17; Ezekiel 1:28.
[2] *The Religious Consciousness*, by J. P. Pratt (New York, The Macmillan Co., 1946). Chapters 1 and 2 are very illuminating on this subject.

controls, and ends all the affairs of life. A Yoruba feels that he is in the presence of his divinity wherever he is and whatever he does. The active existence of the divinity is his controlling thought, whether that means for him a constant source of superstitious dread, or a sense of security which fills him with inward peace. In all undertakings, however trivial or vital, he puts his divinity first and calls upon him for blessing, support, and succour.

Worship in the religion of the Yoruba is essentially ritualistic and liturgical. The rituals follow set, fixed, and traditional patterns. "The way it is done" is the guiding principle whether worship is public or private. These traditional patterns are carefully preserved and systematically followed. Especially is this so because they have acquired magical virtues in consequence of which it is believed that they can only be efficacious when they are correctly conducted.

It is relevant at this point to remark on the personal conditions which qualify a Yoruba for worship. He must be ceremonially clean. This is important both for those who undertake the conduct of worship as it is for all worshippers in general. Ritual defilement may be incurred in several ways, depending on what are *tabu* to the particular divinity who is being worshipped. It is believed, however, that sexual intercourse immediately before worship, or when its "stain" has not been removed by thorough washing, is a thing forbidden by all the divinities. So also is it *tabu* for a worshipper to carry bad medicine on his person. The greatest obstacle to efficacious worship is impurity of heart. Thus moral and ritual cleanness have from time immemorial been accepted as a prerequisite of Yoruba worship.

Now let us give some details about worship. The daily morning worship is simple and usually private in that it is, more often than not, the doing of one person. It takes the form of saying "Good Morning" to the *orìṣà* and of reaffirming man's acknowledgment of him to be the controller of destiny, on the pleasure and blessing of whom depends the worshipper's good fortune for the day and for the future. For this simple worship, the worshipper provides himself with water and kola-nuts.

The worshipper stands before the shrine and begins the worship with the invocation wherein he calls the *orìṣà* by his names and appellations and invites him mercifully to give attention to his "child".[1] During the invocation a rattle may be sounded as if the better to attract the attention

---

[1] Worshippers of a divinity are usually described as his "children"; children are named after such a divinity by his worshippers, e.g. Èṣùbiyi—"Scion of Èṣù": See Chapter 8, p. 84.

of the divinity, and the libation is poured either on the ground or on the shrine. Then the worshipper states the reason why he is there at the shrine: this comprises a statement of the blessings which he desires, and it does not exclude curses upon his enemies. After this, the kola-nut[1] is split, and now comes an anxious moment: for the worshipper expects by the omen of the kola-nut to know whether his worship has been accepted or rejected, whether he meets with the pleasure of the *orìsà* or not, whether all will be well for the day and in the future or not.

When he has obtained a propitious omen, he joyfully concludes the worship by placing a valve or two of the kola-nut on the shrine and eating the rest. He may, if need be, store up some of the kola-nut to be given to suitable visitors, or he may ask anybody who happens to be around to partake of it.

On the sacred day of the *orìsà*, worship is more elaborate and usually involves a community of worshippers. The actual ritual follows practically the same pattern as the daily one, but there are important details which give it distinction. The worshippers are dressed up for the occasion, and there are gifts of food and drink and payment of vows[2] taken to the *orìsà*. There must be as many kola-nuts as there are worshippers, and even additional ones for those who for some reason are not present. The worshippers are presented severally to the *orìsà*. On the presentation of a worshipper, he kneels before the shrine; when the priest has concluded the presentation, the worshipper states his reasons for coming to the *orìsà* on this sacred day; the priest takes over again and restates what the worshipper has said, now making it a petition to the *orìsà*. The splitting and casting of the worshipper's kola-nut is done, and his offering (if any) is made. If all is well by the omen, he stretches out both hands and the priest lays on them the portions of the kola-nut which are his share, during the course of which the priest gives him the final blessing from the *orìsà*. Sometimes, as a part of this final blessing, the priest places an emblem of the *orìsà* on the outstretched hands of the worshipper, and the worshipper touches his forehead and breast with it and returns it, thus accepting the benedictory touch of the divinity. Where this is done, it is after it that the kola-nut pieces will be handed to the worshipper with the final words of blessing.

The main difference between worship on the sacred day and worship during the annual festival is the more elaborate programme connected with annual celebrations. This is an occasion for rejoicing and thanksgiving; people come out in their best and give of their best. The offerings

---

[1] See Chapter 10, p. 135.   [2] See below, pp. 121 ff.

are mostly thankofferings,[1] and the meals[2] constitute an opportunity of communion between the divinity and his "children" on the one hand, and then among the "children" themselves on the other. It is a time for special renewal of covenants.

Moreover, the annual festivals of the principal divinities are usually the concern of the whole community. Here the head of the community is particularly involved. Even though each *orìṣà* has his own high priest, the head of the community is accorded the honour of the *pontifex maximus*[3] and it is he who is ultimately responsible for all that happens during the festival. He also has a special ritual which, personally or by proxy, he must perform during each festival.

During this annual festival, worship is arranged privately in homes, or semi-publicly in shrines belonging to compounds or quarters. At these shrines, people take the opportunity of the annual festival of the divinity to make offerings to the ancestors who had been in the past connected with the worship of the divinity and are in a spiritual way still in communication and communion with the living. There are no separate annual festivals for the ancestors except where they have been deified.

The most significant annual worship takes place in the central shrine of the tutelary divinity of the community. Here the head of the community is present or represented. He is the first to be presented to the *orìṣà* and his own kola-nut is the first to be split and cast. After him come the other worshippers with their kola-nuts, according to their rank and status in the community.

Let us now watch a typical act of worship. We choose that of Ògún. The person on behalf of whom the worship has been arranged comes in with a covered calabash containing kola-nuts. She takes along also a sacrificial victim—a dog, and a roasted yam, a bottle of palm-oil, and a gourd of palm-wine. The priest stands up and faces the shrine. He pours a libation of water or palm-wine and, taking an all-metal hammer from the shrine, he holds it by the head and strikes the handle on the emblems of the divinity, thus making some ringing notes. While he does this, he makes the invocation in these words, *Ògún, ki o mã gbọ́ o, Awó, Lákáaiyé, Ọ̀sìn Imalẹ̀; Awọn-l'-ẹyin-'jú, ègbè l' ẹhìn ọmọ orùnkàn, on'-ilé kángunkàngun tí mbẹ l' ọ́run*—"Attend to us, O Ògún, *Awó*, He-who-is-in-control-all-over-the-world, Chief of the divinities, He-whose-eyeballs-are-rare (to see), Support behind the orphan, the Owner of the innumerable houses of heaven." Then he turns to the worshipper who at a cue states the reason why she comes to Ògún; he takes over again with

---

[1] See below, p. 121.   [2] See below, ibid.   [3] See Chapter 10, p. 132.

these words, *Lágúnjú ọmọ rẹ wa si ọ̀dọ̀ rẹ, o ni òbì, o ni epo, o ni ẹmu, o ni ẹsun 'ṣu, o ni ajá, o ni ki a mú n fún ọ, Lágúnjú nâ l ó mbẹ niwájú rẹ yi: àgàn l' o yà ti 'ò ri (ọmọ) bí, ẹkún ọmọ l' o nsun, àwẹ̀ aìrí-gbé-ddní l' o ngbà; Ògún, jẹk' ó r' ọmọ bi. . . .* "Lágúnjú, your child, is come before you, she brings to you kola-nuts, she brings palm-oil, she brings palm-wine, she brings roasted yam, she brings a dog: she asks that they be presented to you.This is the Lágúnjú before you: barren she is and has no issue; she is in tears because she has no children; she is fasting because she has none to carry in her arms; O Ògún, grant that she may have children. . . ." He then pours the palm-oil and palm-wine on or before the shrine, and casts the kola-nut. If the omen is propitious, he places a portion of the nut on the shrine. Then follows the slaying of the dog: an attendant is handed a scimitar by the priest; two other attendants hold the dog at opposite ends and pull it so that the neck stretches out taut. The attendant who holds the scimitar lifts it and shouts the ritual words thrice, while all those who are present shout back the appropriate response. By the end of the response the third time, he brings down the scimitar with full force and beheads the dog at one stroke.[1] The two parts of the dog are now lifted dripping blood and the whole shrine is smeared and rubbed with the blood. The priest cuts off its extremities and places them on the shrine. He cuts the yam to pieces and lays some of it upon the shrine, placing the rest in a calabash to be shared by the people who are joining in the worship. Lastly, he strikes the emblems again as he did during the invocation and says, *Ògún l' og-bó, o l' atọ́, o l' aìkú, o l' aìrùn, o n' akókò ire; o mu fún ọ*—"Ògún has old age, he has longevity, he has immortality, he has non-corruption, he has time of blessing; he gives them to you". He then stretches out the hammer to the suppliant, who takes it in her outstretched hands, touches her forehead and breast with it, saying, *O t' ara mi o*—"It (the blessing) rests upon me"—and returns it to the priest. Still kneeling with outstretched hands, she receives her own portion of the kola-nut with the final words of blessing from the priest: and so ends the worship.

Frequency of Worship

As we have observed, worship takes place regularly every morning at the shrines. Usually, it takes place before the worshipper speaks to any person.

[1] The ritual demand is that the cutting must be at one stroke; the sacrifice is marred where this is not successful. Then a brick is first cut asunder before another attempt is made at the victim.

There is also regular worship on the sacred days of the divinities. It appears that, originally, the sacred day of each divinity came round every fifth day, and it is possible that the same sacred day was observed for them all. This would be based on the belief that the creation of the earth was completed in four days.[1] There is a saying that *Ifá l' o l' ònì Ifá l 'o l' ọla, Ifá l' o l' ọtũnla, Ifá l' o ni 'jọ mẹrin orìṣà dá 'lé aiyé*—"To *Ifá* belongs today, to *Ifá* belongs tomorrow, to *Ifá* belongs the day after tomorrow, to *Ifá* belongs the four days in which the *Orìṣà* created the earth". Some of the principal divinities still have their sacred days every fifth day. This is so, for example, with Orìṣà-nlá and Ọrunmìlà. But with the bewildering multiplication of the divinities, it became quite impossible to fit every one of them into that pattern; and so while there are those who have the privilege of the original tradition, there are those who have their sacred days on every seventh or ninth day, or even every seventeenth day.

What happened to the sacred day fixtures happened also probably to the annual festivals. A careful calendar has been worked out so that the festivals of the divinities in each locality do not clash. This is necessary as the head of the community is specially concerned, and the whole community interested, in each of the principal festivals. *Gbogbo ọdún ni ọdún ọba*—"All festivals belong to the king". The Head of the community names the date of each festival, or the date is fixed in his name, as the festival approaches. In some places the date on which the festival begins is fixed seventeen days before, and in others nine days. The date naturally varies slightly from year to year because the Yoruba reckon by the appearances of the new moon.

The number of the divinities is such that by the time everyone of them has taken a sacred day and a date for the annual festival the whole cycle of the months and the year should have been covered. Thus, in some deeply religious communities, there is sure to be some ritual celebration going on almost all the time.

Apart from the regular daily or seasonal worship, there are special arrangements made for worship according to the needs of the community. This kind of specially arranged worship is very frequent because, as we have observed, the Yoruba are generally incapable of beginning any venture without consulting the oracle; and the oracle usually directs that one divinity or the other, or an ancestor, should be worshipped or propitiated. Also, people often ask for worship to be arranged in order to make a votive offering, present a thankoffering, or assure themselves of the continued blessing of the divinity. Often also,

[1] Chapter 3, p. 20.

people come before the divinities as suppliants asking for special blessings—children, prosperity, victory over enemies, or any of the manifold things of this life of which they feel in need for their spirit, body, or estate. For all these the people in charge of the cults of the divinities cater and thus keep the attendances at the shrines going all the time. How simple or elaborate this kind of worship is will depend on the prescription by the oracle or the purse of the worshipper.

Music

Music finds an important place in worship in the religion of the Yoruba. The music may be quiet, loud, or noisy; that depends on the kind of worship in which it occurs. It may be just singing; it may be singing accompanied by clapping; or singing accompanied by instruments. Again, the kind of worship decides how full the instrumental accompaniment should be. The instruments may be two pieces of bamboo, sticks, or metal, held by each member of the congregation; it may be a drum; it may be a stick and a gong, or sticks and gongs; it may be all of these together.

In the quiet, daily morning worship, music rarely occurs because the worshipper is more often than not the priest alone, or the priest and one attendant or two. But on the sacred days of the divinities, there is usually singing in the set order of worship and such singing is often accompanied with instruments. How full or loud the instrumental accompaniment is will depend on the rank or status of the particular divinity concerned. On the occasion of an annual festival, however, the set order of worship demands a full accompaniment of instruments.

The liturgical nature of Yoruba rituals makes their language recitative; and Yoruba speech is so tonal that the quick, rhythmical recital of ritual words takes on the nature of chanting. There is no doubt, however, that there is deliberate intonation when it is said that *Nwọn nki orìṣà*—"They chant the praise of the divinity". This is of the nature of an epic; but it can be long drawn-out, depending on how much there is to say about a particular divinity. Every divinity has a set of praise-names with stories which are recited about him in commemoration of his origin, greatness, past deeds, ability and capability.

Hymns occur often in communal worship. Each divinity has his own set hymns which are connected with his cult. These are sung as occasion demands—some only during the sacred day worship, and others during the annual worship; some in times of crisis or at funerals. In the set orders of worship, where they are strictly followed, there are appropriate traditional points at which hymns are sung. When such a place is reached, the hymn is struck up by the officiant or by one of his attendants; or it may be sung antiphonally by a number of officiants, the congregation joining in the chorus. The traditional number of the hymns and the points at which they are sung vary with each liturgy; in some there may be an invocatory song, a hymn of call to worship, a hymn of adoration, a hymn of prayer committing the worshippers to the care of the divinity, and a parting hymn, all set at intervals within the order of worship. In others there may be a set of up to seven hymns coming together at the end of the ritual.

Besides these hymns, lighter songs may occur during the ritual. This is often so during the annual worship when they may be struck up spontaneously by any worshipper after a successful casting of the kola-nut: these are songs of rejoicing that offerings have been accepted.

Let us quote a few examples of Yoruba hymns and songs.

(a) Here is a hymn of adoration in praise of Orìṣà-nlá:

> Ẹni ṣ' ojú, ṣe 'mu,
> Orìṣà ni ma sìn;
> A dá 'ni b' ó ti rí,
> Orìṣà ni ma sìn;
> Ẹni rán mi wá,
> Orìṣà ni ma sìn.

> He who makes eyes, makes nose,
> It is the Orìṣà I will serve;
> He who makes one as he chooses,
> It is the Orìṣà I will serve;
> He who sends me here,
> It is the Orìṣà I will serve.

(b) A hymn of prayer, committing the worshippers to the care of the divinity.

> Baba ọmọ,
> Ṣ' ogùngùn f' ọmọ o,
> Ọmọ l' ogùngùn.

> Father of children!
> Prepare medicine for the children:
> The children have no medicine[1]

[1] This implies that they are entirely dependent upon him.

(c) A song of rejoicing which signifies an assurance of certain blessing:

> *Mo m' ẹiyẹ rú 'bọ,*
> *Mo m' ẹiyẹ̆ rú 'bọ,*
> *Ọràn mi d' ẹ̀yẹ̀-ẹ̀yẹ[1]*
> *Mo m' ẹiyẹ̆ ru 'bọ.*

I make sacrifice of a bird:
I make sacrifice of a bird:
My affairs become very prosperous,
I make sacrifice of a bird.

(d) A parting hymn at the close of the annual worship:

> *A ṣì mã rí 'ra l' ẹ̃mírìn,*
> *Ọdọ̃dún l' ă rí yemẹtì.*

We shall meet again next season,
Annually habitually appears *yemẹtì*.[2]

Music during the solemn rituals at the shrines does not, as a rule, evoke dancing. But there is a place for dancing in the rituals, especially during the sacred day worship and certainly during the annual festival celebrations. Now, ritual dances of this kind are not mere random movements or mere emotional responses to the rhythm of music. They are symbolic and often re-enactments of something sacred, the history of which may still be remembered or may have been forgotten.[3] Most of the dances, except where they are only expressions of religious conviviality, are of fixed patterns and must be done correctly—which foot goes forward first, which movements of the hands and body accompany it, which turns are taken next, and how many times each component of the pattern is to be repeated—all these must be carefully observed. This correctness is more than a matter of form, as we have mentioned; it is a sacred obligation the default in which, the Yoruba believe, may be ruinous to the efficaciousness of the ritual. The "speech" of the musical instruments is often designed to guide the dancers in their movements.

---

[1] Here is a play on the Yoruba words *ẹiyẹ* (bird) and *ẹ̀yẹ* (prosperity) which cannot be reproduced in English. The play on words bears a homoeopathic connotation.
[2] Yemẹtì is an insect found annually on the cotton plant. Here again is a homoeopathic connotation.
[3] See article by H. U. Beier in *Nigeria* (No. 52, 1956), pp. 10 ff.

Prayers

The heart and centre of prayers in the religion of the Yoruba is petition. As we have observed, when the worship is congregational, the worshippers severally present their requests to the divinity through the priest. Where the worship is private, the worshipper does so immediately.

The petitions are largely for what may be described technically as material blessings. They consist usually of asking for protection from sicknesses and death, gifts of longevity, children, prosperity in enterprises, victory over enemies, protection from evil spirits and of relatives near and distant, rectification of unhappy destinies, and abundant provision of material things; blessing on all well-wishers and damnation on all ill-wishers.

Because of this objective petitionary character of prayers in the religion of the Yoruba, the hasty assertion has been made that the Yoruba do not yet know the essential meaning of prayer as communion. Let us be careful here. We must learn to understand our terms. Basically, prayer is not "a state of mind". True prayer cannot be just that even at its "highest". In true prayer, belief in, and knowledge of, the Deity "as personal comes to clear and emphatic expression".[1] Man enters into a personal relationship with the Deity, and in that relationship man as a creature is confronted with the Deity as Creator and "Determiner of Destiny". When this supreme awareness is uppermost, there is set in motion what Farmer describes as "a spontaneous and unbidden impulse" in the heart of man. Admittedly, the objective petitionary character of Yoruba prayers shows that the fulfilment of man's desires, rather than the will of the Deity, is their *esse*—"My will be done", rather than "Thy will be done",[2] but that is because all the time the Yoruba are basing prayer on the fundamental notion that the will of the Deity is supreme anyway and that His will is the ultimate answer to their prayers. We have noticed that their *Àṣẹ*—"May it be sanctioned" or "May it come to pass" is an affirmation of their belief that nothing happens unless He permits it. This is a point at which we need carefully to distinguish between religion and magic and, therefore, between prayers and incantations. The Yoruba presents his petitions— the very word shows the attitude of mind which accompanies the prayer—not with the attitude of one who is bringing divine power

[1] *The World and God*, by H. H. Farmer (London, Nisbet, 1943), Chapter 8, the whole of which is very illuminating on this subject.

[2] *Christianity in Africa*, by Diedrich Westermann (O.U.P., 1926), p. 75.

under control for his own benefit, but as one who asks for a favour the granting of which he knows depends entirely upon the will and pleasure of his "Determiner of Destiny".

In the religion of the Yoruba prayers are undoubtedly deeply tinged with eudaemonism; but eudaemonism is far from all that there is to it. Inasmuch as Yoruba divinities are believed to be not "impersonal" entities, but "personal" beings with each of whom man is in parent–child relations, the Yoruba have been brought into a relationship which is motivated not merely by the desire for material benefits. We have already an expression of that spontaneous religion whereby man is completely dependent upon the Deity because that is the nature of things. This relationship has ample illustration in the "unbidden" confidence with which the Yoruba often regard their divinities as also in the fact that one often meets a devotee who is engrossed by the divinity to the extent that he addresses conversations to him at any time and in any place, just as a person talks to someone with whom he is sitting face to face or side by side.

Prayers are offered, not only at worship, but also at any time and in any place as the worshipper feels or occasion demands. People often stop on their way at shrines to offer brief prayers; or they may speak their prayers in intimate ways to their divinity, whom they believe to be ever-present though unseen, as they walk along the road or as they are engaged in their work. Usually, women are the more religious ones who are more frequently caught in this practice by wayside shrines, sacred trees, sacred brooks, at cross-roads, or at any other places marked with some sacred signs, asking for a blessing on their journey, their work, their wares, their family, or their private undertakings. Ejaculatory prayers at all times form part and parcel of the common life of the Yoruba.

Posture and Attitude at Worship.

The worshipper kneels throughout, facing the shrine. The priest faces the shrine, turning his back to the people and standing erect or bending his body according to the height of the shrine or the tradition of his cult. He faces the worshippers only when he offers them blessing from the divinity or puts in their hands pieces of kola-nuts or portions of the ritual meal. It is a breach of tradition when, in an open-place shrine, the priest is encircled by a throng of pushing and shuffling spectators— which is a thing that not infrequently happens during public festivals these days.

During the conduct of worship, the priest usually bares his head and the upper part of the body, leaving a loin cloth on the lower part. There are cults which demand that all men at worship should also wear nothing on their heads and the upper part of their bodies. As for the women, blouses must be removed, the head bared, wrappers tied above the breast with headties to hold them in place.

Sacrifice

Sacrifice is of the essence of the religion of the Yoruba as it is of every religion the world has ever known. It is inconceivable to have a religion without some form of sacrifice, however modified or refined it may be. Sacrifice is primarily a means of contact or communion between man and the Deity. It is man's best way of maintaining an established relationship between himself and his object of worship. What is offered and how it is offered depends upon the nature of the particular cult as well as the occasion of the sacrifice.

In sacrifice, the Yoruba offer almost all kinds of foods and drinks, and all kinds of living things. Two things must be taken into consideration, however. First, each divinity, by tradition, has his own particular "taste" which must be respected. Therefore, there are foods which are customarily offered to each of them. For example, Orìṣà-nlá delights in snails cooked in shea-butter (although his priests make sure that he has something more substantial from time to time!); Ọrúnmìlà normally prefers his rat and fish to anything else; the staple food of Ṣàngó is ram; Ògún relishes dogs and roasted yams and snails[1]; while Èṣù will do anything for a cock. Every one of the divinities takes kola-nuts; the exception is Ṣàngó who would rather have orógbó ("bitter kola"). Secondly, there are certain foods or drinks which are *tabu* to each divinity. For example, Orìṣà-nlá does not drink palm-wine: it should not be taken near his shrine, and his worshippers should not touch it; Èṣù does not like palm-kernel oil: anyone who brings it near him is therefore asking for trouble upon himself or upon someone else.[2]

For special types of sacrifice as outlined below, the offerings vary according to the type of sacrifice or the prescription of the oracle.

In theory, all sacrifices belong entirely to the divinities. But in practice, worshippers often partake of them, especially of things which can be eaten. These sacrifices of which the worshippers can partake are of the nature of communion. In that case, bits of everything offered are placed on or before the shrine as a token, and then the rest is eaten up by the worshippers. The parts thus left on or before the shrine in case

[1] See Chapter 8, p. 88.　　　[2] See Chapter 8, p. 83.

7. A votary of Ṣàngǒ in a state of possession, Ọ̀yọ́

8. At worship

9. The central shrine of Ògún, Ilé-Ifẹ̀

of animal, bird, or reptile victims, are the entrails and the extremities. When, however, the ritual demand or the oracular behest is that the sacrifice should be given up wholly to the divinity, then the sacrifice is burnt, exposed, or buried.

The highest type of sacrifice among the Yoruba used to be human sacrifice. No one can be quite sure that this sacrifice is not being offered, if secretly and only on urgent occasions even these days, although after the establishment of British rule in the country, it was made illegal. In the old days, human sacrifice by the Yoruba was the climax of sacrifices. The occasion was more often than not a matter of national or communal importance. There were divinities to whom the annual offering must be a human. Such was Ọ̀ràmfẹ̀ of Ile-Ifẹ̀ and of Ondǒ; so also was Ògǔn.[1] The sacrifice was also offered whenever it was believed expedient that someone should die as a sacrifice of appeasement in order that the community might be saved.

The victim of human sacrifice was usually made to bless the people in some prescribed way which bore upon the occasion of the sacrifice. He was then given a special message which he was to deliver on arrival in the presence of the Deity or the divinities. Then followed the actual sacrifice when he was ritually completely buried alive, or buried with just the head showing above the ground; his throat might be cut before he was buried—then his blood would be drained and his extremities with certain members of his body cut and these put together would be exposed in the shrine; his corpse also might be exposed in an open place: there the carrion-birds and the weather would eventually finish off the remains. The greater the avidity with which the carrion-birds disposed of the body, the better omen it was believed to be for the cause for which the sacrifice was offered.

In certain cases, a human who was sacrificed was more than just a victim offered to appease the divinities. He was believed to be going to represent the people before, and carry their petitions to, the higher power. Therefore, before the sacrifice, he was treated with reverence and accorded an extraordinary status. Ironically enough, he was expected to put in every good word possible on behalf of those who offered him up. Because he was an ambassador, he was accompanied in the burial with certain things to be delivered with his message: those were things which were calculated to be efficacious in securing the pleasure of the divinities or the ancestors.

The notion which has been spread abroad that the Yoruba did not, as

[1] See Chapter 8, p. 89.

a rule, offer their own kith and kin in sacrifice is not quite correct. The moral prerequisite to such a sacrifice was that shortly before the sacrifice, a warning must be sounded publicly that there was the likelihood of "someone missing within the next few days" and in order to be safe from such a tragedy, everybody should keep indoors after a certain hour of the night for a specified period. That meant that at certain hours of the night during that period, those who had been prepared to catch a victim would be abroad, and the very first person they met, if he was suitable for their purpose, would be caught, no matter who he might be. Someone, a stranger very likely, usually fell into the trap and was sacrificed. There were, however, specific cases in which the ritual demands were that the victims should be contributed by certain chiefs in the community from the membership of their own compound. In such cases, the victims would be household slaves who had been acquired by purchase or as war captives. Should the oracle be still more definite about the victims, then whatever was mentioned would be sacrificed. There were secret societies the members of which customarily sacrificed in turns their own offspring.

S. S. Farrow observes correctly that "the supreme sacrifice of the Yoruba is, of course, human sacrifice".[1] He seems, however, unable to give this phenomenon in the religion of the Yoruba a correct interpretation. For us who have been brought up in the Christian faith with the all-round freedom which it gives, it is often difficult to interpret sympathetically the cults of other religions. Every worshipping nation of the world has at one time or another offered human sacrifices. That should have warned us that there is something vital in this rudimentarily persistent element in the religions of the world; and should not be sufficient justification for us to call any people low or degraded. The basic purpose of sacrifice is right relationship between man and the Deity; the more urgent the need for the maintenance or restoration of that relationship, the higher the condition man is prepared to fulfil. An Abraham at the point of offering up an only son, or a Jephthah sacrificing an only daughter, or a man of Micah's day asking in perplexity, "Shall I give my first born for my transgression, the fruit of my body for the sin of my soul?", was only a man who had an urge within him to give *the best possible* to the "Determiner of Destiny". Such a person is surely immature in his knowledge of the Deity, but he was not "degraded". Let us make sure that we understand the terms we use. With the development of religion and a clearer knowledge of the

[1] *Faith, Fancies, and Fetich* (London, S.P.C.K., 1926), p. 98.

will of the Deity, man inevitably corrects his interpretation of that will with regard to sacrifice. He knows that the God who is Spirit desires only to be worshipped in spirit and in truth. That does not mean, however, that the sacrifice of human life is excluded. The element remains or religion is emptied of meaning. It only becomes at its highest point sublimated and spiritualised. One must come to the stage at which one realises that the real sacrifice which should be offered is not someone else's life, but the voluntary "laying down" of one's own, following the example of God Himself. "Greater love hath no man than this, that a man lay down his life for his friends"; "I beseech you therefore, brethren, by the mercies of God, to present your bodies a living sacrifice, holy, acceptable to God, which is your reasonable service."[1]

We shall now proceed to look at some major categories of Yoruba sacrifice.

(a) Meal and Drink Offerings:

These begin with the customary libations offered at the shrines daily and the oil poured on the emblems of the divinities. A real offering is offered on the sacred days of the divinities. The meals are of the kind which the worshippers eat in their houses, although they are of richer quality. Primarily the offerings are means of communion between the *orìṣà* and the worshippers who are his "children", and consequently a means of fellowship among the "children" themselves.

The meal is placed before the *orìṣà* and he is besought to accept it. His acceptance of it is ascertained by the casting of the kola-nut. When it is sure that the offering has been accepted, a portion is placed on or before the shrine, and the remainder shared among the worshippers. This ritual is always characterised by a certain form of rejoicing.

(b) Gift or Thankoffering:

There are sacrifices which are offered as gifts to the divinities. By nature the Yoruba are open-handed. That is manifest in every aspect of their life; and it is marked in the way they freely offer things to their *orìṣà* as gifts. They act in this way just as they would to the family elder or village head. At certain times, they feel that it is the right thing to do to take gifts to the *orìṣà*.

Often, offerings are made to the *orìṣà* in appreciation of some success in, or prosperous issue of, an enterprise. Women who have sold well in the market, the person who has been blessed with a much-desired child, one who has received a special mark of divine favour, all want to show

[1] John 15:13; Romans 12:1.

their thanks to the *orìṣà* whom they believe to be the dispenser of their special blessing. The Yoruba abhor ingratitude which with them is a grievous sin. Their keen sense of gratitude they therefore show in their dealings with the being whom they believe to have conducted their destiny prosperously. So an offering of money, ornaments, animals, fowls, or vegetables, is made in thankfulness for favours received. The worshipper may choose his offering, guided by the "taste" of the *orìṣà* or the need of the shrine. If, however, a person has been found ungrateful by the oracle and is therefore under compulsion to make an offering which, in that case, will be both a thankoffering and an appeasement, it is the oracle that will dictate what should be offered.

(c) Votive Offering—*Ẹbọ Ẹ̀jẹ̆*:

People frequently go before the *orìṣà* as suppliants to beg for certain favours in return for which they make a vow to offer something. This kind of sacrifice depends on whatever vow has been made; but it is the strong belief of the Yoruba that whatever is vowed must be fulfilled on pain of serious consequences. There are several Yoruba stories of people who came under disastrous judgments because they failed to redeem their vows. The most popular of such stories is that of Olúrómbí. Olúrómbí wanted a child; and so she presented her petition before an *Iróḳ̀* tree,[1] making a vow that if she had the child, she would make an offering of the very child to the tree-spirit. The child duly arrived; it was a baby of striking loveliness; it grew into a fair, beautiful young person. Olúrómbí remembered her vow but found it impossible to make a sacrifice of such an attractive child, and an only child besides. So she temporised, thinking that she might be able by some means to evade such a costly votive offering. The day of vengeance came upon her suddenly, however. She had been to the market with her comely child and was returning home in the evening, passing by the *Iróḳ̀* tree, when without warning the child left her side and walked straight to the tree. He stood at the foot of the tree and began to sing of the judgment which had overtaken his mother. As he was singing, he was sinking into the ground. Olúrómbí offered any and everything that she could think of to avert the certain calamity of losing her child but it was all to no avail. In the end the child sank completely and disappeared from sight, leaving Olúrómbí childless. The Yoruba think carefully before they make their vows because once made, they are irrevocable.

[1] African Teak. The tree is a sacred tree believed to be inhabited by a powerful spirit.

(d) Propitiation:

Sacrifice in this category is known as *Ẹbọ Ètùtù*—"Sacrifice of appeasement". Usually, this sacrifice is prescribed by the oracle or an *orìṣà* in reply to an enquiry as to what can be done to save the situation during a crisis like an epidemic, famine, drought, or serious illness. When this sacrifice involves a whole community, it can be a very expensive undertaking, as the prescription may involve up to two hundred each of several articles, animate or inanimate, or up to a total of two hundred and one of several articles put together. With an individual, it may be as little as a fowl or a pigeon, or as much as a four-footed animal with some other articles added to it. In the old days, a human offering used to be the main feature of the sacrifice.

As this sacrifice is never shared with the *orìṣà*, it may be buried, burnt, or treated with oil and exposed. The underlying belief of the ritual act is that after such a sacrifice, the manifestation of "the wrath" will be withdrawn.

(e) Substitutionary:

This is known as *A-yẹ̀-'pin-ùn* (*A-yẹ-ipin-ohùn*)—"That which alters an agreement". A little explanation is necessary here. The Yoruba believe that there are companies of *Eléré* or *Emèrè*—"Wandering spirits of children given to the prank of entering into pregnant women and being born only to die for the sheer relish of the mischief".[1] Anyone of them who is being sent on this errand of mischief must covenant with his "companions" that on a named date he would "return to his normal life"; that is, he must die from this world. Whenever anyone believed to be of this company is born, the parents take every care to prevent his "returning". Very often, it is believed, he will "return" in spite of every precaution. However, the oracle usually prescribes a sacrifice whereby a substitute may be offered as a satisfaction for a breach of the covenant, and that is believed to have the effect of preventing the person from being carried away by his "companions". This sacrifice is found necessary when the person is very ill and is in danger of dying, or if there has been an urgent warning by the oracle. It takes its name thus from the purpose it serves—that of altering the agreement made between the person and his "companions".

Another sacrifice under this same category is called *Ba-mi-d'-iya* —"That which bears the punishment which is my due" or "That which bears punishment for me". It is a sacrifice offered when a person

[1] See Chapter 14, p. 196.

is believed to be under the wrath of the *orìṣà* or some malignant spirits. The end of his trouble would have been death; but such a sacrifice, if offered according to prescription, would save him. What is offered therefore is a substitute for him.

In almost every case, a sheep is the victim used as substitute for a human. There are other articles to be added, of course. The sheep and the accompanying articles are rubbed against the body of the suppliant; often his head is gently touched against the head of the sheep to ensure the transfer of his destiny as far as the illness and imminent death are concerned, to the sheep. Then the sheep is treated like a corpse and buried with funeral rites as if it was the suppliant. Occasionally, the sacrifice may be exposed in the bush.

A substitutionary ritual act often involves a change of interest or occupation for the suppliant; and something of value to him is often offered with the sacrifice. There was, for example, a popular stilt-dancer who became grievously ill. When the oracle was consulted about him, it was revealed that he was so ill because the witches were jealous of his popularity and therefore wanted to make a feast of him! A substitutionary sacrifice was therefore prescribed; this was buried, and with it his stilts; and he was forbidden to dance on stilts for ever after.

(f) Preventive—*Ogunkòjà* (*Ogun-kò-jà*)—"That which wards off attacks":

Such a sacrifice is either public or private. It is often a precautionary measure to ward off evil or misfortune. Also, it is offered when there is definite knowledge of an impending disaster. If, for example, a neighbouring village or town is plague-stricken, a sacrifice may be offered to prevent its spread. Sometimes, there may be a prediction that some unnamed trouble may be entering or passing through the community. In that case, a sacrifice is also offered to ensure the protection of the community. The prediction may take such an indefinite form as that "a stranger will be passing through the place and, in order that he may pass through peacefully, let a sacrifice be made!"

The animal victim of this sacrifice may be slain and offered up in the ordinary way; but more often than not, it is buried at the entrance to the town, village, compound, or house. The offering need not be animal, however. The oracles or the priests often prescribe, for example, that each person in the community should rub his body all over with an article—a penny or a head of maize for example—and drop it at a given place from which all will be collected and disposed of according to the particular ritual demand for the occasion. So, preventive sacrifice is either buried, burnt, exposed, or carried away by the priests to be treated as the oracle prescribes.

(g) Foundation

Sacrifice in this category combines the nature of propitiation and preventive. It is to appease the spirit of the earth in order that all may be well with that which is being founded. The sacrifice is offered at the foundation of a house, village, or town. The oracle is first consulted to find out what should be done; and when the required guidance has been obtained, the victims and articles for the sacrifice are taken to the spot where the foundation is to be made and there offered up.

A foundation sacrifice is sometimes called *A-d'-ibodè*—"That which bars the gates". It is a name which implies that the sacrifice is meant to prevent evil from entering the place. In the old days, the victims would be human beings buried alive and armed like sentries guarding all the entrances. Sheep, cows, or oxen take the place of human beings nowadays.

Shrines and Temples

When worship began, man must have worshipped anywhere and everywhere as the "unbidden impulse" seized him in a world which was charged with the all-pervading immanence of the supernatural. It would not be long, however, before he began to mark out certain spots as more significant than others with regard to his religious awareness. While the world around grew progressively familiar, there would be certain phenomena, certain experiences, or certain events, which refused to fit into the category of "the ordinary" and therefore spoke to his mind of some specific Presence which had immediate connection with his notion of the "Determiner of Destiny". Thus he began to associate certain spots with this specific Presence and mark them out from the rest in some recognisable way. Certain rocks, trees, plants, lakes, rivers, streams, the heavenly phenomena, became to him unmistakable repositories of the Presence. He himself created reminders of such spots where they had not been naturally marked.

The earliest shrines, then, must have been either natural or man-made in the sense that stones or sticks were deliberately placed to mark sacred spots. As man was probably on the move most of the time in those early times, it would be necessary for him to create for himself such reminders. But when he began to live a settled life and the character of his object of worship became defined, it dawned upon him that the object of worship could be approached wherever he was; only he had to assure himself of the Presence by finding the same kind of potential repository as had given him his earlier experience. Therefore wherever he saw the same kind of tree, plant, rock, lake, stream, or river, as the earlier one, he regarded it as invested with the virtue of the Presence.

When he began to build dwellings for himself, he reached the stage at which it came to him that the object of his worship could come and dwell with him in his abode, to be part and parcel of his life, acting in the capacity of the President of domestic life and Director of all destiny.

Communal shrines must have come into being very early because man has never been really solitary. While every individual person may worship in his own private way, there has always been the communal significance of worship. That means that shrines which belonged to the whole community as a result of common beliefs came into existence. The social character of worship would inevitably result in the putting up of sacred buildings to hold such emblems of the divinities as should be kept secret and preserved from the common touch or the weather. These buildings would naturally be small, as their sole end was to house the emblems and nothing else besides, except standing room for the custodian of the cultus, with perhaps one or two helpers.

Among the Yoruba, shrines abound all over the land. They exist in all places which are traditionally connected with the presence of the divinities, or such places as have been consecrated to them. Therefore, they are found in traditionally sacred forests. There are divinities which people believe should be better worshipped there than in the towns or houses. Several species of trees are regarded as habitual residences of certain spirits: prominent among these are Ìrókò (African Teak) and Egungun (Silk Cotton Tree). While certain sacred trees are more often than not associated with incorporeal, though powerful spirits, there are others which are usually the sacred emblems of certain principal divinities. Akòko is sacred to Ògŭn, for example. The foot of the sacred tree is the shrine and there acts of worship are performed and sacrifices offered either as prescribed by the oracle or as dictated by the need of the suppliant. Lakes, streams, and rivers have always been associated with divinities and spirits among the Yoruba. The Yoruba believe that in connection with every lake, stream or river, there is a "lord" or "owner". There are therefore water shrines, on a large or a small scale, according to the status of the divinities or spirits whose they are. Among the principal Yoruba riverain divinities are Òṣun and Erinlẹ̀. Several waters are called by the names of the divinities or spirits which people believe to be their "owners". Worship takes place on the bank or at the sources of the waters and offerings are cast into them for the divinities. At cross-roads and by roadsides, and in open places there are shrines especially for "ubiquitous" and wanderer divinities like Èṣù and Ògún.[1] As the divinity of the artisans, Ògún has his shrine in every smithy. There he is the tutelary genius; his shrines are also at the approaches to the shrines of other divinities in some parts of the land, because he is the "way", to and from all divinities.[2]

Almost all the divinities, if not every one of them, have shrines in dwelling houses. In each house, a divinity occupies the central position by virtue of his status as the tutelary "owner" of the place, and is part and parcel of domestic life.

There are divinities and spirits which have their shrines in groves. Such divinities and spirits are, in the main, those whose cults are secret. Orò and Egúngún[3] are principal examples. In those cults, women are excluded while men become members through initiation. Usually, the simple grove is a clearing in the bush; this holds the shrine, and only the initiates may enter there. Often the sacred emblems are kept in a small mud building into which only the priest or the priest with one or two co-officiants usually enters. Large communal groves may have up to three "apartments". There is the large, open place, where all and sundry may come. This may be just outside the entrance to the grove or immediately inside it, beyond the entrance. Even women go as far as this place to hand over their offerings and partake in general worship. Next is an inner clearing which is open to all classes of the initiates. Here certain rituals are performed, and the food brought by the women is properly accepted by the spirit! The third and innermost part is the sacred place which holds the most sacred emblems. This place is forbidden to all except a very few highly privileged people. Where the grove belongs to the *Egúngún* cult,[4] it is there that the regalia of the *egúngún* is put on. There also, the opening and final rituals often take place.

A shrine is primarily the "face"[5] of the divinity. There the divinity is represented by the emblems which are regarded as sufficient reminders of his attributes. For example, the shrine of Ògún as set in the smithy is an elevated place in a corner and contains the emblems which are

[1] See Chapter 8, pp. 80 ff.   [2] Ibid.
[3] See Chapter 14, pp. 192 ff.   [4] Ibid.
[5] Cf. "Peniel"—Genesis 32:30. See also Chapter 14, p. 197.

smith's tools, scraps of iron and (not invariably) a graven emblem in brass on an iron handle stuck in the ground or stood in a corner of the shrine. It is the place where the divinity is called upon and worshipped. It is certain, however, that the Yoruba believe that a shrine is only a "local" meeting-place between the divinity and man. The nature of invocations and the fact that there are usually several shrines to the same divinity in one community, as well as all over the country, show that the Yoruba do not regard any one shrine as the permanent and only abode of the divinity. At the shrine, the divinity gives the people his blessing while the people render him his due in worship.

The Yoruba do not build magnificent temples for their divinities. Their sacred buildings are usually small and are designed primarily to house the communal shrines of the divinities. At worship, only the priest and one or two attendants enter the temple, primarily because there usually, are emblems which only the consecrated persons are allowed to see and, incidentally, because the house cannot contain more than just that few. A large temple is large only because there is an enclosure built round, or a kind of court built as an extension to the small building which *is* the temple. The Yoruba do not build sacred houses in which people can congregate for worship. The place for the congregation is the open air in front of the temple.

10

The Cult of the Divinities
continued

PRIESTHOOD

When the awareness of the Deity first came upon man, he became aware at the same time that there was about Him an atmosphere in which a peculiar property resided, an atmosphere different in quality from that of the natural world in which he lived his commonplace life. His natural instinct warned him that between these two worlds, the world of the supernatural and his own natural world, there was a sharply defined spiritual line of demarcation which could not be crossed except with due and adequate precautions. Something happened at some time in his experience and this put him on his guard by letting him know in terms which could not be mistaken that he could trespass wantonly beyond this demarcation only at his own peril.[1]

At the same time, however, there was an irresistible urge laid upon him to make contact with the supernatural world because his very life depended upon it. There was something inevitable and compulsive about the demand. Thus he discovered to his bewilderment that he must approach that which by nature he felt himself inadequate to approach, and so came up against the formidable situation which Rudolf Otto describes as the *mysterium tremendum et fascinans*[2]—that which bewilders, terrifies, frightens, spells danger, but yet attracts and invites with a "beckoning" which is tantamount to absolute demand. The Yoruba have the saying: *Ibiti ọkà bá p' ẹbu sí, ibẹ̀ ni onjẹ rẹ̀ mã ba a*— "Wherever the cobra lies in wait, there its prey will reach it". We often see a proof of that when a squirrel approaches the lair of a cobra. As soon as it approaches near enough, the awareness of a terrible presence is communicated to it; and as soon as that registers, the squirrel immediately utters shrieks of vexation, fear, and agony, shrieks which

[1] Cf. II Samuel 6:6–9, 13, 14.
[2] *The Idea of The Holy*, by Rudolf Otto (O.U.P., 1943), Chapters 4–6.

rend the air and broadcast to the world at large its presentiment of grave danger. Notwithstanding, it moves towards the cobra as if tied to the end of a string by means of which it is drawn slowly but surely and inexorably. Similarly, the situation which man faced may be summed up in this way: he was forbidden to approach the *sacra* on pain of death; he felt himself inexorably drawn towards the *sacra*.

That is a dilemma which must be resolved; and it was in the attempt to resolve it that the need for an adequate *link* between the object of worship and man manifested itself. And since man felt that he had to deal, not with a vague abstraction, but a Reality with the attributes of a *person*, he naturally thought of a *means* which would be a person— a person sufficiently "conditioned" to make contact with "The Holy" without running the risk of destruction, yet sufficiently "human" to make intimate contact with man and not hurt him. In short, the need for a personal mediator arose.

Thus came into being the priest whose primary function among the Yoruba is that of a mediator. He is a person "in touch" both ways between the object of worship and man: he *knows* them both, *hears* them, and *speaks* on behalf of one to the other. It is his duty to offer up man's worship and to bless man in the name of his object of worship.[1]

It would seem, though, that when worship first began, everybody was his own "priest" in that he expressed his attitude towards the Object of worship as the impulse seized him. This is very much in evidence today among the Yoruba. A devotee of a divinity has a shrine set up in his own house and conducts the routine ritual himself as tradition prescribes. But there is a difference between the ritual which is a mere response to an "unbidden impulse" and the deliberate expression of an attitude. Therefore, even though a devotee may himself undertake the routine ritual in the house, he can do this only because he has already automatically received with his adoption of the divinity the consecration which fits him for the conduct of the ritual. A devotee is an *Olórìṣà*— "One who possesses *orìṣà*"; that is, there is something of the divinity in him and it belongs to his position not only that he should offer worship to the *orìṣà*, but also that he should absorb the *orìṣà* into his personality and manifest him.

The priest presupposes a community, whether that be as small as a family or as large as a clan or town. Thus it is that among the Yoruba the first step in priesthood is found in the family head. To each household are attached some ancestral and tutelary divinity shrines

[1] See Chapter 9.

and the officiant at such domestic shrines is usually the head of the family.

The household grew into the compound—which is usually an oblong or circular enclosure of houses with a common space in the middle and made up in the main of the family which has been extended through procreation, through the living together of blood relations, and the addition to them of "strangers" who came or were brought to dwell among them. In such a compound, there is in the central house, a shrine which is dedicated to the common ancestor. Worship here is undertaken by the supreme head of the extended family who is "father" or "grandfather" to the whole compound community. The whole community is the offspring of the ancestor as well as of the central tutelary divinity. This supreme head is entitled to his priestly function because he is the senior of the blood relations in the extended family and therefore succeeds to the priestly function which used to belong to the common ancestor from whom the family descended.

Next after the compound community is the larger unit known as the ward. The ward is made up of several compounds or families, all of whom need not be blood relations, although it is usual for them to be able to trace some form of relationship in one way or another. Often, of course, the ward has grown, like the compound, out of a nucleus of original dwellers who increased by child-bearing and by the number of "strangers" they acquired. The important binding factor in this case, however, is the common care of surroundings and communal lands. In the olden days, the bond among ward dwellers used to be very strong, almost as strong as that which binds blood relations.

In a ward, the first right to headship goes to the senior member of the stock of the earliest dwellers. But a "stranger", or his offspring, who has been absorbed into the community and has distinguished himself by certain qualities usually qualifies for the headship. To anyone who is so appointed should fall the care of the cults of the ancestor and of the tutelary divinity. Here, however, we see the marked beginning of the separation between the civil headship and the priesthood. First, the question of a common ancestor is almost impossible in the ward except in a case where the ancestor has assumed the status of a divinity; and in that case he is no longer worshipped as an ancestor but as a divinity. Secondly, the cult of the divinity tends to remain with its original "owners";[1] and that means that the cults of the tutelary divinity must remain in charge of these "owners", from among whom the priest is

[1] See below, p. 132.

appointed. Thus, if the head of the ward is not appointed from that group, there come into being two separate heads, one civil and one religious, within the community.

While every member of the ward or compound community is expected to subscribe to the central cult, each household continues its own domestic ritual with its own appointed officiant.

When the cult becomes of town-wide significance, the head of the town assumes the position of the *Pontifex Maximus*. A paramount Yoruba clan-head is virtually a priest-king because he is regarded as "divine" in consequence of his sceptre which is derived from the divinity to whom he is vicegerent.[1] The town belongs to him and so do all the cults. In Ile-Ifè, for example, the Ọni is the *Olórí Àwọn Ìwòrò*— "The head of all the priests". This is so even though he does not now officiate directly at any particular shrine and only performs certain customary rituals as tradition decrees.

It is necessary to modify the impression we have given so far that the head of the family or compound automatically assumes the priestly office. In the case of the ancestral cults, this remains invariably so, except, as we have observed, where the ancestor has become a divinity. In the case of the divinities, however, the situation is rather complicated. Fusion of clans, and intermingling of peoples through marriage and acquisition of "strangers" have been the major causes of the complication. A woman who came into a house with her own cult remains the officiant at the shrine of her divinity because she is the *olórìṣà*, and this line of officiants is continued by her own offspring. The "stranger" (and his offspring after him) who came into a compound with a cult is naturally the officiant at the shrine of his divinity since it is he who *knows* his object of worship. Clans that came into fusion bring their own cults and they remain the sole repositories of the cultus; that is, the priest is chosen from among them. In any one of these cases, whatever might be the relative status of the persons or clans within the community, they retain the guardianship of the cults of which they are the "owners". If such cults become communal property, the whole community still look up to those "owners" for the conduct of their rituals, with the only modification that they now hold the custody and officiate on behalf of the town.

It is in this way that almost every one of the Yoruba divinities is attached to certain lineage "owners" to whom its priesthood belongs exclusively. And it is here that the hereditary character of Yoruba

[1] See Chapters 3, p. 34, and 8, p. 50.

priesthood becomes marked, provided we do not take "heredity" in its strict sense. What it means here is that even though a whole town claims a divinity, it may be generally known that a particular family, living in a particular ward of the town, has exclusive custody of his cult; in which case it is usually unthinkable that without them anything could be done by way of approaching that divinity. Recently, the authority of a Yoruba king was brought to a stalemate on this issue. He, as the head of the clan, had cause to exercise his prerogative by deposing an important chief-priest. As far as the civil side of the matter was concerned, his authority carried. But in appointing a successor, he had to ask the lineage "owners" of the divinity to present another candidate. This they bluntly refused to do on the ground that while the priest whom the king claimed to have deposed still lived, they would not have another one installed. The position at the moment of writing is that each side is standing on its own rights: as far as the king and the civil authority are concerned, the priest is "deposed"; but to the lineage "owners" of the divinity, he remains the priest, still performing his priestly functions for his ward, if not officially for the town.

Besides this loose hereditary character, Yoruba priesthood is hier-archical. As we have observed, the king is the *Pontifex Maximus* under whose superintendence all the cults theoretically are. At the same time, each cult group has its own order of priesthood, which is graded. There is a chief-priest who is assisted by other sub-priests, according to their ranks. Each member of the cult staff is treated according to his status in seating arrangements and in the sharing of emoluments.

There appears to be no specific *call*, in the technical sense, to Yoruba priesthood. The person who succeeds the family priest or the town priest is usually the person next to him in rank. He should have been with the priest and should have "understudied" him by assisting and watching him during the conduct of rituals. If the priest grows to an old age, he normally delegates some of his more strenuous functions to his younger and more able second-in-command. When he dies, the assistant steps in automatically. Thus we can say that there is not what can be described technically as a call to Yoruba priesthood; neither is there any organised training to speak of. A case in point is the episode connected with the "deposed" priest to whom we have referred. When he was "deposed", there were four others who were deposed as well. In those other cases, the lineage "owners" of the cults agreed to the king's behest and presented other candidates who were immediately installed in the places of the deposed ones, without any training, except, perhaps, that someone might tell them what to do during rituals. And yet, the cult concerned in each case is of great significance to the whole community.

Let us observe here that it is a different matter where a devotee is concerned. He is often a person called to belong to the *orìṣà*. Sometimes the *call* comes by possession during which the person becomes ecstatic, and then it is said that the *orìṣà* has taken or possessed him. This may happen at any time, but often it is during some ceremony connected with the *orìṣà*. The person may just be standing apart watching, or be one of the worshippers—often singing and dancing worshippers—when he becomes ecstasised. Thereafter he knows that he is the property of the *orìṣà* to carry out his every behest as vouchsafed to him. The devotee who receives a *call* in this way is the person who really should be called *olórìṣà*—"He who has the *orìṣà*"; for the *orìṣà* abides in him and can express himself through him at any time or place. Often, though, the urge to expression comes more easily during a ritual in which there is loud music, the kind which can induce the ecstatic state in a person already so susceptible. Another way by which a person is called to the worship of the *orìṣà* is through the declaration of the oracle. This often happens when the customary rite is performed immediately after a child's birth; but a grown-up may be so called through a certain untoward event in his life which the diviner interprets as the work of the divinity who is claiming him.

About the new priest, two things must be observed. First, a certain rite must be performed to "remove the hands" of the deceased priest from the cult. Until this is done, the late priest virtually "remains" still in office; and it is believed that if the new priest should then take up the office, he would run into some danger or meet with harm during the execution of his priestly office. Secondly, there must be a gathering of certain elders (priest-makers) to hand over the cult to him. What takes place is simple, although the details vary from one locality to another. But in general it takes this form: the elders assemble and, through their spokesman, call the priest-elect, who goes forward and kneels; then the spokesman says that since so-and-so (naming the late priest) has died, there has been no one in charge of the cultus; that, therefore, they (the elders) could not but appoint someone and since by experience (or connection) the priest-elect is the right person, they are appointing him and handing over to him the tools of the cult. Let him carry on thenceforth the priestly functions; may the divinity accept his offices; may no harm come upon him in consequence of them; may all the children of

10. A ritual dance during the Ògŭn Festival, Ondŏ

11. Offering a sacrifice

12. A popular image of Èṣù (Èṣù Ilare), Ile-Ifẹ̀

the divinity prosper in his time. Then the customary emblems of the divinity are handed to him. In some cases, it may be considered necessary to consult the oracle to find out if anything in particular is necessary to be done before the appointee takes up office; or if any other person within the rank should be chosen. It is unlikely that an appointee should be rejected in a setting like this; but it may be necessary for him to offer a sacrifice of purification. Where the cult has become the concern of the whole town, the installation of the priest usually takes almost the same elaborate form as the installation of a civil chief; and in that case, the priest's appointment must be ratified by the king or the civil authority.

We have said above that the basic function of the Yoruba priest is to be a mediator between the object of worship and the worshippers. As a result of this, he is the person in charge of the shrine. It is he who takes care of the shrine and sees that it is suitably prepared for worship; he consecrates emblems[1] for the shrine, sees that the place is kept clean and supplied regularly with necessary articles, drink and food offerings.

There are several ways by which the priest ascertains the will of his divinity. He may have his guidance through dreams during which it occurs to him that the divinity is asking him to do certain things; this he immediately carries out on waking. The commonest method, however, is divination by kola-nut.[2] This method is employed by practically all the cults.

The kola-nut used must be one which has four valves. Each of the valves has a concave and a convex side, and is described as "male" or "female", depending on its shape on the convex side. In a four-valve kola-nut, the sexes are evenly distributed.

When the kola-nut is split during worship, the cotyledon of one or more of the valves is broken off and thrown outside for Èṣù.[3] Another piece is broken off from the place where the cotyledon has been removed, and this is placed on the ground before the shrine. This piece is believed to be the actual offering for the divinity, because *Èṣẹ́-'bì l' ó nd' ọ́run; b' o ba d' ọ́run tán, odidi ní 'da*—"It is the broken-off piece of kola-nut that gets to heaven; when it has arrived in heaven, then it becomes a whole".

After that preliminary rite, the officiant holds the four valves between his palms, which are held together, and asks such a question as "Is it peace and prosperity?" or "Does the matter for which we are here meet with your favour and approval?", and casts them on the ground.

---

[1] See Chapter 7, p. 63.   [2] See Chapter 9, p. 109.
[3] See Chapter 8, pp. 89 ff.

There is no rule of thumb which is universally operative about the interpretation of the kola-nut omen. It depends largely on the ancestral or cultic tradition, or a combination of both, which obtains in each locality. The traditional principles are specific in each case, although added to them are the broader principles of interpretation which embrace the whole community of cults in each area. Thus, what we have in mind when we refer to the principles of interpretation of the omen, for example, in Ijẹbŭ or Èkìtì or Ile-Ifẹ̀, is the broader principles which are generally accepted in the particular area. In places where people are no longer keen on correct tradition, these broader principles are taken as sufficient.

Let us concentrate on a specific area, Ile-Ifẹ̀, for example. There the omen of the kola-nut is generally interpreted as follows:

(a) When only one valve lies with the convex side up, it signifies "contentment", "satisfaction".

(b) When two valves lie with the convex side up, it signifies "Look forward to some fortune", "prosperity".

(c) When three valves lie with the convex side up, it signifies "wealth", "possessions".

(d) When all the four valves lie with the convex side up, it signifies "peace", "good health".

(e) When all the four valves lie with the concave side up, it signifies "Eat, drink, and be merry", "fortune smiles".

(f) When all the four valves lie in a heap, it signifies "Something good is on the way"; "Expect a very important, fortune-bringing guest: prepare hospitality".

These are too vague to be accepted without further question. Therefore any one of them has to be confirmed and made specific by further casts of the kola-nut. When the kola-nut is thus cast to find out something specific in reference to a former omen, then there is a second list of interpretations which are as follows:

(b), (d), (e), or (f) above signifies "Yes"; while (a) or (c) signifies "No".

But to the priest, the list of interpretations in the two categories is only an aid to the correct omen. What he looks for to begin with is the omen which signifies unequivocal "Yes" according to his own family or cultic tradition. Let us suppose that the omen for him is (b). If, when he casts the kola-nut, he gets the omen (b), then he is satisfied and proceeds with the worship to its conclusion. But supposing that he gets (a) which, although in itself a good omen, is not acceptable for his tradition? What he does then is to collect the valves and recast them, this time addressing the divinity with the question, "The omen says 'contentment': do you mean that 'contentment' is going to be my lot?" If now he gets any one of the "Yes" omens, he is satisfied.

If, however, on casting the kola-nut again, he still gets a "No" omen, then he has to cast it again to find out if there is anything the matter; and if the answer is "Yes", he proceeds to find out by a series of questions what is wrong, and then what should be done about it. This he rounds off by asking, "Will everything be all right once that is done?" and to this he expects an unequivocal "Yes" or he will have to start all over again.

Again, suppose that when he casts his kola-nut, he gets omen (a) three times successively. After the third time, the question he addresses to the divinity is "Is this omen (a) what you wish us to take as your 'Yes' this time?"

But suppose that after he has cast the kola-nut four times the omen is still not auspicious. Then he concludes either that the divinity rejects that particular kola-nut or that the kola-nut is "not good". In pursuance of the first conclusion, he has now to ask the divinity what should be done with the rejected kola-nut—"Is it to be thrown outside or on the dunghill?" If he has to decide that it is the kola-nut that is "not good", he takes it that the reason for its condition is that it fell against a tree on its way to the ground from the kola-tree. There are two ways of treating such a kola-nut; the priest first strikes it against the wall to rectify its "defect". Then he casts it again. If still it brings no "Yes" omen of any kind, then it is abandoned, and another one used instead.

Another way of ascertaining the will of the *orìṣà* is through a medium. This is done very often with the household Èṣù. Usually, a virgin, preferably before she attains puberty, is chosen, and her eyes and ears are treated with a decoction of herbs so that she may be able to *see* and *hear* the divinity. She sits between the *orìṣà* and the client and declares messages from the *orìṣà*. It is not unusual to find a woman of advanced age who has enough *orìṣà* in her to be a medium, but she must have passed the age of, or ceased from, childbearing and sexual habits.

This is not the place for a thesis on the divination connected with the Ọrunmìlà cult, known as *Ifá*. That is an intricate art which is painfully and laboriously learnt before it can be mastered to any appreciable degree. To master it completely is a counsel of perfection. One has to learn the two hundred and fifty-six Odù[1] with the endless stories connected with them, the practical applications of the stories, and the pharmacopoeia which is part of the system, all by heart.

But we have to mention it here because it issues from the cult of Ọrunmìlà, the oracle divinity, who is believed to be the "prophetic" voice of Olódùmarè, declaring His will and behest, as well as the chief "consultant" who gives directions in regard to the relations between the divinities and men.

The person in charge of the cult of Ọrunmìlà is both a hierophant and a priest, although he is known more by the former function of declaring and expounding the mysteries of Ifá. Anybody who has learnt the art of divination by Ifá and has undergone the rite of becoming a votary of Ọrunmìlà automatically becomes a priest-diviner. Ọrunmìlà appears to be the one divinity who is not tied to any particular lineage "owners", although there are family lineages which have practised the art for so long that people have come to look upon them as the lineage "owners" of the cult.

The priest of a central shrine has his distinguishing mark, the type of which depends on which divinity he serves. The priest or priestess of Orìṣà-nlá, for example, is decked in white: that is, white clothes and white beads. In some localities, the priest wears the same insignia as the civil chief—coral beads around the neck, wrists and ankles; or the Itagbè—a specially woven strip of fabric, usually copiously and colour-fully ornamented or all white, with thick tassels at both ends, to be laid on the shoulder or worn tied round the head.

Consonant with the distinguishing marks are the various tabu which are the lot of every priest. These also depend on which divinity it is. The tabu are things "not done" by the priest both in consequence of his attachment to the divinity and for the sake of the efficacy of his ritual performances. They consist of things like food or drink which the divinity does not take[2] and which are therefore forbidden to all his worshippers; or things which make for ceremonial defilement or con-tamination. In every case, a demand is laid upon the priest who is entering upon his sacred office to be sexually clean. That is why the priest should be a person of advanced age and the priestess a person past childbearing and sexual habits. A married priest must be properly washed with water (often with a decoction of herbs) and antiseptic soap

1 See Chapter 1, pp. 7 f.
2 See Chapter 9, p. 118; and Chapter 12, pp. 149 f.

before going into the presence of the divinity. Menstruating women are banned from the shrines.

The priest has always been an important social figure. He is inevitable in the social pattern of the Yoruba since the keynote of their national life is their religion. Virtually nothing is done without the ministration of the priest. For, apart from looking after the "soul" of the community, he features prominently in the installation of kings and the making of chiefs.

II

The Cult of Olódùmarè

We shall open this chapter with three selected quotations to illustrate the general impression which the religion of the Yoruba makes upon foreign investigators with regard to the cult of the Deity.

A. B. Ellis, writing in 1894 said of Olódùmarè, "The native says that he enjoys a life of complete idleness and repose, . . . and passes His time dozing or sleeping. Since he is too lazy or too indifferent to exercise any control over earthly affairs, man on his side does not waste time in endeavouring to propitiate him, but reserves his worship and sacrifice for more active agents."[1]

Leo Frobenius, writing nineteen years later, said: "He is neither worshipped nor considered in any way, but leads an entirely platonic, mythological existence."[2]

E. Geoffrey Parrinder, writing as recently as 1949, said: "The Yoruba call God Ọlọ́run. No cult is offered to him . . ."; and he went on to describe Him as "this supreme but unworshipped God".[3]

Most of the salient points raised by these quotations have been amply answered in the past chapters of this book.[4] The main point to notice here is their specific emphasis that the Yoruba have no cult of Olódùmarè. While it is very likely that Ellis had only mistaken a vivid dream of his own for information by "the natives", that in writing these words Frobenius was only exuding a surfeit of classical education, and that Parrinder's research at this point was incomplete, there is little doubt that the general appearance of things has led to the mistaken notion that Olódùmarè is a "*deus incertus*" and a "*deus remotus*" and is therefore not worshipped at all.[5] Let us therefore examine the reasons for this appearance which has been taken for reality.

[1] *The Yoruba-speaking Peoples* (Chapman and Hall, 1894), p. 34.
[2] *The Voice of Africa* (London, Hutchinson, 1913), Vol. I, p. 198.
[3] *West African Religion* (Epworth Press, 1949), p. 26; but see his *Religion in an African City*, p. 8 f.
[4] See especially Chapters 3–7.
[5] *Africa and Christianity*, by Diedrich Westermann (O.U.P., 1937), p. 74.

First, as we have observed, the objective phenomena in the religion of the Yoruba are the cults of the *orìṣà*.[1] These so predominate the scene that it is difficult for the casual observer to notice that under them, there is one vital cultic basis. There is a pantheon, but it is possible to search through it without meeting Olódùmarè. The reason for that, of course, is not that He does not exist, that He is *incertus* or *remotus*, but that He is just not of the rank and file of the *orìṣà* and therefore is not to be found as one of them.[2]

Secondly, the Yoruba do not erect temples for the cult of Olódùmarè, neither are images dedicated to Him. But in this, they are only being true to their concept of Him. To the question, "To whom will ye liken God? or what likeness will ye compare unto him?",[3] the Yoruba will answer, "No one and Nothing". His attributes exclude any such comparison. He is the King Unique, of superlative and incomparable attributes, One Who cannot be found out by searching, the Invisible and Ever-present One.[4] The Yoruba cannot conceive in what form the Deity of such attributes could be represented in images. Neither can they think of confining within space Him whose appellation is Atẹ́rẹrẹ-k'áiyé—"He who spreads over the whole extent of the earth"; He is so "immense" and "extensive" that that is just unfeasible.

Thirdly, it is true in this case that the people's conception of the position of the Deity has been a reflection of their social pattern. Therefore, a consideration of the social etiquette of the Yoruba with reference to age status will shed light on this subject. In Yoruba etiquette it is considered a thing "not done" for a young person to approach an elder directly when he wants a special favour. Even a son may not go directly to his father to beg for a great favour or apologise for an offence. The young person must approach the elder on such occasions through an intermediary, a friend or a peer of the one who is being approached. It is an observable fact that it is not the custom of the Yoruba to treat familiarly with their kings. In the old days, unless a person belonged to the highest rank in the community, he might never have the slightest chance of seeing the king throughout his lifetime. For example, the Ọ̀ni of Ile-Ifẹ̀, in consequence of his status, used to be held in so much reverence that it was utterly impossible for any, except the very few who were highly privileged, to behold his face or the gates of his palace. About the Aláfin of Ọ̀yọ́, there used to be a popular song: *Ìró l' a ngbọ́, ojú 'ò t' Aláfin*—"We hear only reports, eyes do not reach the Aláfin";

1 Chapters 9 and 10.   2 See Chapters 6 and 7, pp. 49 f.
3 Isaiah 40:18.   4 Chapter 5, pp. 42 ff.

which means that people only heard of him but never saw him. In those days the faces of the great Yoruba kings were veiled whenever they went out of their palaces. The people knew that they had the king, the king was the symbol and genius of their communal cohesion; but his voice and behest came to them through a gradation of civic officers with whom they were in close touch through their own ward or family heads.

When we apply this to the religion of the Yoruba, we can easily see how the superlative status of Olódùmarè has given the casual observer the impression that Olódùmarè is *incertus* and *remotus* and, therefore, never worshipped. The Yoruba appear to be quite satisfied with the divinities with whom they are in immediate touch. But this is only because they believe that once the divinities have been offered their worship, the divinities in their turn will transmit what is necessary of it to Olódùmarè. It is left to the divinities to take what belongs to them by virtue of their position as authorised by Olódùmarè and remit to Him all that is His either to receive or to execute.

It is necessary for us, nevertheless, to reiterate here what we have already observed, that whatever sacrifice or petition is offered to any one of the divinities is considered really accepted only when the Yoruba are assured of the sanction of Olódùmarè.[1]

We will emphasise further that the superlative greatness of Olódùmarè does not preclude direct approach to Him. Although the Yoruba do not build temples for Him, they nevertheless make use of the advantage of His omnipresence—the fact that He is neither restricted nor confined by space and time—to pray to him directly and at any time and place as needs arise. On such occasions, they speak to Him in rather intimate terms; as they sit and ponder over some matter, as their minds work out the details of some enterprise, as they walk along the road or lie in bed, they spontaneously converse with the ever-present, ever-hearing, Olódùmarè.

But there *is* a specific cult of Olódùmarè. Because Olódùmarè cannot be confined into space, the ritualistic worship offered to Him takes place in the open. The worshipper makes a circle of ashes or white chalk; within the circle, which is a symbol of eternity, he pours a libation of cold water, and in the centre he places his kola-nut on cotton wool. He then takes the kola-nut, splits it and holding the valves firmly between the hollow of his palms, he stretches them up and prays to Olódùmarè, offering the kola-nut; then he casts the valves within the circle.[2] Often a white fowl is offered in the same way. In Ile-Ifè, there

[1] See Chapter 6, pp. 52 f.   [2] See Chapter 10, pp. 135 ff.

is a priest-chief whose duty it is to offer this ritual every morning in the name of the Ọ̃ni and of all the people.

It is to be regretted however, that the direct ritualistic worship of Olódùmarè as a regular thing is dying out in Yorubaland. In some parts it is no longer known; in some, it has become the cult of the women. Nevertheless it is often practised under certain circumstances. When two persons enter into a solemn pact, when people have to make a very binding oath or swear over some matter of contention, they go into the open and perform the ritual. Often, also, the oracle declares that an act of worship or a sacrifice should be offered to *Alálàfunfun òkè*, and then the ritual is performed. When the oracle insists that a sacrifice should be offered to Olódùmarè, such a sacrifice is either exposed in the open or sublimated by burning.

We insist, therefore, that the present state of the cult of Olódùmarè is not due to the fact that to the Yoruba He is a *deus incertus* and a *deus remotus*: He is, in fact, very real to the Yoruba, as One without Whom nothing remains. We admit, nevertheless, that the cults of the hitherto ever-increasing intermediary divinities who for practical purposes often become ends in themselves have had an insidiously detrimental effect on His cult as a regular, objective phenomenon in the religious activities of the Yoruba.

Regular remnants of the ancient cult of Olódùmarè are preserved in certain conceptualisations of Him which we find in Jàkŭta—the original Yoruba thunder divinity; Ọràmfè—the special Ifẹ thunder and solar divinity; and Orìṣà-'gbaiye of Ọ̀wọ̀ who has a wider scope in that he represents an abstraction of the totality of Olódùmarè. The cult of each of these divinities, in the main, follows the pattern described above in reference to the cult of the Deity.

12

Olódùmarè and Moral Values

No one knows when the question of morality as a theoretical subject began to exercise the mind of man. There is no doubt, however, that the sense of what to do and what not to do, the practical question as to why certain forms of behaviour are to be preferred to certain others, and the problem of how to live peaceably with another person and be fit to live with, have been with him from the earliest times. Whereas all these began as vague notions, it was not long before they became real factors with which he should reckon if he must live within the community and if the life of the community must be preserved. Thus, by a gradual process they evolved into the definite patterns which we have today as codes of behaviour, as known in the ways and wisdom of each individual nation.

To the question "Whence does morality derive its norm, the force of its demands and sanctions?" the answers have been various. There are those who hold that morality has its origin in society; that is, it is essentially a social phenomenon. Society must keep itself alive and its machinery smooth-running, and to this end it evolves a system of self-preservation. Thus the sense of "Ought" which resides within each person is a result of this system which society created. On this hypothesis, that which we call "conscience" in man is nothing more than the notion, "a complex of residual habits", which society implants in him as it brings him up, feeding him on the milk of approved behaviour and nourishing him on the meat of acceptable character. These notions society tends carefully and strengthens with the dispensation of reward and punishment.

Others have told us that what we call morality is little more than a product of common sense. In order to live, man must adapt himself to his environment. Experience soon taught him what could be done and what must be avoided. A steady accumulation of this experience over a long period has resulted in a very strong sense of what has come to be popularly known as "Right" and "Wrong". But, however strong and imperative this sense may have become in man, it is, nevertheless, at bottom mere common sense. Man put his finger in the fire and burned it; for the future it becomes part of his character to avoid putting his finger in the fire. "Once bitten, twice shy!"

These two schools of thought have been greatly buttressed up in their conceptions of the origin of morality by the kind of practical reasons which have been given to support or account for the adoption or rejection of certain patterns of behaviour. They fix upon these so strongly that they can see no connection at bottom between religion and morality, although they will not deny that religion and morality do interact and influence each other for better, for worse, during the course of man's development. Therefore, they have conveniently overlooked two vital questions. The first school still has to make it explicit why this "mass" which is called society should be so keen on its own preservation. We should have thought that a soulless machine cannot anticipate its own breakdown! What is it that gave society the "sense" of its own value? And to what end is this value being preserved? Why does society not allow its every member to go on eating and drinking and being merry in the way that whims dictate, and then to die any tomorrow? What is it that makes conscience essentially and ultimately individual? And the second school should let us know what it is that puts so much "common sense" in man. Why is it that, like the candle-drawn moth, he does not fly into the flame and be burnt? The answers to these questions are not obvious; and that is because they are bound up with the question of the fundamental nature of man.

Our own view is that morality is basically the fruit of religion and that, to begin with, it was dependent upon it. Man's concept of the Deity has everything to do with what is taken to be the norm of morality. God made man; and it is He who implants in him the sense of right and wrong. This is a fact the validity of which does not depend upon whether man realises and acknowledges it or not. "The sense of obligation to do that which is believed to be right is, in fact, the pressure of God upon every human life. God is made known to all men, even though they may not have learned to call Him God (or may refuse to), and obedience to the behests of conscience is the essential condition of growth in the knowledge of God."[1] "Every human being who is not clearly an imbecile has a knowledge of right and wrong . . . everyone knows that right is not the same thing as wrong. . . . Even though moral philosophers

[1] *Christian Apologetics*, by Alan Richardson (London, S.C.M. Press, 1948), p. 125.

cannot agree upon the explanation of what the difference is, they all perceive that there is a difference between right and wrong. Nor must we allow ourselves to be misled by superficial talk about the relativity of moral standards. It is true that moral standards vary widely from age to age and from place to place . . . yet they all acknowledge, according to their own standards, that there is a difference between right and wrong."[1]

The sense of right and wrong, by the decree of God, has always been part of human nature. Experience comes before theory. That sense was there first before man began to find the reasons why certain modes of behaviour should be preferred to certain others, and the reasons given are often little more than rationalisation. The real truth of the situation is implied in St. Paul's words that the Gentiles "show that what the law required is written on their hearts".[2] Or, in the words of E. O. James, "Sin as a breach of or failure to adhere to the sanctions recognised as the approved standard of social and religious conduct on the part alike of the individual and of society as a whole is a universal phenomenon in human history."[3]

With the Yoruba, morality is certainly the fruit of religion. They do not make any attempt to separate the two; and it is impossible for them to do so without disastrous consequences. What have been named *tabu* took their origin from the fact that people discerned that there were certain things which were morally approved or disapproved by the Deity. So the Yoruba call *tabu Èwọ̀*—"Things forbidden", "Things not done". In the thought of the people, the *tabu* have collectively taken on a special significance by assuming a quasi-personal character in consequence of which it has been given the name *A-kì-'ṣe-e*—"It-is-not-done", "It-is-*tabu*"; and this personification is variously conceived of as the "detective" of Ọ̀runmìlà or as an independent "agent" who is operative in the world by the decree of Olódùmarè. The Yoruba say therefore in the face of a baffling crime or offence, *A-kì-'ṣe-e l' o mã dá 'jọ*—"It-is-*tabu* will judge (track down the offender)", which is as much as to say "Sinners will not go unpunished".

S. S. Farrow has a good chapter on morality in the religion of the Yoruba.[4] But he overstresses what seems to him to be elements of "evil" in the religion. He rebukes one Brinton for regarding these phenomena as "not heartlessness or cruelty" and thinks that Brinton

---

[1] Op. cit., p. 124.   [2] Romans 2:15.
[3] *Comparative Religion* (London, Methuen, 1938), p. 244.
[4] *Faith, Fancies and Fetich*, by S. S. Farrow (London, S.P.C.K., 1926), pp. 143 f.

made such a mistake because he did not live among the "heathen" and enter into their experiences, thoughts, and feelings. The rebuke should belong to S. S. Farrow himself. Although he can claim to have lived among the Yoruba, it is obvious that he did not quite understand why certain things were done or practised because he studied the Yoruba religion subjectively from the standpoint of Christianity and Western culture. It must be the same prejudice which led even Bishop James Johnson to say that Yoruba "heathenism" countenances and encourages revenge, retaliation, jealousy, hatred, ill-will, anger, and wrath.[1] What these two eminent men overlooked is that it has been the pathetic experience of men all down the ages that the ideals set by religion are rarely if ever reached. In one instance only do we know that the will of Man coincided perfectly with the will of God, and that was in Jesus of history. Nevertheless, we do not condemn a religion merely because those who profess it do not live up to its ideals. Cruelty, hatred, jealousy, and other social evils are certainly evident in the life of the Yoruba; but this only shows that they are corporate members of the human race within which sin still has dominion. Let us learn to place things where they belong.

As we talk of these things described as elements of "evil" in the religion of the Yoruba, at once there springs to the mind the practice of human sacrifice,[2] and the severe, atrocious treatment which the Yoruba used to mete out to those who broke the *tabu*. Shocking as these may be, however, we must adopt the right attitude in order to understand why they were done. Here, perhaps more than anywhere else, we need to allow for the imperfection of human conceptions. When a Jephthah offers up a grown-up daughter who was ready for marriage in sacrifice to Yahweh, he thinks and believes in all sincerity that he is giving the best service to his God.[3] For the giving up of a beloved daughter in that way must be indeed a sacrifice and not a pleasurable duty! Similarly in the context in which the Yoruba offer human sacrifices, particularly if the sacrifices are of kith and kin, they do not do it with a sadistic relish; rather, they feel the painful virtue of one who has gone to measureless costs to fulfil an imperative, sacred duty. It is with the development of the mind and spiritual perception that man comes to see that physical human sacrifice is not necessary. What God demands is the offer of one's own life, and that in the spiritual sense, because His demands are purely ethical and spiritual.

The same may be said about the treatment which used to be the lot

---

[1] *Yoruba Heathenism* (England, James Townsend, 1899), p. 51.
[2] See Chapter 9, pp. 118 f.　　　[3] Judges 11:34–40.

of those who broke the *tabu* and were therefore considered as the accursed who were liable to bring disaster upon the whole community. The person who punished such *tabu*-breakers believed that he was really serving the divinity, especially as he usually did so under an oracular sanction which he believed honestly to be beyond question. It is quite a long journey in the history of religion before man reaches the knowledge that judgment and vengeance belong only to God and that in order truly to be able to dispense justice impartially on His behalf, man's will must coincide with His.

It is rather sweeping for anyone to say that the religion of the Yoruba does not give a sense of sin. It is true that the Yoruba have not thought out or stated in a systematic way what they think, believe, and know about this universal scourge; it is true that they have not made out a "theology" of sin; it is nevertheless a betrayal of ignorance to conclude from that that they have no sense of sin. Once a person knows that the Deity will judge; that He judges man by what he is—by his character;[1] once he can be conscious of a guilt which comes out of more than mere ritual failings, he is already at the very threshold of "Against thee and thee only have I sinned".[2] In the final analysis, "the *tabus* embrace everything which can be considered as 'sin'", and convey the sense that in a breach of any of them, one has personally offended someone[3] —the Deity, a divinity, or an ancestor.

Often, reward and punishment on grounds of morality are spoken of as if they had been invented by some far-sighted genius for the purpose of keeping recalcitrant humanity perpetually in check. But it should be obvious that they follow from the very logic of right and wrong as action is followed by reaction. That which is truly right is bound up with goodness as that which by nature is wrong is tied up with evil. Like produces like: and so the consequence of that which is right is good, while the end of that which is wrong is evil. "Men do not gather figs of thistles."[4] Reward and punishment as measured out in this world are only translations to the human plane of that which is of the basic essence of things.

The Yoruba know the distinction between ritual errors which are calculated to be offences against the divinities, derelictions of filial duties which may arouse the anger of the aggrieved ancestors, and the breach of the Deity's behests which is purely a moral issue. Sometimes, of

---

[1] See Chapter 14, pp. 197 ff.   [2] See Psalm 51.
[3] *The Peoples of Southern Nigeria*, by P. A. Talbot (O.U.P., 1926), p. 709.
[4] See Matthew 7:16 ff.

course, it is not easy to draw the line between the merely ritual and the purely ethical, as they are often involved one in the other or, rather, as the ritual may be a means for the easy attainment of the ethical. "At first, doubtless, the abstinence from sexual intercourse, wine, flesh and even bread, and the repeated ablutions before taking part in the rites, were designed to rid the worshipper of ritual impurity, but they acquired a more ethical content in course of time."[1] We shall go further and say that the abstinence has a moral and spiritual basis. By and large, it is believed that each divinity punishes ritual or moral offences which are committed within his province, that each aggrieved ancestor reprimands his own for dereliction of filial duties, and that it is Olódùmarè who judges men purely for what they are; that is, in consequence of their character.

It is to be noted that the same Yoruba word, with its cognate verb, is used for both "sin" and "offence". The word is Ẹ̀ṣẹ̀. This is a word which has been popularised by Christian evangelism and Islam. It is the word used for "sin" in the Yoruba translation of the Bible. The word Èwọ̀ is more comprehensive, however, and goes deeper to the heart of the matter. Obviously, it was connected originally with the breach of "ritual" laws. The phrase j' èwọ̀ (jẹ èwọ̀), means literally "To eat the tabu"; it is a Yoruba expression for "break the tabu" or "commit sin"; and points also to the fact that the tabu among the Yoruba may originally have consisted in things not to be eaten. The word, as we have observed, covers all acts of breach of the moral law, however. Thus, for example, a person j' èwọ̀ by committing adultery, by breaking a covenant, or by beating his parent.

In the ethical system of the Yoruba, covenant plays an important role. In fact, the whole of person-to-person, and divinity-to-person, relations have their basis largely in covenants. The covenant between person and person is usually a parity covenant in that it is "reciprocal—that is, both parties bind themselves to each other by bilateral obligations".[2] It appears that, originally, the Yoruba made this kind of covenant before the tutelary divinity of the Earth, and hence the generic name for covenants—Imùlẹ̀, which means literally, "Drinking the Earth together" or "Drinking together from the Earth". The ritual, in general, is as follows: A shallow hole is dug in the ground; water is poured into it, and a kola-nut split and cast into the water. The two people who are

[1] *Comparative Religion*, by E. O. James (London, Methuen, 1938), p. 267.
[2] *The Living World of the Old Testament*, by B. W. Anderson (London, Longmans, 1959), p. 56.

entering into the covenant kneel face to face with the hole in between them. Then one says, "O Earth . . . come and preside as we make this covenant: if I should break the covenant, may I be carried away by the Earth (may I disappear from the face of the earth)." Then he stoops down and sips some water from the hole, at the same time picking up and eating a piece of the kola-nut. The second person does exactly the same and the covenant is thus concluded.

But although the generic name for the covenant is thus suggestive of a particular ritual, covenant-making actually takes various forms: it may be done before any of the divinities, but especially before Ògùn.[1]

Besides these definitely ritualistic forms of covenant-making, it is believed that to be trusted by a friend, to be bosom friends, to eat together, or to be received hospitably as a guest, is to enter into a covenant which involves moral obligations. A covenant between two parties means, negatively, that they must think or do no evil against each other's body or estate, and positively, that they must co-operate in active good deeds towards each other in every way.

Although every covenant has a ritualistic basis, nevertheless, the obligations which are its outcome are ethical. It would seem that the Yoruba have found it necessary in an imperfect society to introduce this element of subtle "coercion" in order to strengthen their weak will in the performance of their ethical duties.

Someone will say, no doubt, that this kind of ritualistic covenant is not always used for a good end. He will be quite right. We have the examples of certain secret societies whose main purposes, as far as can be ascertained, are anti-social. Members of such societies enter into pacts to co-operate through thick and thin for the achievement of their purposes, and to make sure that no member betrays the others. But that does not invalidate the fact that the original purpose of the covenant is to make sure of good and sound person-to-person relations in the home, in business, in social, and in civic organisations. Any good thing can be abused and the cases to which a demurrer may point here only indicate that the covenant has been put to the wrong use.

The second kind of covenant is the suzerainty covenant. This is rather of a unilateral character. It is "given" by a person in authority to a vassal, and in that case, the terms are dictated by the "giver" while on his own side the "giver" undertakes to afford the vassal protection and security.[2] This is the type of covenant into which a person automatically enters on becoming the worshipper of a divinity. It is described

---

[1] Chapter 8, pp. 85 ff.   [2] Anderson, op. cit.

as *Gbígba èwọ̀*—"Receiving the *èwọ̀*", that is, receiving the list of forbidden things. The terms of the covenant involve certain restrictions from things which are forbidden in consequence of the nature of the divinity and the observance of things which please the divinity and promote good relations between him and the worshipper. The worshipper must keep to the terms of the covenant and let them govern his conduct for ever after.

Let us think of one who becomes a worshipper of Orìṣà-nlá.[1] The person knows at once that Orìṣà-nlá forbids palm-wine to himself and to his worshippers. The orthodox reason is in the myth which has it that Orìṣà-nlá once became drunk with palm-wine and so forfeited his honour of creating the solid earth as well as his seniority over all the other divinities. We have seen, however, that according to the basic belief of the Yoruba, Orìṣà-nlá in actual fact did not forfeit any of his divine attributes.[2] In the theology of the Yoruba, we learn also that Orìṣà-nlá is concerned with man's character since he represents the norm of ethical and ritual purity. The real reason why he forbids palm-wine, therefore, is that wine is an intoxicant which is capable of spoiling man's personality.

Certain investigators have asserted sweepingly that moral sanctions among the Yoruba are vested solely in the ancestors.[3] By what curious way this conclusion is reached it is not altogether easy to tell. This is not to say that there is no truth in the statement. The truth is that the genius of the family, the extended family, or the compact community, is in the ancestor. The ancestor is believed to take an active interest in the family or community and his power over it is now considerably increased as he is no longer restricted by earthly conditions.[4] Matters affecting the family or the community are thus referred to him for sanction or judgment. Therefore, he is naturally brought into the picture as a superintending spirit who gives approval to any proposals or actions which make for the well-being of the community, and shows displeasure at anything which may tend to disrupt it. Thus, in a sense, but only in that sense, he is concerned with the effective discharge of moral obligations. In this connection, he exercises authority within a similarly circumscribed scope as, though considerably more strongly than, an earthly

[1] See Chapter 8, pp. 71 ff.   [2] See Chapter 3, pp. 22 ff.
[3] Ulli Beier maintained this point and even made only one particular cult, the Egúngún, solely responsible in a lecture delivered on "Ethics in Yoruba Religion" to a Conference at University College, Ibadan.
[4] See Chapter 14, pp. 191 ff.

father who is concerned naturally in the welfare of his family and to whom matters are referred for commendation or condemnation. It is for this reason that the Egúngún cult, which materialises the ancestral spirit, is employed in some parts of Yorubaland as an instrument of discipline. So also does the Orò cult fulfil the same purpose.[1] But to hop from this simple truth to the misleading generalisation which asserts or suggests that the only inspiration of the Yoruba towards well-doing are the ancestors is sheer exaggeration.

We are not infrequently treated to the assertion that the *orìṣà* are not interested in moral sanctions.

We have shown that the *orìṣà* are believed to be concerned in the personal relationship which exists among their co-worshippers. Those who as co-worshippers receive a covenant from each *orìṣà* have in effect entered into covenant one with another and are under obligation to maintain good personal relations. "Religion sets its stamp on the culturally valuable attitude and enforces it by public enactment."[2] It is of importance to know that it is generally accepted that a covenant is not a kind of insurance policy which automatically exempts one from the consequences of moral irresponsibility or rashness. For example, at the end of the ritual which confirms a person as a worshipper of Ọrunmìlà, there is a short sermon which runs something like this: *A ti tẹ́ ẹ ná, ki o tún 'ra ẹ tẹ̀; igbà ti ò rọ́, ki o má fi gun ọpẹ; bi o kò ba mọ̀ 'wẹ̀, ki o má jǎ 'lu odò,* etc.—"You have now been confirmed into this cult; you must now undertake a self-confirmation: make sure that the rope is safe before you climb the palm-tree with it; if you cannot swim, do not plunge yourself into a river etc." The short sermon is meant to be taken both literally and metaphorically: the neophyte must not have the mistaken notion that the ritual just concluded insures him automatically against all physical or moral dangers, no matter what he does or omits to do. He has to be vigilant and must always watch his character. There is a saying that *Ẹniti ó rú 'bọ ti kò gba ẽwọ̀, bi ẹni f' owó ẹbọ ṣ' òfò l' o ri*—"One who offers a sacrifice but does not observe the *tabu* is no better than if he has thrown away the money he spent on the sacrifice".

The real weakness of taking the divinities as the norm of moral obligations is that morality as inspired by the cults tends to be restricted

---

[1] See Chapter 14, pp. 192 ff.

[2] See *The Natural and The Supernatural*, by John Oman (Cambridge University Press, 1931), p. 485, for this quotation from *Science, Religion and Reality*, ed. Joseph Needham, p. 61.

OLÓDÙMARÈ AND MORAL VALUES

in its scope and application to a situation in which although the worshippers of the same divinity find themselves under obligation to avoid
every possible harm towards one another in body or estate, and to be
actively good in their personal relations, they may be free to regard
themselves as under no obligation to extend their special "cultic
love" towards anyone who is outside their fraternity. Let us illustrate
from one of the trade-cults. The Yoruba hunters are, in consequence
of their trade, worshippers of Ògǔn.[1] For this reason, they are enjoined
to be in a perfect state of active goodness towards one another, because
otherwise they would excite the displeasure of Ògǔn. They are especially
forbidden to covet or seduce one another's wives. But outside the fraternity, a hunter, *qua* hunter, does not feel bound to observe those moral
obligations. Moreover, the divinities themselves have become so anthro-
pomorphically conceived that it is not all of them who have been models
of good breeding!

Here, therefore, we run inevitably into the problem of right conduct.
It is what comes of trying to derive a norm from a multiplicity of
motives, whether those be human or divine. In one Yoruba poem we
have this plaintive note:

> Olúfọ́n [2] l' ó bí mi,
> Ng ò gbọdọ̀ m' ẹmu;
> Ò'ṣà-Ogìyán[3] l' ó bí mi,
> Ng ò gbọdọ̀ m' òjù[4];
> Ọ̀ṣun 'Pọ̀ndá l' ó gb' ọtí ọkà l' ọwọ́ mi,
> Ẹmu ni nwọ́n ní kí ng mã mu!

> Olúfọ́n it is who gave me birth,
> I must not drink palm-wine;
> Orìṣà-Ogìyán it is who gave me birth,
> I must not drink palm-wine;
> Ọ̀ṣun of Ipọ̀nda, however, forbids me maize wine
> Palm-wine it is which he orders me to drink!

Contradictions and confusion about what should be done or what should
not be done must arise unless there is a central all-governing norm of
morality.

[1] Chapter 8, pp. 85 ff.
[2] Olúfọ́n is the name by which Orìṣà-nlá is known at Ifọn.
[3] Orìṣà-Ògìyán is a branched-off cult from Orìṣà-nlá.
[4] The specific name for the wine obtained from fallen palm trees.

The real source and norm of the unrestricted, universally recognised and binding moral values in the religion of the Yoruba is Olódùmarè. They derive immediately from His own divine nature as revealed to the Yoruba. He is *Ọba Mimọ́, Ọba Pipé*—"Pure King", "Perfect King"; He is *Alálàfunfun-Òkè*—"The One clothed in white, Who dwells above". He is *Ikin n' ifin, Àlà ti kò l' ọnà*—"Essentially White Object, White Material Without Pattern (entirely white)".[1] In Him alone can be resolved the ever-baffling problem of right conduct which we inevitably encounter in the divinities or ancestral sanctions. In order to aid man in ethical living, Olódùmarè has put in him *Ifá àyà*—"The oracle of the heart" or "The oracle which is in the heart". It is this "oracle of the heart" that guides man and determines his ethical life. One is a good or a bad person in accordance as he responds to, or disobeys, the guidance of his inner "oracle". Thus, of a person who behaves shamelessly, callously, or wickedly, the Yoruba say, *Kò n' itìjú, kò n' ifá àyà*—"He has no sense of shame; he has no oracle of the heart". This oracle of the heart is a person's conscience—the law of God written in the heart.[2]

Let us now proceed to analyse the main features of Yoruba ethics.

To the Yoruba, man's character is of supreme importance and it is this which Olódùmarè judges. Thus the demands which Olódùmarè lays upon man are purely ethical. Man's well-being here on earth depends upon his character; his place in the After-Life[3] is determined by Olódùmarè according to his deserts. Olódùmarè is the "Searcher of Hearts" Who sees and knows everything and whose judgment is sure and absolutely inescapable.[4]

Therefore, morality is summed up in Yoruba by the word *Ìwà* which can be translated by the English word "Character". *Ìwà*, according to the Yoruba, is the very stuff which makes life a joy because it is pleasing to God. It is therefore stressed that good character must be the dominant feature of a person's life. In fact, it is the one thing which distinguishes a person from a brute. When the Yoruba say of someone *O ṣ' ènìà*—"He acts the person", "He behaves as a person should", they mean that he shows in his life and personal relations with others the right qualities of a person. The opposite description is *Ki 'ṣ' ènìà; nṣe l' ó f' awọ ènìà bo 'ra*—"He is not a person, he merely assumes the skin of a person". That means that the person is socially unworthy; in consequence of his

---

1 See Chapter 5, pp. 46 f.   2 Romans 2:14 and 15.
3 See Chapter 14, pp. 197 f.
4 See Chapters 5, p. 42; and 14, pp. 197 ff.

character he is not fit to be called a person, even though he goes about in the semblance of one. A person of good character is called *Ọmọlúwàbí* (*Ọmọ-on'-ìwà-ìbí*)—"One who behaves as a well-born"; and a person of bad character is *Ènìa-k' énìa*—"A mere caricature of a person", "a reprobate".

In the *Odù* corpus according to *Ogbè Ègúndá* Ọrunmìlà once sought the means of success in life and was told that the only way was for him to marry *Ìwà*. He accordingly married *Ìwà* and became very successful. Hence everybody has since been seeking after *Ìwà*, with the result that *Ìwà* becomes the mother of many children:

> *Ẹ wá w' ọmọ Ìwà bẹrẹrẹ o,*
> *Ẹ wá w' ọmọ Ìwà bẹrẹrẹ;*
> *Ìwà gbé dání,*
> *Ìwà pọn s' ẹhìn,*
> *Ẹ wá w' ọmọ Ìwà bẹrẹrẹ.*

Come and behold the countless children of *Ìwà*,
Come and behold the countless children of *Ìwà*.
Ìwà carries (children) in (her) arms,
Ìwà carries (children) on (her) back,
Come and behold the countless children of *Ìwà*.

Therefore it is taught that the only essential requisite in life is *Ìwà*. According to another recital under *Ogbè-Ègúndá*,

> *Ìwà nikàn l' ó ṣòro o,*
> *Ìwà nikàn l' ó ṣòro;*
> *Orí kan kì 'buru l' otù Ifẹ,*
> *Ìwà nikàn l' ó ṣòro o.*

Character is all that is requisite,
Character is all that is requisite;
There is no destiny[1] to be called unhappy in Ifẹ city.
Character is all that is requisite.

Another common saying is, *Ẹni l' orí rere ti kò n' ìwà, ìwà l' o mã b' orí rẹ jẹ*—"However happy a person's destiny may be, if he has no character, it is (lack of) character that will ruin his destiny".

[1] See Chapter 13, pp. 171 f.

For the same reason, good character is copiously recommended in the *Odù* corpus. One *Ìrẹtẹ̀-Ìdí* says

> *Ìwà pẹ̀lẹ́ l' okùn aiye*
> *Fi 'rọ́ pẹ́tí l' ọ̀wọ́ ẹni.*
> *O da fun Ọ̀runmìlà*
> *Ti o nlọ fi ìwà pẹ̀lẹ̀*
> *Gba òkùn aiyé l' ọwọ́ ọkàn-le-ní-'rinwó imalẹ̀.*

> Gentle character it is which enables the rope of life
> To stay unbroken in one's hand.
> So declares the oracle to Ọ̀runmìlà
> Who by means of gentle character
> Was going to win the rope of life from the four hundred and one divinities.

Good character is a sufficient armour against any untoward happening in life. Anyone who wears it need not fear anything. It is, therefore, a common saying that *Ìwà rere l' ẹ̀ṣọ́ ènìa*—"It is good character that is man's guard". The bad people, people of evil character, are they who fear needlessly, and it is their sin that causes them needless fear. One of the stories told to inculcate this lesson is that of Aníwọnikùn,[1] who was a person given to incessant but needless fear, all in consequence of a bad conscience: Thus an *Ọ̀wọ́nrín-ṣèdin* says

> *Ẹ jọ' rẹ̀, ẹ jẹ́ ó sá:*
> *Ìwà wọn ni 'mã lé wọn kiri.*
> *O da fun Aníwọníkùn*
> *Ti yi ò mã bẹ̀rù t' ọsán t' òru;*
> *Ō jẹ́ hù 'wà 're,*
> *Ō jẹ́ hù 'wà àtàtà,*
> *Aníwọníkùn, ki o yé 'sa kiri bí ojo.*

> Leave him alone, let him run:
> It is their character that chases them about.
> So declares the oracle about Aníwọníkùn
> Who fears incessantly day and night;
> Will you but practise good character,
> Will you but practise sound character,
> Aníwọníkùn, and stop running about like a coward.

---

[1] The name means literally, "He who has gall (malignity) in his bowels".

The outcome of good character is, of course, good reputation. A person's reputation is described as àlà—"white cloth or clothes". Thus when the Yoruba pray for someone that *Nwọn ò ni 'ta epo s' álà rẹ o*— "May no palm-oil be splashed on your white clothes", they mean "May your reputation be ever good and untarnished." It is a thing of worthy pride and glory when this is so.

As character makes for good social relations, it is laid upon every member of the community to act in such a way as to promote always the good of the whole body. In the old days wicked people were exiled from the community or ostracised from the family; one who had seduced the wife of another must turn and go another way if the offended person walked along the road towards him.

Let us now make a list of the main components of good character:

(a) Chastity before marriage on the part of the woman is essential. A woman who is not virtuous at marriage is a disgrace both to herself and to her family. Chastity in married life is a woman's bounden duty. Although the rule is rather loose as far as the man is concerned, nevertheless, it is forbidden that a man should seduce another man's wife on pain of paying a heavy penalty and, in addition, of having to face grievous consequences. It is realised that the basis of conjugal happiness is in the faithfulness of both parties; that is so, even in a polygamous community.

(b) Hospitality is of great value. The Yoruba are by nature a hospitable race and are particularly hospitable to strangers. Before life became as artificial and sophisticated as it is today in many parts of the country, a traveller need have no fear where to lodge or what to eat if benighted; he was sure to find ready hospitality wherever he called. The Yoruba teach that one should be hospitable because it is right to be so, as also because one can never tell when one might be in need of hospitality oneself. One of our popular sayings is, *Iyán ogún ọdún a mã jó 'ni l' ọwọ́*— "A yam meal of twenty years ago can still be hot to the touch"; and that means, an act of hospitality can have its reward twenty years later.

(c) Obversely, Yoruba ethics are strongly opposed to selfishness. The selfish person is held in contempt and regarded as not deserving of any help in time of difficulty. As the saying goes, *Agbà t' o jẹ à-jẹ-'w'-ẹhìn á ru 'gbá 'ẹ̀ dé 'lé*—"An elder who eats his food without thinking of others will bear his load home himself (no one will help him)".[1] An *Odù* called *Irẹtẹ̀-méjì* tells a story which is designed to inculcate

[1] As a rule, in Yorubaland, when a young person meets an older one bearing a load or carrying an article, he should take it and carry it home for him.

unselfishness. It concerns how once, Ọ̀runmìlà was given to selfishness in consequence of which he became contemptible to his neighbours. It happened that one day as he was going about in the bush, he fell into a deep pit out of which he could not pull himself. There he had to remain until the third day. By the middle of the third day, he heard some foot-falls and recognised them as those of the people of Àrè. Expecting that they would readily come to his rescue, he shouted to them for help. But in reply, they told him that he should remain where he was, and keep "enjoying" the consequence of his selfishness.

He shouted:

> Ọkùnrin Àrè:
> Obìrin Àrè;
> À-t' òni m' òni,
> À-t' àna m' àna,
> Ẹrungbọ̀n ìjẹ́ta;
> Aládé mbẹ ninú ọ̀fìn,
> O nyí gbiri!

> Men of Àrè!
> Women of Àrè!
> It has been all day today,
> It has been since yesterday,
> It is now practically the third day,
> The crowned one has been in the pit,
> Rolling about!

They replied:

> Igbàtí o njẹ apá ajá,
> Tal' o ké sí
> Igbàtí o njẹ igẹ̀ àgbò,
> Tal' o pè?
> Igbàtí o nf' apá òbúkọ wà 'kọ mu,
> Tal' o rí ọ?
> Nje Ọkùnrin Àrè!
> Obìrin Àrè!
> À-t' òni m' òni,
> À-t' àna m' àna,
> Ẹrungbọ̀n ijẹ́ta:
> Jẹki Aládé jokǒ s' inú ọ̀fùn
> K' ó mã yí gbiri.

When you were feeding on dog's arms,
Whom did you invite?
When you were eating ram's breast,
Whom did you call?
When you were having corn-porridge with a he-goat's arm,
Who saw you?
Now "Men of Àrè!
Women of Àrè!
It has been all day today,
It has been since yesterday,
It is now practically the third day":
Let the crowned one remain in the pit,
Rolling about.

(d) Kindness involving generosity is accounted a great virtue and greatly to be cultivated. The kind have the unfailing blessing of Olódùmarè and of men always. We shall quote a few selections of Yoruba sayings on this topic:

Igbá olõre kì 'fó,
Àwo olõre kì 'fà ya
T' owó t' ọmọ ní 'ya 'lé olõre.

The calabash of the kind breaks not,
The dish of the kind splits not,
It is both money and children that flow into the house of the kind.

This means that no mishaps befall the kind; his lot is always material blessing.

Õre l' õre 'wọ́ tọ̀.

Kindness begets kindness.

Ilé olõre ki 'wó tán;
Ti o-ṣ'-ìkà kì 'wó kù.

The house of the kind does not break down completely;
That of the wicked does not break down incompletely.

That is, the kind unfailingly have help in time of need while the wicked do not.

It is admitted, though, that there are times when one may be involved in trouble through kindness. But that is in consequence of the wicked people of the world who are always envious of the good. Because of this likely involvement in trouble through acts of kindness, some extremists have said that kindness is not worthwhile. Hence this kind of saying which is a contradiction of all that we have said on kindness so far:

Ŏre n' igún ṣè t' ó fi pá l' orí;
Ŏre l' àkàlàmàgbò ṣe t' ó yọ gẹ̀gẹ̀ l' ọ̀rùn;
K' ẹni ó má mà ṣ' ŏre mọ́ o.

It was in consequence of kindness that the vulture became bald;[1]
It was in consequence of kindness that the hornbill developed goitre;
Let us for that reason refrain from rendering kindness.

On the whole, however, the Yoruba believe that kindness pays in the end, whatever may be its immediate outcome. Therefore, one must go on being kind whatever happens. At the worst, *Inú 're kì 'pa 'ni, wàhálà ni 'kó bá 'ni*—"Kindness does not kill: it can only involve one in trouble".

(e) It is obvious then that wickedness should be roundly condemned. The law of retributive justice[2] operates in such a way as to bring back the reward of wickedness, not only upon the wicked, but also upon his offspring. *Ẹnití ó bá da ẽrú ni ẽrú 'tọ̀*—"The ashes blow after the person who throws them"; that means, the effect of wickedness ultimately falls back upon the wicked; and *Ẹnití ó bá gbin èbù ìkà, orí ọmọ rẹ̀ ni yí ó hù lé*—"He who sows the seed of wickedness, it is on his children's head that it will grow"; that is, his children will reap the harvest in suffering.

For this cause also, to demand or accept reparation from a neighbour for the loss or damage of property is considered mean and wicked. Besides the fact that such a demand creates strained relations, it breeds such bitterness in the heart that if in future a chance of retaliation presents itself, the situation can be terrible.

The following story is told to show what the repercussion of cruelty may be upon its perpetrator:

A man lent his neighbour an earthenware pot which had lost its bottom for the purpose of protecting a young kola plant from the animals. When the kola plant had grown into a tree so that it was

---

[1] See Chapter 6, p. 51.   [2] See above, p. 146.

impossible to remove the pot without breaking it, the man went and demanded his pot, stipulating that he wanted it back exactly as he had lent it to his neighbour. Everything was done to convince him that it was unfair for him to make such a demand, but all to no avail; he insisted on recovering his pot "unbroken". In the end, the kola tree had to be destroyed so that his pot might be returned to him. Not very long afterwards, this same man had a baby and borrowed a neck-ring which belonged to the neighbour to whom he had behaved so badly. The neighbour took this as an opportunity of teaching him a lesson which he would not easily forget. He therefore waited until the child grew up to an age when the ring could not possibly be removed from his neck without either first cutting the ring or removing the head. Then he went and demanded his ring, stipulating that he wanted it back uncut. Of course, there was no other way of doing that apart from decapitating the child, and that was what happened in the end! This story sounds fantastic, of course; but it is meant to inculcate in the most forceful way the lesson that acts of cruelty usually reflect with terrible consequence upon the doer; for *Enití ó kọ́ d' óró kì 'mọ̀ ọ 'dá, bí ẹnití o dá a k' ẹ̀hìn*—"He who first commits an atrocious act towards a neighbour cannot anticipate the bitterness of the revenge which will bring back retaliation".

Nevertheless, retaliation is forbidden because it is wrong. To retaliate is to become involved in wickedness just as much as the first offender. *Bi o bá rí òkù o-ṣ'-ìkà n' lẹ̀, bi o bá f' ẹsẹ̀ tà á, ìkà wá di méjì*—"If you see the corpse of the wicked and kick it, there are now two who are wicked".

(f) Truth and rectitude are placed very high among the essential virtues. It is believed that the truthful and upright have the unfailing support and blessing of the divinities. We have the popular song from an *Odù* called *Ètúrúpọ̀n-méjì:*

> *Ṣ' òtítọ́; ṣe rere,*
> *Ṣ' òtítọ́ o, ṣe rere;*
> *Ẹni s' òtítọ́*
> *N' ímalẹ̀ ígbè.*

> Be truthful, do good;
> Be truthful, do good;
> It is the truthful
> That the divinities support.

Ọ̀runmìlà is often saluted as *A-f'-òtítọ́-gb'-aiyé, ọmọ Àjàlọ́run*—"The offspring of the Chief of Heaven, who wins the earth by means of rectitude ". It is taught that one should be truthful and practise rectitude as one's days are thus prolonged on earth:

Òtítọ́ șíșe nìkan ni kì 'mú ni 'kú,
Ṣùgbọ́n tí-'mú ni 'hu ewú ori nẹnẹ.

It is only rectitude that prevents one from dying young,
And enables one to grow exceedingly hoary.

Thus rectitude pays a good dividend in the end. *Òtítọ́ inú ni à-jẹ-kù ju irọ́ lọ*—"Rectitude rather than falsehood pays the dividend". Consequently, lying and falsehood are considered damnable. In the old days, the lips of liars were carved out by way of punishment and as a warning to others. In Ijẹ̀bǔ-òde area, the people whose lips had been removed in that way were settled in a quarter by themselves and employed as state executioners.

(g) Yoruba ethics forbid stealing. In the old days, thieves were pilloried and then killed. The belief is strong among the Yoruba that even if the thief escapes the notice of men he cannot escape the judgment of Olódùmarè. *A-m'-ōkùn-ș'olè, bi ojú ọba aiye 'ò ri i, t' Ọba Ọ̀run nwò o*—"He who steals under concealment (secretly), even though the eyes of the earthly ruler do not see him, those of the King in Heaven are looking at him". In those old days, people used to leave articles of food for sale at cross-roads or by roadsides without anybody to watch them. The owner had only to indicate the prices by pebble signs and any traveller who wanted any took what he wanted and left the price on the stall. Neither article nor money was stolen. A hungry traveller who had no money was permitted to take of the fruits or yams of a farm, provided he ate what was taken on the spot.

(h) Covenant-breaking and falsehood are condemned. A covenant-breaker is considered not only worthless but also accursed.[1] The one who is given to falsehood, it is believed, cannot prosper ultimately. On this topic, there are several sayings of which we shall quote only a few by way of illustrations.

Ẹni ti ó bá da 'lẹ̀, a bá 'lẹ̀ lọ.

The covenant-breaker will disappear with the earth
(will be carried away by the earth).

The worship and sacrifices of both the liar and the covenant-breaker are never acceptable, while those of the good-natured are always accepted.

[1] See above, pp. 149 ff.

Thus an *Òfún-Ètùrà* says,

> *Èké pa 'bì o dí;*
> *Ọ-dà-'lẹ̀ pa 'bì, é yàn;*
> *Oní-nú-'re pa 'bì,*
> *O yè peregede.*

The liar casts the kola-nut,[1] it is unauspicious;
The covenant-breaker casts the kola-nut, it gives bad omen;
The good-natured casts the kola-nut,
It is plainly auspicious.

In the *Odù* corpus, there is an *Èjì-Ogbè* which tells a story that the four hundred and one divinities accused Ọ̀runmìlà falsely before Olódùmarè. Because he was innocent, he turned upon them with the following imprecation:

> *Àṣẹ d' ọwọ́, ilẹ̀ a jọ mu;*
> *Àṣẹ d' ọwọ́ ilẹ̀, a jọ mu;*
> *A jọ gb' orí ilẹ̀, a j' eku,*
> *A jọ gb' orí ilẹ̀, a j' ẹja*
> *A jọ gb' orí ilẹ̀, a jẹ 'kòkò igbin,*
> *Aṣe d' ọwọ́ ilẹ̀ a jọ mu.*[2]

Judgment belongs to the earth upon which we covenanted,
Judgment belongs to the earth upon which we covenanted;
We were together upon the earth and ate rats,
We were together upon the earth and ate fish,
We were together upon the earth and ate snails,
Judgment belongs to the earth upon which we covenanted.

Another story in *Ètùrúpọ̀n-Ọ̀kànràn* from the *Odù* corpus tells of a first-assistant-chief of the Ọ̀runmìlà cult who seduced the wife of his chief. For a while both he and the woman kept the matter secret; then he became very ill and had to make a confession of his secret sin. As a result we have the following:

> *Èké 'ò sunwọ̀n ara ẹni*
> *Ọ̀-dà-'lẹ̀ 'ò sunwọ̀n ara ènìa;*
> *B' ọmọdé bá nyọ́ 'lẹ̀ dà,*
> *Ohun abẹ-'nu a mã yọ́ wọn ṣe,*
> *O dá fún ajùbọ̀ná*
> *Ti o lọ nfẹ obìrin olúwo*

---

[1] See Chapter 10, pp. 135 f.
[2] See above, pp. 149 f.; and Psalm 41:9, John 18:18.

Falsehood is not right for one,
Covenant-breaking is good for no man;
If the young surreptitiously break covenant
Ills surreptitious will befall them.
So declared the oracle for the *ajùbọnà*
Who went and seduced the wife of the *olúwo*.[1]

And it is important to observe the rule against falsehood and covenant-breaking on account of one's end. Thus, an *Ọyẹ̀kú-méjì* says,

K' á má ṣ' èkĕ ẹgbẹ́;
K' a má dà 'lẹ̀ ọgbà;
Nitorí à-ti-sùn ara ẹni ni.

Let us not lie against a companion;
Let us not break covenant with an associate;
That is on account of our sleeping (dying).[2]

(i) Hypocrisy is unmanly and reprovable. A hypocrite as well as hypocrisy is called *àgàbàgebè*—"One who moves in zigzags" (probably one who attempts to climb a ladder and a mound simultaneously), one whose character is unpredictable. Olódùmarè forbids such a character— *Àgàbàgebè? Ọlọrun kò fẹ́ bẹ̃*—"Hypocrisy? Ọlọrun forbids it". It is definitely enjoined upon all, according to another *Ọyẹ̀kú-méjì* that,

Ẹni tí ó bá nṣ' akin,
K' ó má m' óhùn ṣ' ojo;
Ẹni tí ó bá nṣ' ojo,
K' o má m' ohùn ṣ' akin.

He who is brave,
Let him not declare himself cowardly;
He who is cowardly
Let him not declare himself brave.

(j) It is the responsibility of the Yoruba man to give protection to the woman as the weaker sex. When men and women walk together, the woman should be allowed to go in front and the man behind her so as to afford her protection and defence should there be a sudden danger. In any crises, women should be sheltered and afforded the first chance

---

[1] The *Olúwo* is a head priest of Ọrunmìlà and the *Ajùbọnà* his second-in-command.
[2] See Chapter 14, pp. 197 f.

of escape, if need be. It is mean and immoral to outrage a defenceless woman. In one Yoruba saying, someone makes the wistful complaint, *Ọba 'ò jẹ́kí nwọn ṣi 'gun ìlú 'bìrin ki ng bá wọn lọ*—"O that the king might permit an attack on a women's city so that I might accompany them (the attackers)".

(k) Honour and due respect to old age is the duty of every Yoruba person. The young must respect the elder because of their seniority as well as because of their riper and richer experience from which the young should profit. So it is taught.

> *Ọmọdé, ẹ wo 'lẹ̀ f' agbà;*
> *Àgbà ni 'gba ni;*
> *N' ijọ́ a rí jẹ,*
> *Àgbà ni 'gba ni;*
> *N' ijọ́ aìrí jẹ,*
> *Àgbà ni 'gba ni.*

Young ones, do obeisance to the elders:
It is the elders who come to the rescue;
The day one has plenty to eat,
It is the elders who come to the rescue;
The day one has nought to eat,
It is the elders who come to the rescue.

From the store of their experience the elders can make the young gifts of much needed wisdom and guidance for the purpose of tackling life's difficulties.

> *Ọjọ́ 'ò t' ọjọ́, ọjọ 'ò t' ọ́jọ̀,*
> *Ti mo r' òde rè 'ká 'ṣin;*
> *Mo dúró-dúró, ọwọ mi 'ò to 'ṣin.*
> *Mo bẹ̀rẹ̀-bẹ̀rẹ̀, ọwọ mi 'ò to 'ṣin;*
> *Awọn àgbà kan, àgbà kàn*
> *Ni nwọn wá kọ́ mi pé ki ndúbù yẹ̀kẹ́:*
> *Igbàtí mo dúbù yẹ̀kẹ́*
> *Ni gbogbo iṣin wá nkán sí mi l' ẹ́nu*

That was a day of days
When I went out to pluck *iṣin*:[1]
I stood upright all I could, my hands did not reach the *iṣin*;
I stooped down all I could, my hands did not reach the *iṣin*;

[1] This is a fleshy, juicy, edible fruit which enjoyes the name of *Sapindaceae* in R. C. Abraham's *Dictionary of Modern Yoruba* (1958).

Some veritable elder
It was who came and taught me to lean sideways;
It was when I leant sideways
That *iṣin* in countless numbers dropped their juice in my mouth.

The elders also must afford the young care and protection and not count them as of no consequence. In life, both age and youth are complementary in helpfulness.

Ọwọ́ ọmọdé 'ò to pẹpẹ;
T' àgbàlagbà kò wọ kèrègbè.

The hand of the young does not reach the high shelf,
That of the elder does not go into the gourd[1]

Yoruba ethics sums up what man-to-man relations should be in this:

Bí a bá ṣẹ́ 'gi n' igbó,
K' a f' ọ̀ràn ro ara ẹni wò!

Whenever a person breaks a stick in the forest,
Let him consider what it would feel like if it were himself (that was thus broken).

And

Bí o ti ndun ọmọ eku,
Bẹ̃ nâ l' ó ndun ọmọ ẹiyẹ

As sensitive to pain as are rats' little ones,
So sensitive to pain are birds' little ones.

All these approximate to what has been described as the "Golden Rule"—"Do unto others as ye would that they should do unto you". Yoruba elders teach that if everyone would first think in this way before acting, there would be perfectly good relations and happiness.

This array of the constituents of moral values in the religion of the Yoruba are sufficiently impressive to convince even the most sceptical that the Yoruba are a people endowed with a strong sense of Right and Wrong, and that this sense has been implanted in their "inward parts" by the Author of life Himself. Even though there are certain things in the practical life of the people which are incompatible with these values, it is now clear to us that the religion *per se* could not have been the causative of such things.

[1] The rind of the gourd is used for carrying oil, water, or palm-wine.

This brings us to the crucial question, however. Why is it that in spite of this knowledge of Right and Wrong and an impressive system of moral values, man can still be in the state of "I delight in the law of God, in my inmost self, but I see in my members another law at war with the law of my mind and making me captive to the law of sin which dwells in my members"?[1] The answer is that here, in the realm of moral values more than anywhere else, mere knowledge is not power. Merely to know that "Thou shalt not kill", "Thou shalt not commit adultery", "Thou shalt not steal", does not make a saint of man. He has his innate propensities to reckon with, and these have the inveterate habit of leading him to commit what St. Paul describes as "things which are not becoming" or "things which are not natural".[2] As Franz Cumont says, "It is not sufficient for a religion to classify moral values; but in order to be effective it must furnish motives for putting them into practice".[3] We shall go further and say that it must furnish a motive power for putting them into practice. For, are there not already those motives which are implied in the system of Reward and Punishment, divine and human, and in a strong belief in an After-Life which is the scene of retribution? Those motives are there; but they are not enough, as they usually lead only to "prudential morality". In any case, they only appeal, in the final analysis, to man's egocentricity; and man's egocentricity is a factor which may cause him to take punishment merely to exercise his sovereign rights, or choose hell on a self-assertive decision that it is better to reign in hell than to serve in heaven.

What man needs is a clear knowledge that he is made for his Maker and that his supreme duty is to dedicate his entire life to Him. To do this, he needs the enabling grace of God. Here we must agree with S. S. Farrow that the major defect of the religion of the Yoruba is that "It has no conception of divine grace working effectually in them that believe". For, what the religion really presents is a picture of the goodness of God on one hand and the demand of strict rectitude and justice on the other. Man confronted by these two sides of Reality which, unfortunately, appear to him to be separate entities, is at a loss what exactly to do. He wants to bask in the sunshine of God's goodness: at the same time he is harrassed by the chilling demand of strict rectitude and justice. As the latter becomes more real and urgent to him as in

> The flashing of the lightning free,
> The whirling wind's tempestuous shocks,

[1] Romans 7:22, 23 (R.S.V.).   [2] Romans 1:28 ff.
[3] *Oriental Religions in Roman Paganism* (Dover, 1956), p. 157.

in epidemics of smallpox or phenomena of similar nature, it confronts him with a daunting "must!". It occurs to him that this demand confronts him in the nature of practically autonomous divinities who represent "the Wrath". It does not occur to him that the God who demands righteousness is Himself the righteous God who alone is the Enabler of Righteousness in man. The goodness and severity of God are thus dangerously put asunder. And since the law must be fulfilled and he cannot and does not know how to fulfil it adequately, he finds apparent compensation in sacrifices of propitiation and prevention, and in magic. Somehow, he derives a kind of gloomy relief from these, provided he keeps up the rituals in perpetuity. In effect, man has unwittingly devised his own means of salvation and seeks by them to evade the consequences of his shortcomings or the violations of moral values. In his heart of hearts, however, and through the concrete exhibits relating to his moral failure which stare him in the face, he knows that "... to obey is better than sacrifice, and to hearken than the fat of rams".[1] The means of this obedience is the urgent quest of his soul; its unattainability under the present system is his perpetual embarrassment. And here we see the failure of a religion the sole repositories of whose theology are the priests.[2]

[1] I Samuel 15:22.   [2] See Chapter 15.

13

Olódùmarè and Man's Destiny

Every religion has to face the question of man's relationship to the Power that rules the Universe. "What is man?" and "To what end was man made?" are questions which demand doctrinal answers. And such answers depend upon man's conception of the Ruler of the Universe, while upon the answers themselves depends man's attitude to life.

To the question "What is man?" the Yoruba will answer off-handedly that man is body plus *èmí*, the English approximation to which is "spirit". The body is the concrete, tangible thing of flesh and bones which we know through the senses, which can be described in a general way, or analytically by anatomy. *Èmí* is invisible and intangible;[1] it is that which gives life to the whole body, and thus can be described through its causal functions. Its presence in, or absence from, the body is known only by the fact that a person is alive or dead. While the body can be created, and is created, by a divinity, it is Olódùmarè alone who puts the *èmí* into man, thus giving him life and being.[2]

Èmí is closely associated with the breath and the whole mechanism of breathing which are its most expressive manifestation. But although the fact that a man breathes shows that *èmí* is in him, the breath is not *èmí*. *Èmí* is causative of breath and so it is the "breather", that which breathes in man. The breath is *èmí*—"that which is breathed". Thus we say of a person who is just dead, *Èmí rè ti bó*—"His *èmí* has slipped off", or "*Èmí rè ti ló*—"His *èmí* is gone"; that is, the spirit has left the body; we say also under the same circumstances *Èmí ti tán nínú rè*—"There is no more breath in him". *Èmí* is also used for "life" as the bare fact of animate existence.

What we have said so far is not the end of the matter. Anyone who

---

[1] It is believed that *èmí* can assume a visible, tangible form as when it comes out of the witch, takes wings and flies like a bird! It is said that if the "bird" could be caught and killed, that is the end simultaneously of the witch also. *Èmí* can also become visible as an apparition.

[2] See Chapter 3, p. 21; Psalm 104; 29, 30.

knows the Yoruba intimately cannot escape the haunting feeling that in their thought there is more to man than just body and spirit. We are therefore led to ask the question "Do the Yoruba have souls?" or "Are they truly no more than mere 'burnt-out husks of men'"?[1]

In the Yoruba Bible, the word ọkàn is used to translate the English word "soul". This, however, is rather inaccurate. Ọkàn is accurately translated "the heart". This, according to the Yoruba, is the seat of the emotion and psychic energy. We describe the brave person as O ní ọkàn —"He has a 'heart'"; and the timid person as Kò ní ọkàn—"He has no 'heart'". To encourage a person is Ki i l' ọkàn or Mú u l' ọkàn le— "Strengthen his 'heart'" or "'Strengthen him in the heart'". Within this context, practically all the internal organs of the body taken together or severally have emotional or psychical functions attributed to them.[2] When we say of a person, Inũ rẹ̀ le, or Inũ rẹ̀ di—"His 'inside' is hard", or "His 'inside' is inscrutable", we mean that "He is obdurate" or "He is not open-hearted". A person's intestines are regarded as the source of strength and resourcefulness. Thus when a person is described as Kò n' ífun nínú—"He has no intestines", it means that he is not strong; he has no resilience. An o-n'-ífun kan—"a person with only one intestine"—is a person who is not resourceful or one who has no initiative.

But all the internal organs of man taken together or severally function only as the seats of man's psychical or physical actions or reactions. None of them together or severally constitute the soul.

Do the Yoruba then have any concrete conception of the soul? What do they call "the soul" if they have any, and know that they do? The soul, to the Yoruba, is the "inner person": their name for it is Orí.[3] This is the personality-soul.

Orí is the word for the physical "head". To the Yoruba, however, the physical, visible orí is a symbol of orí-inú—"the internal head", or "the inner person". And this is the very essence of personality. In the belief of the Yoruba, it is this orí that rules, controls, and guides the "life" and activities of the person.

Here we need to re-emphasize the connection between orí, the essence

[1] See The Voice of Africa, by Leo Frobenius (London, Hutchinson, 1913), p. XIII.
[2] Cf. The Christian Doctrine of Man, by H. Wheeler Robinson (Edinburgh, T. and T. Clark, 1943), Chapter I, pp. 1–27.
[3] We must sound the warning that the idea of the orí as the personality-soul is rather indeterminate so far as the oral traditions are concerned. But one gets it clearly through patient detective work!

of being and Orìṣè, the "Head-Source" of being.[1] Orìṣè is Olódùmarè Himself, as we have observed. The *orí* which is the essence of personality, the personality-soul in man, derives directly from Olódùmarè Whose sole prerogative it is to put it in man, because He is the One Inexhaustible Source of being. This means that apart from Him, man cannot be alive. The Yoruba is well aware of the fact that "in Him we live and move and have our being. . . . For we ourselves are also His offspring".[2]

In the act of taking the destiny which we shall describe presently, it is the *orí* that kneels down and chooses it.[3] It is also the *orí* that comes into the world to fulfil a destiny—hence the song:

> *Ohun orí wá ṣe*
> *Kò mà ni 'ṣ' alaì ṣe e o.*

> What the *orí* comes to fulfil
> It cannot but fulfil it.

What makes for the individuality of each *orí* is its quality. Generally, a prosperous person is called *Olórí-'re (Olórí rere)*—"One who possesses good *orí*", while one who is unfortunate in life is described as *Olorí burúkú*—"One who possesses a bad *orí*". This is more than saying that a person is "lucky" or "unlucky". It is a matter which is inextricably bound up with the person's destiny. While because of its pure origin no *orí* is essentially bad, the person's destiny is a factor which may affect it for the worse because it is partly the *orí*'s own responsibility. We may find T. R. Glover's account of the *genius* in Roman Religion illuminating both at this point and in reference to other points in our observation of *orí*.—"Why there should be such difference even between twin brothers,

> *He* only knows whose influence at our birth
> O'errules each mortal's planet upon earth,
> The attendant genius, temper-moulding pow'r,
> That stamps the colour of man's natal hour."[4]

A person's destiny is known as *Ìpín-orí—(Ìpònrí)*—"The *orí*'s portion or lot". It is usually abbreviated as *Ìpín*—"Portion". But sometimes, in consequence of the connection between *orí* and *ìpín*, destiny is loosely designated *orí*, which makes *ìpín* and *orí* synonymous in popular speech. Thus we say *orí burúkú kò gbó ọ̀ṣẹ*—"A bad *orí* cannot be

---

[1] See Chapter 7, pp. 60 f.   [2] Acts 17:28.   [3] See below, pp. 173 f.
[4] *The Conflict of Religions in the Early Roman Empire* (Methuen, 1932), p. 15.

rectified with soap (by washing)".[1] What this means, strictly, is that a bad portion which is already allotted to the *orí* cannot be rectified with medicine. Of an unsuccessful person it is said, *Orí inú rè l' ó ba t' òde jé*— "It is his internal *orí* that spoils the external one for him"; that is, the bad quality of his *orí* reflects on his external activities. Still, strictly, this means that it is the portion which his *orí* holds that conditions the person's life.

The idea of the *orí* is further complicated when it is conceived as a semi-split entity[2] in consequence of which it is at the same time the essence of the personality and the person's guardian or protector. There sneaks in here rather indeterminately the conception of the "double" or "guardian angel". We see this illustrated in the little sermon to the new bride on going to the husband's house: *Mú orí lọ, má m' ẹwà lọ; òjó l' ẹwà 'bọ, orí ni bá ni gbé 'lé ọkọ*—"Take *orí* along, do not take beauty along; beauty returns in a day (is ephemeral); it is *orí* that abides with one in the husband's house". This refers certainly to the inner quality which makes for conjugal success; but it has a hint of the *orí* as a semi-separate entity from the personality-soul. Further, we have the suggestion in the prayer for a person who is going on an enterprise, *Ki orí kí o sìn ẹ́ lọ o*—"May *orí* go with you"; or in the oft-heard saying that a person is sure to return unsuccessful from an enterprise if he does not consult *orí* before he sets out.

Orí in its totality is an object of worship. There are two reasons for this. First, as it is the essence of personality, it must be kept in good condition so that it may be well with the person. Secondly, one must be on good terms with it, so that it may favour one. In support of the first reason, the Yoruba sometimes speak as if the *orí* is all that it is necessary to worship. An *Odù, Òṣé-'Túrá*, speaks in rebuke of *Ọlọ́yọ̀ ti ó f' orí ara rè s' ilè ti ó nbọ ìdí àdǒ: ṣùgbọ́n orí ní 'gbe 'ni, àdǒ ò gbe 'ni: njẹ́ orí l' à bá bọ ti a bá f' òrìṣà s' ilè*—"Ọlọ́yọ̀ who neglects his own *orí* and makes offering to *àdǒ*[3]: but it is the *orí* that favours one, *àdǒ*

---

[1] The Yoruba use medicated soap for many purposes which range from curative to magical.

[2] See Chapter 14, p. 195 for a reference to the "subliminal self".
Cf. also the Syrian Gnostic's Hymn of the Soul, . . . according to the quotation by T. R. Glover:

It was myself that I saw before me as in a mirror;
Two in number we stood, but only one in appearance.

Ibid.

[3] *Àdǒ* is the hollowed rind of the small gourd which is used as a receptacle for pulverised medicine. A fairly large, long-necked one may be strung with cowries and used as the emblem of an object of worship. And there are types of medicine which need regular offerings.

OLÓDÙMARÈ AND MAN'S DESTINY

does not; it is rather the orí that should be worshipped and orìṣà left out".

Yet, often when the Yoruba refer to the "double" or the "counterpart" whom they designate Ẹnìkejì, they are speaking in clear terms of an entity other than the personality-soul but which yet has a strong influence on its destiny. He is variously described as a person's "guardian angel"; a person's surety in heaven, or the one who loaned to a person certain essential things which makes it possible for him to enter the earth and live on it. This last conception means very likely that a person lives on earth by drawing upon certain virtues the source of which is in his heavenly counterpart.[1]

To make an offering to the orí, the physical orí is the common emblem.[2] Kola-nuts, fish, fowl, or an animal victim may be offered. A piece of the kola-nut or fish is stuck on the forehead, while the blood of the fowl or animal is smeared on it. The physical orí also serves often, though not always, as the emblem for the ẹnìkejì. More often than not, the sacrifice to the ẹnìkejì is exposed in the backyard or any open place which the oracle may prescribe.

A person makes offerings not only to his own orí but also to his parent's orí. Here, still more, is emphasised the conception of a "guardian angel". The emblem for the father's orí is, generally, the big toe of the right foot, while that to the mother's orí is the big toe of the left foot. A young woman in difficulty is often asked to make an offering to Ọkọ òrun—"The husband which is in heaven (her husband's ẹnìkejì)". Thus, it is not only a person's own orí or ẹnìkejì, but also another's, that can be his guardian, enabler, and protector.

To the Yoruba, the end for which a person is made is inextricably bound up with his destiny. They believe that man's doings on earth have been predestined by Olódùmarè. According to the general conception, a person obtains his destiny in one of three ways. He kneels down and *chooses* his destiny: for a destiny which comes upon a person in this way we have the name À-kúnlẹ̀-yàn—"That-which-is-chosen-kneeling"; or he kneels down and *receives* his destiny; for this we have the name À-kúnlẹ̀-gbà—"That-which-is-received-kneeling"; or his destiny is *affixed* to him; for this we have the name À-yàn-mọ́—"That which is affixed to one". Thus we have a trimorphous conception of destiny the sustaining motif of which is that the person who is coming into the world must kneel before the High Authority Who is Olódùmarè for its

---

[1] See below, p. 182, for further discussion on Ẹnìkejì.
[2] See the *History of the Yorubas*, by Samuel Johnson, pp. 27, 48.

conferment. Whatever is thus conferred is unalterable and becomes one's portion throughout life. That is what the person goes into the world to fulfil.

It is not clearly stated in the oral traditions what the pre-existent state of the person is before he comes into the world. But it occurs in the sayings that it is the * orí* that kneels before Olódùmarè to choose, receive, or have the destiny affixed to it.[1] The general picture, therefore, is of a complete "person" kneeling before Olódùmarè to choose or receive.

When the rite before Olódùmarè is completed, the person starts on his way into the world. He arrives at the gates between heaven and earth, and encounters the *On'íbodè*—"The Gate-Keeper"—to whom he must answer some questions before he passes through. The questions and answers go as follows:

> ONÍBODÈ: Where are you going?
> PERSON: I am going into the world.
> ONÍBODÈ: What are you going to do?
> PERSON: I am going to be born to a man named X, of a woman named Y, in the town of Z. I shall be an only son. I shall grow up to be handsome and in favour with everybody; everything I touch will prosper; when I am twenty-five, my father will die and when I am fifty, my mother will die. I shall build a large house and possess a large prosperous farm; and be the father of a large family through my twenty wives; When I am sixty years old, two of my children will have a quarrel and one will be killed. At the age of ninety, I shall be ill for a short while and then die peacefully in my house, to be mourned by all and to be accorded a grand burial.
> ONÍBODÈ: *To!* (It is sealed!).

And so the person passes into the world with his destiny doubly sealed. By passing into the world, he forgets at once what has happened to him in heaven, including the contents of his destiny.

How the "finished" person becomes a thing in the womb, born of a woman, we are not told in the oral traditions. But even though the Yoruba know that conception results from sexual intercourse, yet they think that each person is a new creation which in some inexplicable way enters the womb to be born after the due period of gestation. A father insists on making sure that a child is his own and does not belong

[1] Cf. Plato: *The Republic*, translated by Dr. A. D. Lindsay (Everyman's Library, No. 64), pp. 322 ff.

to another man by looking at the child carefully and establishing some points of lineage resemblance while at the same time thinking that the child is a newly created, newly predestined being.

We have said that by the very nature of the destiny, it is unalterable especially as it has been doubly sealed, i.e. in the act of its conferment and finally at the "gates". It appears, then, that there is nothing anybody can do about it thenceforth. There are several sayings to support this belief. Here are a few.

A-kunlè-yàn ni a-d'-aiyé-bá;
A kunlè a yàn 'pĭn,
A d' aiyé tán ojú nro ni.

That-which-is-chosen-kneeling is that-which-is-found-on-getting-
    to-the-world;
We knelt down and chose a portion,
We get to the world and are not pleased.

A-kunlè-gbà l' o wà l' ǫwǫ ̀ èdǎ:
Kò s' ǫgbǫ́n owó,
Kò s' ǫgbǫ́n ǫmǫ.

That-which-is-chosen-kneeling is what the creature holds:
There is no (other) means of (possessing) money,
There is no (other) means of (possessing) children.

A-yàn-mǫ 'ò gb' õgùn.

That-which-is-affixed-to-one cannot be rectified with medicine.

In the *Odù* which is called *Ogbè-Âtĕ*, there is mentioned in this con-nection one Lábòdé, ǫmǫ Ǫtúnba:—Lábòdé, the son of Ǫtúnba: *Nwǫn ni gbogbo aiyé a mã bù u kù; ṣugbǫn Ajàlǫ́run a mã bù kún u*—"It is said that the whole world[1] will do their best to thwart him; but the Chief-in-Heaven will keep blessing him". And there is a popular song which says:

Igi t' Ǫlǫ́run gbìn,
Kò s' ǫni t' o lè fà a tu.

[1] See below, pp. 176 ff.

The tree which Ọlọrun plants,
None can uproot it.

It seems therefore that once the matter of a person's destiny is settled in heaven, that is the end of it.

In the light of the practical experiences of the Yoruba, however, the conception of the unalterability of destiny is considerably modified; in the business of daily living, the Yoruba act in the apparent belief that given certain conditions, a person's destiny can be altered. And it can be altered in the following ways:

(a) By the aid of Ọ̀runmìlà. We have observed that the major reason why a person becomes a votary of Ọ̀runmìlà is that a happy destiny may be preserved or an unhappy one rectified.[1] An item in the order of the ritual by which a votary is made contains a dialogue between the priest and the suppliant which, in general, runs as follows (the priest begins by pointing to each of the articles brought by the suppliant):

> PRIEST: *Tal' ó ni eku?*
> SUPPLIANT: *T' emi o.*
> PRIEST: *Tal' ó ni ẹja?*
> SUPPLIANT: *T' emi o.*
> PRIEST: *Tal' o ni ãka?*
> SUPPLIANT: *T' emi o.*
> PRIEST: *Kil' o mú nwọn wá fún?*
> SUPPLIANT: *Ki ng l' owó m' ówó,*
> *Ki ng bi 'mọ lé 'mọ,*
> *Ki ng kọ 'le mọ 'le,*
> *Ki ng f' atitàn s' ẹhìn,*
> *Ki ng ṣẹ́ 'gun ọ̀tǎ,*
> *Ki ng r' ẹhìn odì,*
> *Ki ng ni aiku ṣ' ẹgbọn iwà,*
> *L' ohun ti mo ṣe mu wọn wa.*

> PRIEST: Whose are the rats?
> SUPPLIANT: Mine.
> PRIEST: Whose are the fish?
> SUPPLIANT: Mine.
> PRIEST: Whose is the hedgehog?

[1] See Chapter 8, p. 77.

SUPPLIANT: Mine.

PRIEST: Why do you bring them?

SUPPLIANT: That I may have money upon money (plenty of money),

That I may have children upon children (in increasing numbers),

That I may build houses upon houses (many houses),

That I may extend the boundaries of my property,

That I may be victorious over all foes,

That I may see the end of all who bear me malice,[1]

That I may possess immortality[2] which is the best of all earthly goods,

Those are the reasons why I bring them.

We see already in this that the suppliant is taking steps through the agency of Ọrunmìlà to influence his destiny. Throughout the course of life, one is to serve Ọrunmìlà, or one's tutelary divinity, by consultation or worship so that a good portion may be ensured.

(b) A person's destiny may be altered for the worse by *Ọmọ Ar'-aiyé* —"Children of the World". The Yoruba use the phrase-name to describe the persons in whom the evil powers of the world are apparently vested, just in the same sense as they operate through the men of the world who "loved the darkness rather than the light; for their works were evil"; or "the power of darkness".[3] *Ọmọ Ar'-aiyé* includes witches, secret cults with a bias towards evil practices, any who are given to evil practices or machinations. The Yoruba believe that *ọmọ ar'-aiyé* is a dreadful reality. Thus they say *Ọmọ ar'-aiyé ogun*—"'The children of the world' are an army"; that is, they are ever given to incessant warfare against anyone who, or anything which, does not conform to their standard. They are believed to have the power of spoiling any person's lot, however good it may have been to begin with. Hence Alágẹmọ-tẹ́rẹ́kangẹ̀, who came into this world and found himself confronted with *Ogun ọmọ ar'-aiyé* ("The army of the 'children of the world'") pleaded, *Ẹ jẹ́' mi j' iṣẹ ti Olódùmarè rán mi*—"Let me fulfil the mission

---

[1] *Ọtă* and *Odì* are also used metaphorically in some part of Yorubaland to designate respectively one's father and mother. One is congratulated as *O ṣe 'gun ọta, o r' ẹhìn odì*—"He has been victorious over his foes and seen the end of her who bore him malice"—when one has lived to perform successfully the funeral rites of both parents.

[2] What is really meant here is "longevity". In the belief of the Yoruba, immortality belongs to After-Life, and is not a thing of this world. See Chapter 14, p. 176.

[3] John 3:19; Luke 22:53, Colossians 1:13.

committed to me by Olódùmarè". A Yoruba ballad carries the plaintive note of pleading:

Ẹ má pè mi n' ipè ẹ p' agbe,
K' ágbe o tó 'd' aláró igbó;
Ẹ má pè mi n' ipè ẹ p' àlùkò,
K' álùkò o tó 'd' olósùn ẹ̀gàn;
Ẹ má pè mi n' ipè e p' òbùrő,
K' òbùrő o tó 'd' alâwí-rìn ẹiyẹ ninu oko.

Do not telepathise[1] me as you did *agbe*,
So that *agbe* became the indigo-coloured one of the forest;
Do not telepathise me as you did *àlùkò*,
So that *àlùkò* became the camwood-coloured one of the wilderness;
Do not telepathise me as you did *óbùrő*,[2]
So that *óbùrő* became the vagrant-babbler of the groves.

Another designation for the agents of evil in the world is *Elénìnì*—"The implacable, causeless, sadistic foes who oppose people relentlessly and spoil every opportunity of their success". They can debar *orí* from carrying out its destiny. In *Ogbè-Èdì* we have the words *Orí kunlẹ̀ o yàn 'wà, elénìnì 'ò jẹ k' o ṣe e*— "*Orí* knelt and chose the portion, *elénìnì* hinder it from its fulfilment".

Ọmọ ar'-aiyé and *Elénìnì* draw their power from the evil principle · which is described comprehensively as *Aiyé*—"The World".[3] Here resides the concentrated power of evil. We have seen this power partially manifested in *Èṣù*; but we know that *Èṣù* is not essentially evil.[4] In the notion of the human choice of *ìpín* there is a suggestion also that a person's failure or happiness may be his own responsibility.[5] In *aiyé*, however, we meet unmitigated evil in its essence, malignant, obstructing, spoiling, out-and-out diabolic.[6] It is not at all clear from the oral traditions what will account for this "power". But if a Yoruba is

[1] The Yoruba believe in the possibility of telepathy. It is said to be one of the deadliest weapons in the hands of *Ọmọ ar'-aiyé*.

[2] *Agbe*, *àlùkò* and *óbùrő* are birds. The first two are said to belong to the cuckoo family. *Agbe* is given the name *Blue Touraco Musophagidae* in A. C. Abraham's *Dictionary of Modern Yoruba*. Apparently, they were either not birds but human beings originally, or if birds, they were not of the present colour, according to the folk-tales.

[3] Cf. Matthew 18:7; John 15:33; 1 John 3:13.

[4] See Chapter 8, pp. 83.

[5] See below, p. 179.

[6] That is as far as the conception of *Aiyé* goes within this context. There is a cult of *Aiyé* in *Igbó-ọrà* where *Aiyé* is an ancestress.

pressed for an explanation of its being, he will certainly make Olódùmarè responsible. This is not because Olódùmarè ever has, or ever
can harbour evil in his nature, but because the Yoruba believe that all
things which are in the world originated from Him.[1] The Yoruba
elders will certainly say that ultimately it is Olódùmarè who gives
ọmọ ar'-aiyé their power. If, however, we ask further, "What purpose does aiyé serve?" we shall find that we have reached a cul-de-
sac. The Yoruba do not bother themselves with such a question. They
accept aiyé as an urgent factor to be reckoned with in their lives and go
about finding ways and means of meeting the situation. It is an accepted
fact to the Yoruba that Aiyé n' ipá—"Aiyé is malignantly powerful".
The Yoruba explain any condition of malaise, any baffling untoward
happening or persistent misfortune in the life of a person by saying
Aiyé l' o nbá a jà—"It is aiyé that is afflicting him". The power of aiyé
for evil is so great that it can alter the course or operation of nature.
Therefore it is said:

> Bi ẹ r' aiyé, ẹ sá f' aiyé,
> Bi ẹ r' aiyé, ẹ sá f' aiyé:
> Ìṣẹ̀ṣẹ̀ w' aiyé ijímèrè dúdú,
> Aiyé nã l' ó t' aṣọ ijímèrè b' epo;
> Aiyé nã l' ó p' ògìdǎn
> Ògìdǎn olólà ijù;
> Bi ẹ r' aiyé, ẹ sá f' aiyé.

If you encounter aiyé, flee from aiyé,[2]
If you encounter aiyé, flee from aiyé:
The primeval ijímèrè[3] was black,
This aiyé it is that soaked ijímèrè's clothes in palm-oil;
This aiyé it is that slew ògìdǎn,
Ògìdǎn the surgeon[4] of the wilderness;
If you encounter aiyé, flee from aiyé.

(c) A person's destiny can be affected for the worse by his character.
The Yoruba believe that a good destiny unsupported by character is

---

[1] Cf. Isaiah 45:7—"I form the light, and create darkness; I make peace, and
create evil: I am the Lord, that doeth all these things" (R.V.).

[2] "Do not show familiarity or audacity towards aiyé."

[3] Ijímèrè is the red monkey. The implication here is that its red colour (because
dyed in palm-oil) is contrary to what it should have been.

[4] Ògìdǎn, olólà ijù is a praise-title of the leopard. Olólà in Yoruba is one who
circumcises and cuts clan marks and tattoos. The leopard bears the title because
it is capable of tearing its victim according to impulse.

worthless.[1] Destiny can also be spoiled by one's action, especially by acts of rashness and impatience. In the *Odù* corpus, an *Ọbàrà-ọ̀yẹ̀kù* tells a story of someone who aspired to climb the coconut tree to the very top. He was told that it had been laid down that he could do it; but he must be very careful not to be misled by the pride of his achievement and attempt to jump from tree to tree. This warning he did not heed: in the attempt to jump from one tree to another he fell and died. In this connection, people are especially warned against impatience, as by it a person may easily forfeit the good fortune which is in store for him. Another *Odù* recital tells of one *A-lu-kósó-Aiyé*[2] who lived a life of wretchedness up to the age of forty, when he got tired of it and decided to commit suicide. In the attempt, he only swooned and thought that he stood before *On'íbodè* who demanded why he should appear un-bidden at the "gate". He made his complaint, in answer to which *On'íbodè* only locked him up in a room and instructed him to keep listening. Before long, there were footfalls and he knew that those who were travelling into the world had arrived. He heard each of them recite what his destiny would be, and how it was sealed finally by *On'-íbodè*. When they had all gone away, *On'íbodè* sang:

> *Alukósó-Aiyé,*
> *Ṣe o ngbọ́ o?*
> *B' aiyé ṣe nyẹ ni mà rẹ̆ o.*

> Alukósó-Aiyé,
> Have you been listening?
> This shows how one's life is ordered.

Thus *Alukósó-Aiyé* learnt that, so far, things had happened to him on earth according to his destiny. Next, *On'íbodè* led him out and showed him an enclosure which contained a wealth of cattle, and a room full of earthly goods. All those, he was told, were to be his after the age of forty, according to his destiny. Now, however, he had forfeited every future benefit by his impatience. The story concludes that at the sight of all the wealth, *Alukósó-Aiyé* burst into tears, and pleaded so strongly that Olódùmarè allowed him another lease of ten years in which to enjoy his predestined fortune!

[1] See Chapter 12, p. 155.

[2] *Alukósó* is the title of a drummer, particularly in the ancient Ọ̀yọ́ govern-ment, who woke up the king at 4 o'clock every morning. See *The History of the Yorubas*, by Rev. S. Johnson (Lagos, C.M.S., 1937), p. 58.

In this emphasis on character in relation to destiny, there sneaks in
the paradox of human responsibility in a system of apparently cast-iron
predestination. We have the hint already in the conception of destiny
as a thing "chosen" by the person. With the element of character
involved, a person is not allowed to expect an automatic fulfilment of a
good destiny. He must co-operate to make his destiny successful by
acquiring and practising good character.

(d) An unhappy destiny may be rectified if it can be ascertained what
it is. We have referred to the work of Ọrunmìlà in this connection.[1]
We need only to add the following. On the third day after a child's
birth, the oracle is consulted for it. This rite is called *Ikọ-'sẹ̀-w'-áiyé* or
Ẹ̀sẹ̀-n-t'-aiyé—"The first step into the world". The main purpose is to
find out what sort of child it is, what are *tabu* to it, what things are to be
done in order to preserve its good destiny or to rectify an unhappy one.
The third day is not the only time the oracle is consulted for this purpose; it is done during any crisis in the person's life. Often, when during
an illness the oracle declares that the person's life is going to be termi-
nated in fulfilment of his destiny, a substitutionary sacrifice[2] is prescribed as a remedy against the operation of the destiny. Apparently,
there are several other ways of making sure what the destiny is and doing
something remedial to forestall an unhappy fulfilment.

Here is a story which our elders will claim to be quite historical. There
was a man named Atele who was much troubled by *Àbíkú*[3]; that is, his
wife had babies which died in immediate successions not long after
their birth. Atele tried several ways of rectifying the situation but failed.
He therefore decided to trace the cause to its source. So he set out for
Ajiran.

Ajiran is a village which has gathered round itself the legend of being
a "gate" between heaven and earth. Through it new "persons" enter
the earth and returning "persons" enter into heaven. The *On'íbodè*
there is Ojòmǔ, who is also the head of the little town, and who bears
the cognomen of *A-y-ọ̀run-bọ̀* (*A-yún-ọ̀run-bọ̀*)—"He who goes to
heaven and returns". In some parts of Yorubaland, people apostro-
phise him during burial rituals that he may open the "gate" for the
good to enter heaven, lest they should be kept waiting. To this personage
Atele went with his problem. Atele himself must have been a man of
some distinction to have been able to do this.

Ojòmǔ listened sympathetically to his story, gave him hospitality for

[1] Chapters 8, pp. 77 ff. and above, p. 176.
[2] Chapter 9, pp. 123 f.   [3] See Chapter 9, pp. 123 f.

the night, and promised him a solution to it the following morning, which happened to be the sacred day at Ajiran. Very early that morning, Ojòmŭ hid Atele under the stool upon which he customarily sat for the sacred day ritual. At the appointed time, the new "persons" who were going to the earth assembled and each of them answered his catechism in a way which made his destiny clear. One of the "persons" who thus assembled was the one who was going to be born to Atele. The most significant among the things that he said, as far as Atele was concerned, was that on his marriage day, in the evening just before the bride was brought in, he would go into the bush to ease himself and would be bitten by a snake and would die and return to heaven.

Atele went back to his home town of Ipẹru with the secret locked up in his breast. The marriage day duly arrived, and in the evening, just before the bride was brought in, Atele's son said that he was going into the bush to ease himself. But his father had been watchful all along; he appealed to him to stay in the house and use any receptacle he chose for his purpose. The son was adamant: into the bush he must go! The father then gave up but insisted on following him into the bush. When they arrived at the spot chosen by his son, just before he stepped into the bush, the father lighted the place with a torch, saw a large snake, and killed it. Thus Atele rectified the destiny of his son who in consequence lived to a ripe old age.

(e) A person's destiny can be affected for the worse by the machinations of the Ẹnìkéjì. This, as we have observed, is one of the reasons why the ẹnìkéjì must be kept in a state of peaceful contentment through regular offerings. A recital, Ogbè-Ègŭndá, in the Odù corpus states that one who is born under that particular Odù must offer constant sacrifices to the ẹnìkéjì; for otherwise, he will be deprived of half of his every earthly possession, which means that he cannot really prosper. Incidentally, anyone born under this Odù must not give his confidence to a woman!

·   ·   ·   ·   ·

These can be all summed up in this way. The Yoruba believe generally that everybody coming into the world is predestined by Olódùmarè. The destiny is doubly sealed and therefore unalterable. Whatever a person does achieve, or whatever happens to him, is a precise working out of his destiny.

Nevertheless, the Yoruba act in the belief that given certain conditions,

13. A sacred lake, Àyè (Èkìtì)

14. The priestess of Odùdúwà, Igbó-Ọrà

a person's destiny may be altered. They therefore take steps to see that a happy destiny is not spoilt and that an unhappy one is rectified.

The paradox involved in this two-sided conception is accepted by the Yoruba without question. They offer neither explanation nor rationalisation about it. It just means that in an inexplicable way, what happens to a person may be simultaneously the result of *Bi ó ti gbà a*—"As he received it (was destined)", and *A-f'-ọwọ́-fà*—"that which he brings upon himself" and *Oró aiyé*—"the venom of *aiyé*".[1]

On the whole, the Yoruba teach caution and patience as one goes on in life. They desire long life and pray for it as they feel that it is seldom that the morning really shows the day with regard to the working out of destiny. Thus, they would consider of no lasting importance whatever misfortune or prosperity attends a person's early life, and wait with patience, and something of foreboding, for the "evening of life". They pray, *Ki a má fi ọrọ p' ìtàn*—"That our opulence may not become history"; and say *Ọmọ 'ò l' ayọ̀ lé, ẹni ọmọ sin 'l ó bí 'mọ*—"There is little cause for joy in children; he who is buried by children is he who really has children"; that is, he cannot really call them his own until they survive him.

There is no need to act in heat and haste: a person may miss the good things which come with the "evening of life" if he does. Therefore, we have the warning as contained in *Ogbè-méjì* that:

> *K' a má fi kán'jú-kán 'jú j' aiyé;*
> *K' a má fi wàrà-wàrà n' okùn ọrọ̀;*
> *Ohun à bǎ fi ṣ' àgbà,*
> *K' a má fi ṣe 'bi 'nu;*
> *Bi a bá de 'bi t' o tùtù,*
> *K' a simi-simi;*
> *K' a wo 'wajú ọjọ́ lọ tìtì:*
> *K' a tun bọ̀ wá r' ẹhìn ọràn wò,*
> *Nitori à-ti-sùn ara ẹni ni.*

> Let us not run the world hastily;
> Let us not grasp at the rope of wealth impatiently;
> What should be treated with mature judgment,
> Let us not treat in a fit of temper;

[1] I think this is the problem with which Meyer Fortes is trying to grapple in his book with the curious title of *Oedipus and Job* (Cambridge University Press, 1959).

Whenever we arrive at a cool place,
Let us rest sufficiently well;
Let us give prolonged attention to the future,
And then let us give due regard to the consequence of things,
And that is on account of our sleeping (end).

The *Odù* corpus is full of messages of hope to people who are despairing of life: such people should wait hopefully and patiently as things may surely turn out prosperously in the end. For example, we have it in *Irẹtẹ̀-Iwòrì* that

A-ṣọ́n-'kọ-sùn ni t' ọ̀n pọ́n;
Ẹni ti o tá ewé orí, ewo ni k' o ṣe?
O dá fún Ọ̀tẹ̀wòrì t' o sọ wipé
On nre egbè rè 'so:
Ọ̀tẹ̀wòrì ma ti 'so;
Nwọn nmú ewe ire oyè nbọ̀.

He who eats his corn-meal without stew complains of his hard lot;
What should he do that only has the wrapping-leaves to scrape?
So declared the oracle to Ọ̀tẹ̀wòrì
Who decided to go into the bush and hang:
Ọ̀tẹ̀wòrì, do not hang yet;
Leaves of chieftaincy are being brought (for you).[1]

It is probably this hope to the very end which makes the Yoruba value old age so much. In spite of the strong belief in predestiny, it is considered a grave tragedy to die young. So they pray, *Ki a gbó fun ikú jẹ*—"May we be sufficiently ripe before we are eaten up by death", and seek by all means to attain long life, which is their eternal desire and longing. Therefore do we have it in *Idĭ-méjì* that,

Ng bǎ r' ógbó, ng bǎ gbó;
Ng bǎ r' atọ́, ng bǎ tọ;
Ng bǎ d' àgbà bi Ẹléjù
Ma yọ̀ ṣèṣè.

If I possess the means of old age, I *will* be old;
If I possess the means of long life, I *will* live long;
If I can be as old as Ẹléjù
I will rejoice exceedingly.

---

[1] He will soon be made a chief.

OLÓDÙMARÈ AND MAN'S DESTINY

And with the desire for old age goes the prayer that the old age may be one of blessedness and prosperity, and not one of wretchedness.

K' a mă kŭ ni kékeré;
K' a mă d' àgbàlagbà òṣì;
K' a mă f' òpǎ tan 'lẹ̀
Ni 'bi ijẹ ẹbọ.

That we may not die young;
That we may not attain an old age of wretchedness;
That we may not scratch the ground with a stick
In the place of sacrifices.[1]

[1] The Yoruba dread an old age in which the aged have to beg for their living or go about the public shrines where sacrifices are placed in search of coins or other articles which may be turned into means of livelihood.

14

Olódùmarè and Man's Final Destiny

We concluded the last chapter on the fact that the Yoruba regard the end of life here on earth as of serious importance. That end, of course, involves the question of what becomes of man after the present life. Every religion has to face this eschatological question and, here again, the answer depends upon man's conception of the Deity.

The matter of man's final destiny is divided up naturally under the two headings of Death and After-Life, the latter of which involves a look at the idea of Judgment. We shall examine the whole eschatology of the Yoruba under these headings, therefore.

Death

The fact of death is a baffling and disturbing question-mark written conspicuously on the face of things. Man has been forced, therefore, since he became acquainted with it, to apply his mind to the question of its origin and purpose. In this, the Yoruba as corporate members of the human race are no exception; for, from the evidence at our disposal, we find that it is a subject to which they have given careful thought. Their name for it is *Ikú*, which besides being their designation for "dying" stands also, and more importantly, as the name for the personified power, the agent which the Yoruba believe to be responsible, under commission from Olódùmarè, for killing and removing people from this earth. The question of the beginning of his operation in the lives of men is one to which they have attached little importance, although they have naturally showed some curiosity about it. There is a conception of its beginning which says that *Ikú* began to kill only when he was grossly offended; that is, when his mother was killed at Ejìgbò-Mẹkùn market. This is contained in the *Odù, Ọyẹkú-méjì*:

> *Nwọn pa ìyǎ ikú*
> *S' ọjà Ejìgbò-Mẹkùn:*
> *Ikú gbọ́ n'lé,*
> *Ikú han bi àgọn Il'ọ́yẹ́,*

Ikú han bi ẹyin arawo;
O f' ọká ṣe kẹ́sẹ́,
O f' erè ṣe bàtà,
O f' akèrekère ṣ' òjǎ;
Ikú ta orí ìgbǎ,
Igbǎ gbìrì' à n'lẹ̀;
Ikú ta orí ẹ̀gungun,
Ẹ̀gungun gbìrì' à n'lẹ̀.

Ikú's mother was killed
In Ejìgbò-Mẹkùn market:
Ikú heard it in the house,
Ikú screeched like the *àgọn*[1] of Il'ọ́yè̀,
Ikú rang out like an *arawo*'s[2] egg;
He made cobras his spurs,
He made boas his shoes,
He made scorpions his girdle;
Ikú fell upon the Locust Bean Tree,
The Locust Bean Tree fell prone to the ground;
Ikú fell upon the White Silk Cotton Tree,
The White Silk Cotton Tree fell prone to the ground.

This is saying that death began to kill because Death's mother was killed! It is no wonder then that this is not the orthodox belief of the Yoruba about the origin of death.

The common, orthodox belief is that *Ikú* is a creation of Olódùmarè: he was made for the specific purpose of recalling any person whose time on earth is fulfilled. Hence he is known as *Òjiṣẹ́ Ọrun*—"Heaven's Bailiff". When they think of death as "dying", then they describe it as a "debt"—the debt which everyone must pay. This is as much as to say that death is the inevitable and ultimate lot of every person who comes into the world.

The Yoruba act in the belief that death is meant for the aged and that given the right conditions, every person should live to a ripe old age. Therefore, when a young person dies, they consider it to be a tragedy and enter into mourning. On the other hand, the death of an aged person is an occasion for rejoicing because the person has only been recalled home and his children live to bury him. Because of the emphasised belief that

---

1 *Àgọn* is a re-enactment of the origin of a Yoruba secret cult. The "character" is not to be seen by anyone and screeches its messages in unnatural tones to create the illusion of a non-human agent.

2 *Arawo* is a carnivorous bird.

187

death is meant primarily to recall home the aged, the Yoruba sometimes say that *Ikú kì 'pa ni, ayọ̀ l' o npa ni*—"Ikú does not kill: it is excesses that kill". This, of course, refers to the death which overtakes a person violently or prematurely through his own inordinate actions[1] and differentiates between that and the kind of death which is "normal" and "natural"—the home-call of the aged.

Although death is inevitable and unpreventable, the Yoruba believe or act in the belief that it can be deferred. It can be deferred through the intervention of Ọrunmìlà,[2] or any other divinity. There is a myth which has it that *Ikú*'s secret, which was naturally a source of discomfort to all men, was not known at first. Eventually, however, Èṣù[3] cunningly bribed *Ikú*'s son who in consequence revealed to him that the means by which *Ikú* slew was a club. That was the indispensable source of his power over men: deprive him of it and he became powerless. Èṣù's next move in order to achieve the much desired end was to bribe Ajàpă (the Tortoise, the most popular and subtle hero of Yoruba fables) to help him. Ajàpă set to work at once and by a clever stratagem snatched away the club from *Ikú*. *Ikú* at once became powerless as predicted and everybody rejoiced that *Ajàpă gb' òrúkú l' ọwọ́ ikú, aiye Ifẹ̀ d 'ọ̀fẹ̆*— "Ajàpă has deprived *Ikú* of his club: the Ifẹ̀[4] are liberated from anxiety". Later on, however, *Ikú* made a pact with Ọrunmìlà on the condition that Ọrunmìlà would help him to recover his club, and that he would respect the intervention of Ọrunmìlà whenever any of his victims placed himself under the latter's protection. The myth concludes by saying that, thenceforth, *Ikú* takes away only those who do not put themselves under the protection of Ọrunmìlà[5] or those who are absolutely ready to go home.[6]

At bottom, however, the Yoruba know that little can be done even to defer death when *Ikú* is really ready. Hence the saying, *Arùn l' a 'wò, a kì 'wo ikú*—"It is sickness that can be healed; death cannot be healed"; that is, one can treat sickness with medicine, but not so death. An *Odù* recital under *Iròsùn-Oṣó* begins with the three lines,

> *Aìdé Ikú l' à nb' ọsun*
> *Aìdé Ikú l' à nb' ọṣà;*
> *B' Ikú bá dé, Ikú 'ò gb' ẹbọ.*

---

[1] See Chapter 13, pp. 179 f. [2] Ibid., p. 176.
[3] See Chapter 8, pp. 81 f.
[4] Ifẹ̀, being the "centre", represents the Yoruba World.
[5] The myth is more to emphasise the importance and power of Ọrunmìlà rather than to explain death.
[6] See below, pp. 196 f.

It is when *Ikú* is not yet ready that it works to propitiate Ọsun;
It is when *Ikú* is not yet ready that it works to propitiate *orìṣà*;
When *Ikú* is really ready, *Ikú* does not yield to sacrifices.

Another *Odù-Iwòrì-Ọsǎ* says:

> *Ikú ìbǎ gb' owó,*
> *Owó l' à bǎ san;*
> *Òjìṣẹ́ Ọrun kì 'gb' owó*

If *Ikú* would accept ransom,
It is ransom we would have paid;
Heaven's Bailiff does not accept ransom.

Thus, it is the belief of the Yoruba that sooner or later, everyone must die. Death is the inevitable conclusion to man's earthly existence.

After-Life

What becomes of man after death? This, again, is a question which has haunted every religion all down the ages. "After death, what?" is a poser on the face of life itself. And all religion, each in its own way and according to its conception of the essential constitution of life, has found an answer. To the question, the Yoruba are definite in their answer.

Death is not the end of life. It is only a means whereby the present earthly existence is changed for another. After death, therefore, man passes into a "life beyond" which is called *Ẹ̀hìn-Ìwà*—"After-Life". This *Ẹ̀hìn-Ìwà* is of more vital importance than the present life, however prosperous this one may have been. The Yoruba thus speak of *Ẹ̀hìn-Ìwà ti 'ṣ' ẹgbọ́n ònì*—"After-Life which is the superior of Today (the present)". Whatever is done in the present life, therefore, must be done with due regard to this great future: *Nitorí Ẹ̀hìn-Ìwà l' a ṣe nṣe ònì l' ōre*—"It is on account of After-Life that we treat Today hospitably (that we make a good use of the present and do not abuse it)". In After-Life, those who have finished here go on living. This belief is attested in several ways.

(a) *Joy or Fear of Anticipation.* The Yoruba aged look forward with longing or dread in anticipation of what may be awaiting them in the new life where they are bound to fare according to their deserts. It is a common occurrence to hear the aged saying *Mo nre 'lé*—"I am going Home" or *Ilé ti yá*—"I am ready for Home", meaning that they are prepared to die and enter into After-Life. When an ageing person is heard talking abstractedly by himself, it is generally believed that he is talking to his associates or relatives who have gone before. If asked, he himself will sometimes confirm that. The Yoruba say of such aged people that they no longer hear what we say here, their conversation being with those who are on "the other side".

(b) *Burial and Funeral Rites*. These are observed with varying details from place to place; but the underlying motive as well as the general routine is the same. The rites are such as make it plain that the survivors believe strongly that the deceased is only making a journey, though a final one, into another life. Immediately a person dies, the first rite is to slay a fowl which is called *Adìẹ-ìrànò*—"The fare-fowl". This is meant to make the road easy for him. When the corpse is laid in state, a yam meal is prepared and a portion of it placed at the foot of the bier: this is food for the deceased. During the actual burial, the children and relatives of the deceased gather round, each of them bringing clothes, fowls, or animals. The body is wrapped in all the clothes which are meant for the deceased person's use in the next life. When the corpse is lowered into the grave, the survivors draw near it, each according to his family status and each bringing an animal victim, usually a goat: he offers his gift through the officiant, asking that the deceased person should accept it, and praying him not to sleep in *Ọrun*,[1] but to open his eyes wide and always look after his children, taking good care of them, providing for their needs, and aiding them in their difficulties. People other than the children or relatives of the deceased also send messages, oral or material, through the deceased to their own folk who have gone before.

The officiant now descends into the grave and performs the rite of slaying a victim, splitting the kola-nuts, and placing certain articles, including food and condiments beside the body. This rite is known as *Bíbá òkú ya 'hùn*—"Entering into a covenant with the deceased". The essential part of the rite is therefore to say farewell to the deceased, impressing it upon him that now that he is no longer in his former earthly state, his duty is one of protection and care over his children, relatives, and associates; he is not to molest anyone or allow himself to be employed on any errand of malice; he is to go on now to partake only of the blissful life of heaven, and not be side-tracked into partaking of anything unworthy.[2]

Several days after the burial, there is another rite known as *Fífa ẹ̀gún òkú wọ 'le*—"Bringing the spirit of the deceased into the house". By

---

[1] See below, p. 197.   [2] See below, p. 199.

this, it is believed, the survivors will again be able to have intimate intercourse with the deceased. The rite takes place at night when all lights have been extinguished. As a result of it, a shrine is made in one corner or at the foot of the central wall of the house; this is a specific meeting-place between the deceased and his children. Thenceforth, there they go and make offerings to him, speak to him, beg special favours of him, enter into covenants with one another or swear over bones of contention. Of course, apart from this place, the Yoruba feel that they can talk to a deceased person anywhere and everywhere in a general way, as they believe that he can be anywhere he chooses, now that he is free from the limitations imposed by this physical life.

(c) *Dreams and Appearances.* The Yoruba believe that the deceased can be seen in dreams or trances, and that they can impart information or explanation, or give instructions, on any matters about which the family is in a serious predicament. They can also send messages through other persons or through certain cults to their folk. Along the road or in lonely places, or during the night, it is believed that the deceased can appear to a person either to give guidance or aid, or to molest. A Yoruba dirge which we can quote as an illustration is as follows:

> *O di gbéré!*
> *O d' à-rìn-nà-kò!*
> *O d' oju àlǎ!*

> It is a long farewell!
> It is now a matter of meeting along the road,
> It is now in dreams (that we shall meet).

Of course, there are those voices in the wilderness which hold that though the deceased continue to live in After-Life, they have nothing more to do with those who are still here. Such is the view expressed in such a saying as *Ẹnit' o kú kò w' ẹ̀hin mọ́*—"The deceased does not mind the things that are left behind"; or *Ẹnit' o kú ti re Òkè-Odò: o ti f' ọwọ́ rọ igi igbàgbé*—"The deceased has gone to the other side of the river: he has laid his hand on the tree of oblivion" (has forgotten all that he left behind). Such a view gains adherents especially when things do not go on well with the survivors and the ancestors appear to be deaf to their prayers. But it is very far from being a generally accepted view, or one which persists even with its authors.

(d) *Communion with the Ancestors.* We are now in the position to see the real meaning of the phenomenon which has been given the name

of "Ancestor Worship", the main cause of which is the invincible conviction that those who have departed from this world have only changed
this life for another. In consequence of going into that life, they have
been released from all the restraints imposed by this earth; thus they
are possessors of limitless potentialities which they can exploit for the
benefit or to the detriment of those who still live on earth. For that
reason, it is necessary to keep them in a state of peaceful contentment.
But this is only incidental. Primarily "Ancestor Worship" is an extension into infinity of the family activities of the earth. Those who die
do not remain in the grave. Their body will rot away indeed, but they
remain their essential selves apart from the "bodies of earth". In fact,
the Yoruba believe that the deceased stand apart and watch all the performances of the burial and funeral rites. They do not leave the house or
its premises until a few days after the burial, and that after the comple-
tion of certain essential rites. It is in consequence of the belief that the
deceased are really never in the grave that the Yoruba have no doctrine
of the Resurrection of the Body; that is, not in the dramatic, eschatological sense of the graves giving up their dead at the consummation of
all things. To the Yoruba, what takes place happens immediately after
death—the deceased, after all the necessary rituals have been performed, passes through the gate into the presence of Olódùmarè to
receive whatever judgment awaits him. As the deceased are never really
in the grave, they still remain the fathers or mothers which they were
before their death, capable of exercising their parental functions,
though now in a more powerful and unhampered way, over their
survivors. The Yoruba say still *Bàbǎ mi*—"My father", or *Ìyǎ mi*—
"My mother", when they speak about their deceased parents. Although
they speak of bringing the spirit of the deceased into the house, they
rarely say that "I am going to speak to the 'spirit' of my father"; what
they say is, "I am going to speak to my father". Thus the deceased
continue to have the title of relationship which they had borne as heads
of families while they were on earth. This shows that "Ancestor Worship" is a wrong nomenclature for that which in fact is no "worship"
but a manifestation of an unbroken family relationship between the
parent who has departed from this world and the offspring who are
still here. This is a view which is further attested by an *Odù* under
Ogbe-Irosùn which has it that a person should render his filial duties
to a deceased parent in order that he may have children to look after him.

   (e) *Egúngún and Orò.* These two cults are means of demonstrating in
a still more concrete way the belief that those who depart from this earth

continue in existence elsewhere and are actively "in touch" with those
who are still here.

Egúngún designates the spirit of the deceased with whom intercourse
is held at the ancestral shrine. It materialises in a robed figure which is
designed specially to give the impression that the deceased is making a
temporary reappearance on earth. This reappearance may be that of a
specific ancestor. Where this is to be the case, a rite of "creating" the
egúngún takes place on the fortieth day after the burial; and after that,
the reappearance takes place periodically, once a year or more often.
Egúngún also symbolises just the broad, general conception that there
is After-Life and that between those who have gone there and those
who are still on earth there is a close, active bond. In this case, the
Egúngún is just *Ará-Ọrun*—"Visitor from heaven".

In order to preserve the illusion that the *Egúngún* is *ará ọrun*, the
character is completely sealed up in an outfit which nevertheless does
not conceal his main physical features. He only sees through a thick,
closely-woven net and speaks in a "piping, treble voice". No one, except
the authorised few, may come close to, or touch him.

The distinctive characteristics of *Orò* is his "voice" which is the
"bull-roarer", and the fact that, by and large, he operates only in the
grove and is abroad only at night. There are only a few localities where
he materialises in a masked figure: in those places women are shut in
when *Orò* is abroad.

Orò, like *Egúngún*, may represent a specific ancestor; but he is more
of a general symbol.

Both *Egúngún* and *Orò* used to operate as instruments of discipline
and execution in the Yoruba governments of the old days.[1]

The Yoruba emphasise the conception that both *Egúngún* and *Orò*
sprang from a common motive. To support this, there is a story, among
others, which has it that *Egúngún* and *Orò* were full brothers, *Orò*
being the older. They were both tillers of the soil and it was the duty of
their wives to sell the products of their farms in the market. But whereas
the wife of *Egúngún* was very thrifty and able, therefore, to put by
enough money to buy clothes for her husband, *Orò*'s wife was a spend-
thrift who could not resist the attractions of food and trifles. The day
came when *Egúngún* put on his clothes and asked *Orò* to go out with
him, but there were no clothes for *Orò* to put on. That opened *Orò*'s
eyes to the faults of his wife; whereupon he reached for a whip and
began to flog her. The wife contrived, however, to escape after what he

[1] See Chapter 12, p. 151.

considered to be only a few lashes. He was affronted; especially as he could not run after her because he was naked. Thus he began his endless call—the "voice" which we hear is that call to Bunńbun, his wife, to return for the full count of her well-deserved lashes. This story circulates, of course, only in those places where *Orò* never materialises in masked figures. But the motif is clear: it purports to show that *Egúngún* and *Orò* are twin brothers.

(f) *Partial Reincarnation.* It is almost certain that there is no belief in reincarnation in the classical sense among the Yoruba; that is, in the sense that "Reincarnation is the passage of the soul from one body to another . . . the lot of the soul in each being determined by its behaviour in a former life".[1] The Yoruba speak of *Á-tún-wá*—"Another coming"; but, in reality, there appears to be nothing like it in a specific sense.

The specific belief of the Yoruba about those who depart from this world is that once they have entered After-Life, there they remain, and there the survivors and their children after them can keep unbroken intercourse with them, especially if they have been good persons while on earth and were ripe for death when they died.

Nevertheless, we find ourselves confronted with the paradox involved in the belief of the Yoruba that the deceased persons do "reincarnate" in their grandchildren and great-grandchildren. In the first place, it is believed that in spite of this reincarnation, the deceased continue to live in After-Life; those who are still in the world can have communion with them, and they are there with all their ancestral qualities unimpaired. Secondly, it is believed that they do "reincarnate", not only in one grandchild or great-grandchild, but also in several contemporary grandchildren and great-grandchildren who are brothers and sisters and cousins, aunts and nephews, uncles and nieces, *ad infinitum.* Yet, in spite of these repeated "rebirths" which should be rather exhausting, the deceased contrive to remain in full *life* and *vigour* in the After-Life.

In order to have some light on this paradox, it will help us to examine first the process by which a "reincarnated" ancestor is identified.

When the child is three months old, the oracle is consulted: this rite is known as *Mímọ orí ọmọ* "Knowing the child's *orí*", or *Gbígbọ́ orí ọmọ*—"Hearing the child's *orí*".[2] By that the oracle declares which ancestor has "reincarnated". Now, this is significant: according to this

[1] *Encyclopaedia of Religion and Ethics*—Vol. 12, p. 425.
[2] See Chapter 13, pp. 171 ff.

rite, to know the child's *orí* is to know which ancestor has "reincarnated". It is to be noted also that the "reincarnation" of an ancestor is known as *Yíya ọmọ*—"Turning to be a child", or "becoming incarnate".[1] It is taken as a good omen in fulfilment of the blessing which the well-wishers invoke upon the survivors who have successfully accomplished the burial and funeral rites of a parent: *A yà l' ọ́wọ́ rẹ o*—"May he 'turn to be' (children) for you"; *A ya 'mọ fun ọ o*—"May he 'become' children for you". There is also the prayer that *Awọ́yà a kún orí ẹni o*—"May his 'turning-to-be' (children) fill the mat (increase and multiply)".

It would seem, then, that here we have a clear belief that the ancestor's *orí* does transmigrate into the body of a new creation. We are disconcerted, however, by the fact that according to this system, no one grandchild may have the monopoly of the ancestral *orí*; and in that case we have to choose between the impossibility of a transmigrating of the *orí* and the possibility that the *orí* can "dole out" itself *ad infinitum*. Neither of which alternatives appears to be leading us anywhere.

Thus *Mímọ orí* or *Gbígbọ́ orí* and *Yíya ọmọ* cannot be taken as establishing a belief in reincarnation in the technical sense. All it appears to establish is the belief in the concrete fact that there are certain dominant lineage characteristics which keep recurring through births and thus ensuring the continuity of the vital existence of the family or clan. This view is substantiated by the fact that it is not unknown among the Yoruba that the oracle has declared that a child is a "turning-to-be" of a person who is still living: such a person is known as *A-f'-aìkú-yà*—"One who 'turns-to-be' (a child) without dying".

When all these things have been said, we must admit, in conclusion, that there are many things about ourselves which we do not yet know. It may well be that in regard to this matter there are possibilities which are yet beyond our comprehension. Let us note with interest, therefore, F. W. H. Myers' hypothesis of the "subliminal self", which William James modifies, and from which stems the idea "that there is more life in our total soul than we are aware of"; and that "therefore . . . some other portion of our self may reincarnate".[2] The names Babátúndé—"Father returns" and Yétúndé—"Mother returns", and other names

---

[1] Geoffrey Parrinder translates *Yìyà* as "The shooting forth of a branch" in his *West African Psychology* (Lutterworth, 1951), p. 123.

[2] *West African Psychology*, by E. Geoffrey Parrinder, p. 220. For an illuminating discussion on this subject of the "subliminal self", see *The Religions Consciousness*, by J. B. Pratt (New York, Macmillan, 1946), pp. 46 ff.

in the same category which specify the return of particular ancestors, are very suggestive. For while *Gbígbó orí* and *Yíya ọmọ* may include several persons as "partial-reincarnations" together of the same ancestor or ancestress, neither of these names is repeated in more than one child. Babátúndé is the name of a baby boy born immediately after the death of his grandfather and Yétúndé the name of the girl born immediately after the death of her grandmother. No other child after either of these two may bear Babátúndé or Yétúndé (or any other one of the names with the same connotation) in reference to the same ancestor or ancestress.

We must come back to the point of this discussion, which is not the resolution of a paradox but the fact that there *is* this apparent paradox which is one of the solid grounds on which the Yoruba base their belief in the concrete reality of After-Life.

Our next question now is, "Where is it, this After-Life?" Generally, one may say that there are slightly varying opinions on the matter. There are those who believe that to die is only to change places on this earth. The deceased continues in existence in another country or region far away from his former one. He settles down in his new environment by beginning life all over again; he may get married and have children, build houses, start a business and carry on a new, but normal, existence until he either dies again or moves because his whereabouts have been discovered by people who knew him in his former life. Stories in support of this belief abound among the Yoruba. It is, of course, a belief which some would explain as resulting from "the phantasm of the dying".

A slightly modified form of this belief is that it is only the wicked and those whose days on earth are not yet fulfilled, and, therefore, cannot be received back into heaven, who continue like that in some part of the earth. This explains how the mind of the Yoruba could accommodate the belief that Ajiran[1] and Ile-Ifẹ̀[2] and a few other special places in Yorubaland are dwelling places of the "deceased". It partly answers the major question involved in the belief of the Yoruba in the existence of *Elérě* or *Emèrè* who are believed to be the cause of the *àbíkú* phenomenon,[3] which is the one clear notion of metempsychosis in the belief of the Yoruba.

The real orthodox belief of the Yoruba on the matter of After-Life, however, is that there is a definite place, other than this earth, where the

[1] See Chapter 13, pp. 181 f.   [2] See Chapter 2, pp. 13 f.
[3] See Chapter 9, p. 123.

deceased go. The general name for the place is Ọ̀run, the original meaning of which appears to be "the face of" and therefore "the place of
worship" and hence, the "abode of the Deity".[1] Ọ̀run in a general
sense thus means "Heaven", or "Paradise", where Olódùmarè and
the orìṣà dwell.

With reference to After-Life, the Yoruba speak of two Ọ̀run. The
first one is Ọ̀run Rere, Ọ̀run Funfun, Ọ̀run Bàbá Ẹni—"Good Ọ̀run",
"White Ọ̀run", "Our Father's Ọ̀run", and the second is Ọ̀run Buburu
(buruku), Ọ̀run Àpâdì—"Bad Ọ̀run", "Ọ̀run of Potsherds"[2]—"This
is a celestial rubbish-heap, like the midden-heap of every village, where
broken pots are thrown . . .; or it may be compared to a kiln where there
are charred fragments of pots, hot and dry".[3]

The deceased are allocated to either of the two places by the deciding
factor of Judgment by Olódùmarè. We have already observed that one
of the factors which makes Him an urgent reality to the Yoruba is His
impartial judgment.[4] It is their strong conviction that sinners will not
go unpunished and that judgment attends every form of sin. They often
say of one who suffers without relief, Ìwà rẹ̀ l' o nf' ìyà jẹ́—"It is his
character that brings affliction upon him"; or Aò mọ ohun tí ó ti ṣe tí
Ọlọ́run nfi ẹgba rẹ̀ nà a—"We do not know the reason why Olódùmarè
afflicts him".

But the judgment which the Yoruba fears most is the one which
awaits every person, first at the end of life on earth, involving the agony
of dying, and then in After-Life when the final verdict of Olódùmarè
will be known.

The Yoruba will quote frightful examples of persons whose ends
on earth were tragic in consequence of their bad character. Some of
these had appeared to evade the consequences of their actions; but as
the end of their lives drew near, they had been visited by certain adver-
sities like wretched blindness or losses of favourite children, and had
ended finally with miserable deaths and unceremonial burials. There
were some of them who had been stung by so much remorse and
appalled by the anticipation of what might be awaiting them at the
other end that, during their death-throes, they had involuntarily made
detailed confessions of their past wickedness. For this reason, whenever

[1] See Chapter 9, p. 127.
[2] It seems that the notion of Ọ̀run iná—"hell of fire"—is not originally
Yoruba and has been introduced by Islam and Christianity.
[3] West African Psychology, p. 107.
[4] See Chapters 5, p. 42; and 12, pp. 148 ff.

the Yoruba think of the end, they think twice before they act. Here are two quotations from the *Odù* corpus—

Ètùra-méjì:

 Iró pípa kì 'wipe k' a ma l' owó l' ọwọ,
 Ilẹ̀ dídà kì 'wipe k' a mâ d' àgbà,
 Ṣùgbọ́n ọjọ́ à-ti-sùn l' ẹbọ.

Lying does not debar one from becoming rich,
Covenant-breaking does not debar one from reaching old age;
But the day of sleeping, there awaits trouble!

Ọ̀yẹ̀kŭ-méjì:

 K' ẹni hù 'wà gbẹ̀dẹ̀gbẹ̀dẹ̀,
 K' ẹni lè kú pẹ̀lẹ́pẹ̀lẹ́;
 K' ọmọ ẹni lè n' ọwọ́ gbọgbọgbọ
 Le 'ni sin.

Let us behave gently,
That we may die peacefully;
That our children may stretch out their hands
Upon us in burial.

 We have mentioned *Akíṣe*—"It-is-*tabu*", the personalised retributive principle set in operation by Olódùmarè to track down the sinner.[1] Other names for him are *Ẹlẹ́san*—"The Avenger", *Abèrè*—"He-who-queries". In one of these three capacities, he manifests himself in an unmistakable way to the sinner. An *Odù* under *Irẹ̀tẹ̀-Èdì* has the saying,

 Ẹlẹ́san a san, á, k' à ṣài sán;
 Abèrè a bèrè, k' à ṣài bèrè
 O dá fun Ọrunmìlà
 T' ó ṣe kìlọ̀kìlọ̀ fun ọmọ rẹ̀
 T' akọ t' abo.

The Avenger will avenge, he cannot but avenge;
He-who-queries will query, he cannot but query,
This is the oracle's declaration for Ọrunmìlà
Who gave strict warning to his children,
Male and female.

[1] See Chapter 12, p. 146.

15. Olúorogbo (centre) with two others from his temple, Ile-Ifẹ̀

16. The temple of Orị̀à-nlá, Ãyè (Èkìtì)

17. Methodist Chapel, Teacher Training College, Ìfàkì

When the person reaches After-Life, there he faces the final judgment. He has now to give an account of how he has used his earthly life, particularly with reference to his character. The judgment is before Olódùmarè, although it is sometimes said that it will take place before Ọbàtálá, which comes to the same thing, since Ọbàtálá is only a deputy of Olódùmarè.

Gbogbo ohun ti a bá ṣe l' aiye,
L' a o kunlẹ̀ rò l' ọ́run.

All that we do on earth,
We shall account for kneeling in heaven.

A ó ro 'jọ́ l' ẹsẹ̀ Èdùmàrè.
or
A ó ro 'jọ́ l' ẹsẹ̀ Ọbàtala l' ọrun.

We shall state our case at the feet of Olódùmarè.
or
We shall state our case before Ọbàtálá in heaven.

Thus, a person is allocated a place in the good *Ọrun*, the *Ọrun* of the Fathers, or consigned to the *Ọrun* of potsherds according to the verdict of Olódùmarè. That is his final destiny.

In conclusion, let us consider the quality of life in the After-Life. Generally, the Yoruba think that the wicked man suffers endless wretchedness in his *Ọrun*. Life there appears dreary and not even up to the standard of the worst on this earth. In the final words of farewell to the deceased, we catch a hint of what it is like:

Má mà j' ọ̀kùn,
Má mà j' ekòlọ̌,
Ohun ti nwọn njẹ l' Ọrun,
Ni kí o mã bá wọn jẹ.

Be sure you do not feed on centipedes,
Be sure you do not feed on earthworms,
What people feed on in *Ọrun*,
That should you feed on.

That means that he should go to heaven where the inhabitants feed on good things and not to the wrong place. To this some will reply;

Má j' ọkùn,
Má j' ekòlǒ,
Ilé aiyé ni 'ti 'ba ni 'lọ.

Do not feed on centipedes,
Do not feed on earthworms!
That depends on one's character while on earth.

The vague hint of metamorphosis or transmigration of souls, which are both doctrines alien to the Yoruba, strictly speaking, is found in this connection. Apart from the possibility of a life of unrelieved wretchedness, there is also the possibility of one's becoming transmuted into a lower creature. There is a Yoruba dirge which says:

O kú tán,
O d' ewúrẹ́ olú-j'-ewé;
O kú tán,
O d' àgùtàn olù-j'imọ̀;
O kú tán,
O d' alãmọ̀ ti 'jẹun l' ẹ̀bǎ ògiri.

He is dead,
He becomes a goat that feeds on leaves;
He is dead,
He becomes a sheep that feeds on palm-leaves;
He is dead,
He becomes a lizard that feeds along the walls.

Apart from the hint of judgment, there is also in this a note of uncertainty about the lot of the deceased; for this dirge is often of a piece with the one quoted immediately before it, that one coming at its tail end.

On the whole, however, the Yoruba is definite about the final lot of the good. They go to the Good *Ọrun*. As they enter through the gates all their relatives and associates who have gone before come to meet them in rejoicing welcome. If a person was genuinely prosperous and happy on earth, the life in heaven will be for him an enlarged copy of his former happy one. In fact, life in *Ọrun* is the larger and freer copy of this one, minus all the earthly sorrows and toils, with amenities for peaceful enjoyment considerably enhanced. The choicest benefit of getting to heaven for the Yoruba is that they will become reunited with their relatives and associates who have gone before.

Ọrun Bàbá Ẹni is, therefore, a place where the weary are at rest and
the good enjoy in the company of their own kin the reward of goodness.
This is certainly something which gives confidence and comfort as one
considers the end of life. With this belief, the good Yoruba can face the
prospect of After-Life with longing, knowing that Ọrun is only the place
where he will live *anew*, and that back "At Home"

> *Ikú pa Abírí, Abírí kú,*
> *Ẹ ni kò si nkan;*
> *Ikú pa Abìrĭ, Abìrĭ r' ọrun,*
> *Ẹ ni kò si nkan;*
> *Ibití Ikú ti pa Ọgíní*
> *Láì ẹiyẹ 'ò de bẹ̀ jẹ;*
> *Ẹ ṣì tún nwipé kò si nkan!*
> *Nwọn ni, Kò si nkan:*
> *Ṣe Awo kì 'kú*
> *Awo kì 'rùn*
> *Nṣe l' awo mã nlọ si Ìtunlà*
> *Ìtunlà, ilé awo.*

> *Ikú* slew Abírí, Abírí died,
> You say there's nothing wrong;
> *Ikú* slew Abìrĭ, Abìrĭ went to heaven;
> You say there's nothing wrong;
> The place where *Ikú* slew Ọgíní
> Never again do birds go there to feed;
> You still say there's nothing wrong!
> They answer, "There's nothing wrong:
> For the initiate never dies,
> The initiate never sees corruption,
> The initiate only goes to *Ìtunlà*,[1]
> *Ìtunlà*, the home of the initiate".[2]

[1] *Ìtunlà* means "Place of endless, true living" or "Place of renewed living".
[2] "Awo"—"The initiate-in-mystery"—is, strictly speaking, a member of
one of the secret societies. It means in this context those who have known the
secret of living and have therefore conducted their lives successfully.

15

Change or Decay?

Throughout this book, one fact stands out with unmistakable clearness: that is, Olódùmarè is of vital, absolutely indispensable, significance to the Yoruba. It is well that this has been emphasised; because in that way we have seen justice done to the one essential Factor by which the life and belief of the Yoruba cohere and have sustenance; by it we have come to the indubitable knowledge that it is a wrong notion to describe or refer to Olódùmarè in any way which suggests that He is a *deus incertus* or *deus remotus*, since He is so urgently real.

In consequence of the position and status of Olódùmarè, and the added evidence which we have gathered, we can with confidence predicate that the religion of the Yoruba was, or consisted in, a "Primitive Monotheism". We notice with interest that other investigators before us have been confronted impressively by this fact.[1]

The question of the historical origin of this monotheism, or of how "pure" it was originally, is a rather debatable one to pursue, one which is quite capable of leading us astray in a wilderness of theories and conjectures. Nevertheless, we have every confidence in stating categorically that the ultimate origin of such a lofty conception can be none other than the revelation of the living God Himself Who has never left Himself without witness in any age or generation. As to the question of its primitive purity, we can only repeat here that there are Yoruba elders who have the notion that the crowd of divinities which now inhabit their pantheon is a later accretion the effect of which has not altogether been to the benefit of their religion.[2] And we have implied the possibility that the present position in which Olódùmarè appears in the system is a later development when we stated that it is a reflection of the social pattern of the Yoruba.[3]

Now, if the religion as it is now is a departure for the worse from a

---

[1] *Faith, Fancies, and Fetich*, by S. S. Farrow (S.P.C.K., 1926), pp. 23 ff. and 157.

[2] Chapter 7, pp. 68 ff.   [3] Chapter 11, pp. 141 f.

primitive state of purity, our next assignment is to find out the cause of its retrogression. From what we know of the whole system, it appears that its main weakness is that the sole repositories of its doctrines and traditions are the priests upon whose individual character or calibre depends its ordering. And these priests are guided in their task by several motives which range in descending order of importance from spiritual awareness, cultic exigencies or expediencies, social contingencies, clan assertiveness, to personal profit. This makes it possible for them to multiply cults in such a way that we have today a pantheon of innumerable divinities.[1] The priests acted on the impulse of their guiding motives, and the people who *must* worship and be led in spiritual matters follow as a matter of course the only lead available to them. There arose no "prophets" to awaken and keep alive in the people the sense of the primitive purity of their religion and save the religion from the retrogression which thus became inevitable. This lack of prophecy as a thing which stands apart from the set-up of cults with the main function of emphasising with reiterated force that which is the substance of the religion, is our main explanation of the fate which has now overtaken it.

Under the present circumstances, it is rather dubious if we could speak "of the religion of the Yoruba" as a precise term. What we have seems to be a mixed bag of individual cults out of which everyone chooses according to lineage or family traditions, or as the circumstances of life dictate.[2] Nevertheless, the one "Bag" which holds the individual cults together (if we may continue the metaphor) is Olódùmarè. Thus, if we speak of "The religion of the Yoruba", we can only do so in reference to the fact that Olódùmarè is the core which gives meaning and coherence to the whole system. This is what the Yoruba themselves will say if they are to describe their religion in a precise term.

The complication involved in all that we have said so far makes the question of what name to give to the religion rather debatable. "Polytheism" is certainly not the suitable name, however much the appearance of things may suggest it; for, strictly speaking, "polytheism" presupposes a pantheon in which Olódùmarè would be one (whatever His status) among many, whereas He is not.[3] He is apart as "wholly other", His relationship to the divinities being that of the sovereignty by which He orders His dominion in which they are included. Strictly speaking, no divinity of the Yoruba pantheon can fulfil a capricious will unless he is permitted to do so by Olódùmarè, whether by direct authorisation or

[1] Chapter 7, p. 69. [2] See Chapter 13.
[3] See Chapter 7, p. 62.

by connivance. At bottom, as we have observed, the soul of the religion, that which makes it a coherent whole, is the monotheism which is implied in Olódùmarè. But since that monotheism has been attenuated through the many divinities whose cults form the objective phenomena of the religion, the matter of finding a descriptive name for it has been a problem for honest and conscientious investigators. Geoffrey Parrinder, when faced with this problem, says, "It would be useful to devise a term which would denote religions that have a supreme God and also worship other gods."[1] For the purpose of a descriptive label, we would like to suggest such a startling thing as "Diffused Monotheism": this has the advantage of showing that the religion is monotheism, though it is a monotheism in which the good Deity delegates certain portions of His authority to certain divine functionaries who work as they are commissioned by Him. For a proper name we unhesitatingly say that there can be none other but *"Olodumareism"*. The world is already crowded with "isms", we know; but this is a vitally meaningful one to appreciate the full import of which will benefit the world immeasurably.

Besides the internal weakness which makes for its retrogression, the religion of the Yoruba has been affected by the incursions of two world religions—Christianity and Islam—which came into the country with their attendant cultures. It is difficult at the moment to say exactly when the two religions first made their contacts with the country; their coming is bound up with the early history of the Yoruba, the material for writing which the historians are still collecting. But as we study the religion and culture of the Yoruba, we come upon certain elements which appear to us to be foreign to the general character of their traditions.

Let us take two important examples.

First we shall look at the cult of Olúorogbo[2] in Ile-Ifè. The story of this divinity is connected with an historical crisis in the life of the Ifè. Between the Ifè and the Igbò there had been continual warfare in consequence of which the former were subjugated. This was not because in physical force the Igbò were superior to the Ifè, but because the Igbò appeared each time to have certain supernatural allies fighting for them; and, of course, the appearance of these usually scared away the Ifè warriors or created in them such fears as paralysed their forces.

There happened to be one Ifè woman, Mòrèmi by name, who had

[1] *Religion In An African City* (O.U.P., 1953), p. 11.
[2] See Chapter 8, p. 105.

cause to suspect that the "supernatural" allies of the Igbò were not as unhuman as they looked: there was a ruse somewhere, and if that ruse could be found out, the Igbò would be easily forestalled and defeated. Thus she decided that the trick must be known and assigned herself the difficult and perilous task of finding it out. In preparation for her enterprise, she went to the river Esìnmìrìn and made a covenant with its divinity that if he gave her success in her venture, she would make him the choicest offering on her return. This concluded, she got herself captured by the Igbò; and because she was a woman of striking loveliness, she readily found favour with their king to whom she became a favourite wife. With this vantage position secured, she found the rest of her work easy; by such ingenuity as only a woman of her calibre knows how to employ, she soon learnt the ways and wisdom of the people, among which was the object of her enterprise—the "mysterious" stratagem which had repeatedly won the Igbò their victory over the Ifè. Having accomplished her end, she escaped and went back to Ile-Ifè where she taught her people that their reply to the next attack by the Igbò should be lighted torches, because their stratagem consisted mainly in masquerading a number of their warriors under a covering of grass and thus making them look unhuman. The Ifè confidently awaited the next attack by the Igbò and things worked out as directed by Mọrèmi, with the result that the Igbò were completely routed and subjugated.

Mọrèmi now went to the river Esìnmìrìn to fulfil her vow. According to the oracle, the only offering that the river divinity would accept was her only son, Olúorogbo. Him she offered, therefore. Olúorogbo rose from the dead, however, and went by a rope to heaven.

There have been various comments on this story. Let us quote from the more recent ones. S. O. Biobaku thinks that "Mọrèmi sounds suspiciously like Mariam (or Mary) and might well be Jephthah or Delilah; and the sacrifice of an only son who rose from death recalls Jesus Christ and the Christian story of the redemption of man".[1] H. U. Beier, on the other hand, warns that "the sacrifice of the only son is nothing peculiar to Yoruba mythology or Christian. . . . The resemblance between the names of Mọrèmi and Mary does not seem very convincing".[2]

So much for the representative opinions of investigators on the subject. What is the actual belief of the Yoruba in reference to the story ? The Yoruba believe that Olúorogbo is indeed a saviour of his people.

[1] *ODU* (Journal of Yoruba and Related Studies, January 1955, No. 1), p. 16.
[2] Op. cit., p. 19.

But the whole set-up of his cult is very suggestive of Christian influence. His priest often relates about him stories which are identical with or, at least, very similar to, those about Jesus Christ. Olúorogbo is described as On'iwe ọ̀run—"The bookish one who is in heaven" because, according to the oral traditions, he was the originator of bocks and of writing. Therefore, a part of the ritual at his shrine is to scratch the ground in imitation of writing.

There is no doubt about the evidence, then, that the cult of Olúorogbo may have been coloured by a foreign element which very likely was Christianity. This refers us to our suggestion in Chapter 8 that Olúorogbo is probably a development from Ẹ̀là.[1] There may well be something in the suggestion of R. E. Dennett that there were probably at one time in Ile-Ifẹ̀ two churches, one dedicated to Mary and one to Jesus Christ.[2]

Next, let us consider the cult of Orìṣà-nlá. We are told that in Ile-Ifẹ̀, one of the emblems in the shrine of this arch-divinity of Yorubaland used to be a "bundle" made up of books. During the early morning procession which opens the annual festival, the priests shout at intervals. O r' iyè-é? Iyè rí ọ?[3] (O r' ìwé? Ìwé ri ọ) "Do you see books?" "Do books see you?" This, we are told is an obscure reference to the bundle of books which used to be carried in the procession. It would be the same bundle of books which has been referred to as Ìdì in connection with the early history of the Yoruba.[4] An Ifẹ̀ informant related that when he was a student of the divinity school at Kudẹtì in Ibadan, he was presented with a book taken out of the shrine of Orìṣà-nlá by a priest who accompanied the gift with the remark, "This is one of the things we worship here". He claimed to have recognised the book as a Bible written in a "strange" character which he thought was Hebrew or Greek. However, he kept the book for a long time until an unscrupulous investigator with whom he had close dealings stole it from him![5] About books in the temple of Orìṣà-nlá in Ile-Ifẹ̀ we have made a close investigation recently, and it does not seem that there are any more books to be found there.

There is another piece of evidence which is historically significant.

---

[1] pp. 101 f.   [2] *Nigerian Studies* (London, Macmillan, 1910), p. 24.
[3] This kind of shout is an element in a ritual procession in Yorubaland when sacred cult objects which the uninitiated must not see are being carried in the procession. The Ògbóni cult in Abẹokuta and Ijebuland is very much noted for this. The shout is to warn the uninitiated to keep away as he would be in danger of his life by looking unworthily at the *sacra*.
[4] *The History of the Yorubas* (Lagos, C.M.S. Bookshop, 1937), pp. 4 and 7.
[5] There was much pilfering of relics in this country in the past.

In Ile-Ifẹ̀, there are two localities which are called respectively Òkè Itàpǎ—"The Hill of Revolt", and Òkè Ìlérí—"The Hill of the Vow"; and this is the story of how they received their names. There came into Ile-Ifẹ̀ a religion or culture which for a painful period eclipsed the religion of the land because those who brought it along were more powerful than the indigenous people. (This may very likely have reference to something of a different origin from the Odùdúwà cult.[1] We have a strong suspicion that this religion was Christianity or something with a strong tinge of it since, according to tradition, it is very much connected with "books".) However, the Ifẹ̀ only bore the imposition grudgingly until they were strong enough to cast off its yoke. When they were sure that they could do this successfully, they appointed a day on which they all assembled and unanimously took a resolution that they repudiated the alien thing. It is the spot on which the resolution was registered that is called Òkè Itàpǎ, which signifies that it was there that the Ifẹ̀ revolted against the alien imposition. From Òkè Itàpǎ, they proceeded in a body to another chosen spot where they "burnt" (some elders say "buried") all the available literature in the town. After this holocaust of books, they unanimously made a solemn vow the purpose of which was to seal the resolution already made on Òkè Itàpǎ. Hence the second place is called Òkè Ìlérí—"The Hill of the Vow". To mark this final break with the alien thing and a return to their own indigenous cult, the Ifẹ̀ immediately established the temple of Orìṣà-nlá, the arch-divinity, on Òkè Itàpǎ and there it stands today.

About the actual contact of missions with Nigeria of which we have records, there are the following facts. G. P. Groves speaks of the missionary activities of the Portuguese and of the Spanish in Benin between 1485 and 1655.[2] So does the Encyclopaedia of Religion and Ethics speak of missionary activities in Benin, Angola, Upper and Lower Guinea, at about the same time.[3] It is not unlikely that ramifications of those early missions reached the Yoruba country, particularly Ile-Ifẹ̀, which is only 180 miles away from Benin.

Nevertheless, we have to take into account the opinion of such an authority as Leon Underwood[4] that Ifẹ̀ art is prior and superior to that of Benin, and that Benin art appears to have been a development of that of the school of Ifẹ̀. When we combine this with the story of the destruction of books related above, it seems clear that a completely

---

[1] See Chapter 3, pp. 22 ff.
[2] The Planting of Christianity in Africa (London, Lutterworth, 1948), p. 127.
[3] Vol. 8, p. 722.   [4] Bronzes of West Africa (Tiranti, 1949).

separate contact from outside had reached Ile-Ifẹ several hundred years ago. This is not to suggest that the origin of the literature should necessarily be identical with that of the bronzes.

One question which still baffles investigation is that of the extinction of sculptors and artists such as produced the works which are now being excavated in Ile-Ifẹ. In connection with this, there is an interesting story told by some Ifẹ elders. It is said that the sculptors and artists used to be in a class by themselves, forming a kind of lineage guild. And they used to make not only bronze or terracotta heads, but also sizeable and life-like effigies of kings.[1] It happened that once a much-beloved king died; and for some reason his immediate courtiers did not wish to announce his death. They therefore created the impression that he was still alive by installing an effigy of him in a dark corner of the state room of the palace, and to this the chiefs and courtiers unsuspectingly did homage. But it did not take long before the deception was exposed. The next king was so aggrieved because he had been unduly kept waiting for the throne that he ordered a wholesale slaughter of all the members of the lineage of artists and sculptors, so that such a deception might never again be possible. And that, the story concludes, is the reason why there is a complete extinction of those ancient artists and sculptors.

It should be noted that there is no point of this story that is fantastic. Every point of it might be historically true. In the old days, artisanship went by clan or family lineages in Yorubaland. There are houses or quarters which are named after the trade for which those who lived there were famous. Examples are Ile Asúdẹ—"The house of those who smelt brass"—in Ile-Ifẹ; Idúmàgbẹ̀dẹ—"The ward of smiths"—in Ondǒ; Idǒmòwǒ—the clan whose trade were brass cult effigies—in Ṣagamu. Also, in those days, very few persons could see the face of the king, and thus it would be possible in a fairly dark room to keep up such a deception for a short while, at least. The wholesale extermination of a clan, especially if the membership was not very large, would not be impossible, especially if a tyrannical ruler had the sanction of the oracle and the backing of the people. Whether the story is an historical account of what actually caused the extinction of the sculptors and artists of the old school of Ifẹ or not is another matter. The fact as we now have it is that there are none left to continue the work of that good old school.

For the time being, then, all that we know for certain is that there are traces in the Yoruba cults of ancient cultures for which the calibre of the present indigenous people does not fully account. It is also clear that

[1] Some of the recent finds at Ile-Ifẹ would belong to this category.

before the present system of education was introduced into the country, the present Yoruba race could neither read nor write in the Western sense of the terms: they either conveyed their messages orally or communicated with their distant folk by a system of material symbols.[1]

Christianity came again into Yorubaland, according to recorded history, in 1841, pioneered through the slaves who were liberated in Sierra Leone. It came accompanied by Western culture and dressed up in European garb. Its influence for good in the country has been incalculable: it has enlarged men's visions, freed their minds of superstitious shackles, and liberated their spirits from unnecessary fears. In that way, it has given them a progressive outlook and a sense of personal values. Directly or indirectly, it has helped to emphasise the belief of the Yoruba in the Supreme God and has impressed upon them the sacredness of human life and human responsibility, thus making for ameliorative adjustments in personal relations. Its work was greatly facilitated by the Pax Britannica, as it had the backing of the law in waging war against those things which, according to its own light, were considered idolatrous evils.

Islam came through the Sudan via Northern Nigeria. This is another religion which confirms the belief of the Yoruba in regard to the Deity. It also enhances their belief about predestiny into Islamic fatalism, with the result that one can hear the Yoruba saying now that "We are God's chickens: He can do with us at will whatever His unquestionable sovereignty decrees".

Both religions have had a weakening effect on the hold which the indigenous cults used to have on the Yoruba. Christianity is the religion of the "enlightened" and both it and Islam are "fashionable". There are many who seek to belong to one or other of them for that reason alone. As the Christian missionaries were afforded the opportunity of working upon the minds of many modern Yoruba from childhood through the church schools, they have used that opportunity, not only to preach the Gospel, but also to pooh-pooh the ways and wisdom of the land and to decry almost everything Yoruba as worthless and unbecoming, with the result that the educated young Yoruba have, through Western educational indoctrination, lost interest in the cults as such, even though they are still rather curiously bound by some of the superstitions. In this way, a partial death of the cults has been caused.

Moreover, the change in outlook occasioned by the new religions,

[1] See *The Religion of the Yorubas*, by J. Olumide Lucas, pp. 409 ff.

especially by Christianity, has affected the cults themselves. It is only in appearance that they are now conservative. In reality, they have undergone many internal changes. Earlier in this book, we emphasised the fact that in Yoruba liturgical rituals, everything must proceed correctly according to the traditional patterns.[1] That is still so in theory; but what is happening now, in fact, is that the officiants have unwittingly drifted away from what the past generations of worshippers would accept as correct traditions. The "correctness" now depends upon the imperfect knowledge of "the way things are done" in reference to both the language and the ordering of the liturgies which a people with half-hearted zeal for learning the traditions possess. It is not unusual these days to meet with astounding ignorance of the whys and wherefores of the cults in the people who by tradition become chief-priests.

This is inevitable, of course, in a system in which the attainment of official priesthood is not by discipline. Apart from the weakness involved in the possibility that a person could become a priest without systematic training, some of the present repositories of the cultus are people who returned home after a long absence abroad, during which period they have lost touch with what was being done. The old generation of priests is thus fast dying out without transmitting their knowledge about the cults to the young.

To this, we shall add changes in political systems caused by Western influence. There was a time when the king *must* be present during certain rituals. Now, however, he can perform his part of such rituals by proxy or not at all. One instance was the occasion of the lament which I heard from the Ògŭn worshippers in Ondǒ that they had to omit a certain part of an important ritual because their king had ceased to take any interest in that particular ceremony. On another occasion of great significance to the town, the Ǫni of Ile-Ifẹ̀ had to decide at the last minute that he would not attend a ceremony because of a likely political riot which his appearance might cause. These are things which used to be unheard of; but, as everywhere, things are changing and the Yoruba *orìṣà* system with them.

Silent witnesses to the decline in the power of the cults are the shrines and temples which all over the country are in a sorry state of neglect. This evidence strikes one forcibly as one goes about even in such an important cult centre as Ile-Ifẹ̀. At the moment of writing, the temple of Odùdúwà, which is especially connected with the institution of kingship, is a disgraceful, dilapidated sight.

[1] Chapter 3, p. 9.

There has also been a remarkable change in moral values all over the land. Western influence has not been altogether beneficial to the people: the Yoruba have been taught too many things! The Pax Britannica makes it possible for a daylight burglar to escape his well-merited punishment if he and his lawyer are sufficiently clever about it—the judge is so bound by the paradox of objective justice that even though he knows in his heart of hearts that the accused before him has committed the crime for which he is arraigned, yet he will let him go scot-free if the law is on his side. Christianity, by a miscarriage of purpose, makes its own contribution to the detrimental changes in moral values. Somehow, it has replaced the old fear of the divinities with the relieving but harmful notion of a God Who is a sentimental Old Man, ever ready to forgive perhaps even more than man is prone to sin, the God in whom "goodness and severity" have been put asunder. So also does Islam unwittingly create the erroneous impression that the fulfilment of the obligatory duties and acts of penance by good works are sufficient for the purpose of winning heaven. The result of all these is that our "enlightened" products of the two "fashionable" religions can now steal without any twinge of moral compunction those articles of food placed for sale at crossroads and by roadsides, which used to be quite safe; they can now cheerfully appropriate other persons' property; they can break covenants, or promises made on oath, with brazen indifference; all these they feel free to do where those who have been brought up in the old ways and wisdom still shake and tremble at the mere thought of such things.[1]

Nigeria is truly "overhung ... by a Twilight of the Gods".[2] The days of the cults in their old, conservative forms are numbered. But it is not easy to say that the cults are dying out completely. While their outward forms are undergoing radical changes, nationalism is seeking to maintain their spirit. Long before what can be described technically as nationalism began, there had been signs of revolt against what people have come to regard as foreign religion and culture and voices in the wilderness have been raised as a signal for a return to the old ways and wisdom of the fathers.

We see signs of this revolt in the syncretistic sects which have come into being, beginning about 1925, and which have since spread all over the country like the seed of contagion. The initial motive-spring of the sects was the spiritual dissatisfaction which the Nigerians began to have

1 See Chapter 12, p. 146.
2 *Religion in An African City*, by Geoffrey Parrinder, p. 6.

with the kind of Christian worship which the Church offers them. The main attraction of the sects consists in their apparently successful attempt to make the best of two worlds by syncretising Christianity with some dominant practices of the national cults. The end product of this syncretism is a church whose characteristics are frothy, ecstatic ritual, seeing of visions and dreaming of dreams, making of predictions and prescriptions, mass hysteria which gives birth to babbling of incoherent things as symptoms of possession by the Spirit. All these naturally make them popular with the mass who like neglected hungry sheep flock where they find promises of nourishment.

There is, however, a definite groping after a national religion or, shall we say, a nationalistic one, based upon the *orìṣà* system. For this reason, there has been a movement for some time now to give the cult of Ọrunmìlà[1] a "new look". This seems to be the only cult which at the moment is undergoing a radical reorganisation. The priest-diviners cling to it because it is their means of livelihood. They also know and are disturbed by the fact that there abound everywhere charlatans who are making a "racket" of divination. Conferences of the *baba'láwo* are now being held from time to time, and meeting houses are being built; all with the purpose of establishing the cult properly.

We notice also a recrudescence of the old socio-religious *Ògbóni* cult in the thing that has been given the specious name of Reformed Ògbóni Fraternity.[2] While the *Ògbóni* still maintains a shadow of its former glory, this branch has sprung from it, masquerading under a "reformed" exterior which does not quite conceal its origin. But it is definitely a national reply to the attitude which has inconsistently decried all Yoruba cults as things of the devil while yet sponsoring the European lodges.

The Reformed Ògbóni fraternity has many advertised baits by which it lures the unwary into its meshes. These are principally (a) that it was originated by a highly intelligent, astute, ex-priest of the Anglican Church in compensation for the loss of his priestly dignity; (b) that it knows no religious distinctions—Christians, Moslems, and "heathens" can come into it and find "fellowship"; (c) its claim to make people better fulfillers of God's will than either Christianity or Islam could ever make them because within its fold the initiated would find enlightenment and help in every difficulty which they might bring upon themselves or which the world[3] might impose upon them.

[1] See Chapter 8, p. 75.   [2] See Chapter 3, p. 24.
[3] See Chapter 13, p. 177.

Three factors have incapacitated the R.O.F. so far:

(a) There has been very strong opposition to it almost from the beginning. It was the Moslems who first became quite unequivocal in their stand against it: it was laid down that every Moslem had to choose between the Islamic faith and it, and that there could be no compromise. This was because Islam detected rather early its menace to its own fundamental tenets and officially legislated against it. Since that definite pronouncement has been made no Moslem *may* become a member of the R.O.F.

On the whole, the opposition of the Church to the R.O.F. has been curiously half-hearted and ineffectual. This may be due to the fact that many of the Church leaders have become entangled in its meshes and now lack both the courage and the grace which should have enabled them to extricate themselves.

(b) Many of its members have been disillusioned; although it is laid upon every member to make "converts" into the cult, those members who are honest would rather drop just enough hints to make their folk know that they would not advise it. Besides, the cult has antagonised those who are not its members by its alleged policy of victimisation which finds its way into the civil service and mercantile houses of the country.

(c) The cult is not sufficiently intellectually equipped to appeal to those who are serious minded and in pursuit of knowledge and the solution of the mysteries of life. Within its thin esoteric shell, there is little for the teeth of the serious enquirer. It is this intellectual lack that prevents the R.O.F. from presenting us with a Yoruba Gnosticism. Those whose quest is esoteric knowledge can find little appeal in feasting and excesses, in low jests, or in minding the machinery of vindictiveness and victimisation.

Our next question concerns the future of Yoruba cults. This is not an easy question because the answer can be little more than speculation. It is obvious, however, that at the moment the wind is blowing in two directions the latter of which may be a consequence of the former.

First, the process of atrophy which has attacked the cults is sure to continue with the conspiracy of factors which make for general lack of interest by the educated children of the land in them. We find that most of our university students today are extremely ignorant about the cults. This is a general fact which may be traced everywhere in the country.

As a result of the atrophy which is overtaking the ancient cults and the consequent vacuum which is being created, there is likely to be a concerted alliance between nationalism and intellect in order to formulate something of a specifically nationalistic character out of the present system. We have mentioned the Reformed Ògbóni Fraternity. In the same way as the Ògbóni cult has been "reformed", any one of the cults, or an amalgam of several cults, may be dressed up in a new garb or be given a new shape to bring it "up-to-date". What is likely to happen may be inferred from what is already taking place. In 1943, Mr. A. Fagbenro-Beyioku delivered a lecture entitled *Orunmilaism, The Basis of Jesusism*.[1] The main purport of this was to propound a theory that Ọrunmìlà, the oracle divinity was the prophet of God to the Yoruba (or rather, the Africans), even in the same way as Jesus Christ was the prophet of God to the Jews; and, moreover, Ọrunmìlà was of a higher status than Jesus Christ inasmuch as the latter derived from the former. Even before this lecture, a "church" known as *Ijọ Ọrunmìlà*—"The Church of Ọrunmìlà" had come into being with branches in many parts of the country. This "church" orders its worship after the Christian pattern, with a specific liturgy directed to Olódùmarè through Ọrunmìlà. And it should be noted that this reordering of the liturgy of the cult has done no violence in any way to the religion of the Yoruba: it is only a resetting of the pattern while its main core is maintained.

About four years ago, the Nigerian Broadcasting Corporation set up a small committee to examine the question whether *Orunmilaism* was the "religion" of the Yoruba (or, in fact, of the Africans) or not. The occasion of the committee was a strong request from the worshippers of Ọrunmìlà that their religion should be accorded equal recognition with Christianity and Islam; that is, they wanted their cult to feature on the national broadcasting programmes. The committee easily decided against the claim of *Orunmilaism* by showing from incontrovertible facts that since Ọrunmìlà was just one, though a principal one, among the divinities in the Yoruba pantheon, no one cult among the many could claim to be the "religion" of the Yoruba, not to speak of the whole of Africa. But it was quite obvious that if that committee had not been formed and its work so thoroughly done, the Nigerian Broadcasting Corporation would have been misled easily into making itself a means of subtle propaganda for the establishment and propagation of a nationalistic religion based on a deliberate heresy such as we have outlined above. The situation was really saved by an executive officer of the Corporation who was sufficiently vigilant to detect the implication

[1] Lagos, Tika-Tore Press.

of what was being proposed and demurred very strongly even while others, some of whom partly instigated the request, hailed it with nationalistic fervour and were for granting it forthwith.

We notice also that the *Odù* corpus is being adulterated to the end that Ọrunmìlà may have conferred on him a status which makes him higher and the progenitor of both Jesus Christ and Muhammad. An interesting one among the newly hatched recitals is the one which carries the story that there was a woman named Mọrówà in the days of old. This woman was barren; but she was determined, notwithstanding, to have a child. To that end, therefore, she approached Ọrunmìlà one evening and appealed to him for a medicine to open her womb. Ọrunmìlà consented to cure her of her sterility, but told her to return for the medicine the following morning, as it was already evening and "the herbs had slept (*Ewé ti sùn*)". Mọrówà was, however, for receiving the medicine that evening. Ọrunmìlà appealed to her again to let the herbs sleep (*J'ewé sùn = Jẹki ewé sùn*—"Let the herbs sleep") and return for her medicine in the morning. Mọrówà still would not go and, as a result, of her importunity, Ọrunmìlà had to go into the garden, collect the required herbs and dispense the medicine for her. As a result, Mọrówà became pregnant and a baby boy duly arrived. Ọrunmìlà now decreed that the boy must be named J'-ewé-sùn ("Let the herbs sleep"), for a perpetual remembrance of her importunity. Thus, the story concludes, was Jesus (Jesu in Yoruba, which is, according to this story, an ellipsis of *J'ewé-sùn*—"Let the herbs sleep") born of Mary (Mọrówà being a corruption of Maria which is the Yoruba for Mary according to the Yoruba Bible) through the ministration of Ọrunmìlà. A fantastic story born of a riotous imagination, no doubt! But it just shows the extent to which things can be carried.

In conclusion, let us emphasise the fact that a vacuum is being created with regard to religion in Yorubaland. And there are contending forces for the filling of the vacuum. Of all the forces at work, Christianity, by its unique and universal message, stands the best chance of fulfilling that which is implied in the Yoruba concept of God, and that for the benefit of the people and country. This, however, depends as in every age and land upon the vision, spiritual stamina, and faithfulness of those who are charged with its message.

Index of Subjects

INDEX OF SUBJECTS

Index of Proper Names